Great Power Policies Towards Central Europe 1914–1945

EDITED BY

ALIAKSANDR PIAHANAU

E-INTERNATIONAL RELATIONS PUBLISHING

E-International Relations
www.E-IR.info
Bristol, England
2019

ISBN 978-1-910814-45-1

This book is published under a Creative Commons CC BY-NC 4.0 license. You are free to:

- **Share** – copy and redistribute the material in any medium or format
- **Adapt** – remix, transform, and build upon the material

Under the following terms:

- **Attribution** – You must give appropriate credit, provide a link to the license and indicate if changes were made. You may do so in any reasonable manner, but not in any way that suggests the licensor endorses you or your use.
- **Non-Commercial** – You may not use the material for commercial purposes.

Any of the above conditions can be waived if you get permission. Please contact info@e-ir.info for any such enquiries, including for licensing and translation requests.

Other than the terms noted above, there are no restrictions placed on the use and dissemination of this book for student learning materials/ scholarly use.

Production: William Kakenmaster
Cover Image: Andrey_Kuzmin / Keport via Depositphotos

A catalogue record for this book is available from the British Library.

E-IR Edited Collections

Series Editors: Stephen McGlinchey, Marianna Karakoulaki and Agnieszka Pikulicka-Wilczewska
Books Editor: Cameran Clayton
Copy-editing: Corey McCabe and Farah Saleem
Editorial assistance: Jakob R. Avgustin, Hayden Paulsen, Christian Marks, Fernanda de Castro Brandão Martins and Alex Tanchev.

E-IR's Edited Collections are open access scholarly books presented in a format that preferences brevity and accessibility while retaining academic conventions. Each book is available in print and digital versions, and is published under a Creative Commons license. As E-International Relations is committed to open access in the fullest sense, free electronic versions of all of our books, including this one, are available on our website.

Find out more at: http://www.e-ir.info/publications

About the E-International Relations website

E-International Relations (www.E-IR.info) is the world's leading open access website for students and scholars of international politics, reaching over 3.5 million readers each year. E-IR's daily publications feature expert articles, blogs, reviews and interviews – as well as student learning resources. The website is run by a registered non-profit organisation based in Bristol, UK and staffed with an all-volunteer team of students and scholars.

Acknowledgments

The preparation of this book has greatly benefited from the help of many individuals and organisations. The idea of making this volume was born and tested at two special panels dedicated to the 'great power policies towards Central Europe,' which were part of the 4th and 5th International Congresses of the Belarusian Studies in Kaunas, Lithuania in October 2014 and October 2015. I wish to thank the Congress Organising Committee and the paper contributors, who supported the project from the beginning. However, this collection would have never been achieved without assistance of Dr. Raisa Barash, Dr. Andras Becker and Silvana Vulcan, who helped with the translation of some papers into English, and also of Linda Ouma and Nicolas Vahdias, who pointed out some language shortcomings. Last, but not least, I feel indebted to the E-International Relations team whose assistance was crucial in finalising this book.

Abstract

This book provides an overview of the various forms and trajectories of Great Power policy towards Central Europe between 1914 and 1945. This involves the analyses of diplomatic, military, economic and cultural perspectives of Germany, Russia, Britain, and the USA towards Hungary, Poland, the Baltic States, Czechoslovakia and Romania. The contributions of established, as well as emerging, historians from different parts of Europe enriches the English language scholarship on the history of the international relations of the region. The volume is designed to be accessible and informative to both historians and wider audiences.

Aliaksandr Piahanau received his PhD from Toulouse University, France.

Contributors

Sorin Arhire is a Lecturer at the '1 Decembrie 1918' University of Alba Iulia, Romania.

Ivan Basenko is a PhD Candidate at the National University of Kyiv Mohyla Academy, Ukraine.

Agne Cepinskyte holds a PhD in International Relations from King's College London, UK.

Oleg Ken (1960–2007) was a Professor at Herzen University and European University, Saint Petersburg, Russia.

Tamás Magyarics is a Professor at Eötvös Loránd University, Budapest, and a Hungarian diplomat.

Halina Parafianowicz is a Professor at the Institute of History and Political Science of the Białystok University, Poland.

Alexander Rupasov is a Senior Researcher at the Institute of History in Saint-Petersburg of the Russian Academy of Sciences.

Ignác Romsics is a member of the Hungarian Academy of Sciences. He teaches at the Esterházy Károly University, Eger, Hungary.

Artem Zorin is an Associate Professor in Vyatka State University, Russia.

Contents

INTRODUCTION
  Aliaksandr Piahanau   1

PART ONE - GEOPOLITICS AND SECURITY

1. HUNGARY'S PLACE IN GERMAN SOUTH-EAST EUROPEAN POLICY, 1919–1944
   Ignác Romsics   7

2. MOSCOW AND THE BALTIC STATES: EXPERIENCE OF RELATIONSHIPS, 1917–1939
   Oleg Ken and Alexander Rupasov   43

PART TWO - ECONOMY AND DIPLOMACY

3. BALANCING IN CENTRAL EUROPE: GREAT BRITAIN AND HUNGARY IN THE 1920S
   Tamás Magyarics   77

4. BRITISH POLICY TOWARDS ROMANIA, 1936–41
   Sorin Arhire   91

5. AMERICAN POLICY TOWARDS CZECHOSLOVAKIA, 1918–1945
   Artem Zorin   107

PART THREE - PROPAGANDA AND PERCEPTIONS

6. THE GREAT WAR AND THE POLISH QUESTION IN IMPERIAL RUSSIA: A CASE STUDY OF ITS REFLECTIONS IN KIEV'S PRESS, 1914–1917
   Ivan Basenko   129

7. THE BALTIC DREAM OF A 'HANDICAPPED' GREAT POWER: THE WEIMAR REPUBLIC'S POLICIES TOWARDS THE BALTIC-GERMANS
   Agne Cepinskyte   153

8. HERBERT C. HOOVER AND POLAND, 1929–1933: BETWEEN MYTH AND REALITY
   Halina Parafianowicz   176

NOTE ON INDEXING   199

Introduction

ALIAKSANDR PIAHANAU

In the first half of the 20th century Central Europe repeatedly set the stage for Great Power rivalry and conflict, as well as political, economic and cultural exchange. With a touch of irony, contemporary Hungarian writer Lajos Grendel described the region as a mere sum of small landlocked countries that could be occupied by foreign armies from any direction and whose inhabitants and governments faced multiple foreign interferences during their lifespans. Indeed, during the Great War, the interwar period and World War 2, the area situated between Germany and Russia became the target of covert or direct expansion.

The context of Great Power meddling in Central Europe in the period 1914–45 offers numerous perspectives. The multiple and often conflicting regional viewpoints about national identity, frontier and territory had not only underpinned regional interstate antagonisms, but at the same time provided a platform for Great Power interference. This collection of studies provides an overview of the various forms and trajectories of Great Power policies towards Central Europe between 1914 and 1945. This involves the analyses of perspectives, such as the diplomatic, military, economic or cultural policy of Weimar and Nazi Germany, tsarist and Bolshevik Russia, Great Britain, and the US on Central European countries, like Hungary, Poland, Latvia, Lithuania, Estonia, Czechoslovakia and Romania. The contributions of established as well as emerging historians from different parts of Europe are aimed at enriching the English language scholarship on the history of international relations.

The volume is divided into three parts and, in total, contains eight papers. The first part, entitled 'Geopolitics and Security,' illustrates how two European continental powers – Germany and Russia, whose frontiers set the limits of Central Europe, programmed their regional agenda and tried to implement it. Their ultimate objective was the expansion of influence in the region. The Great War brought military defeat, political and economic weakness, international humiliation and isolation for both powers. Despite the fact that they fought in different camps during the war, Moscow and Berlin soon entered into cooperative relations that lasted until the early 1930s and which were briefly re-established in the first years of World War 2. Using the examples of Hungary and the three Baltic countries, this part illustrates how the German *Reich* and the USSR built relations with the small regional countries, assuring their loyalty through classic 'carrot and stick' methods.

The opening paper is written by Ignác Romsics, in which he analyses German foreign political thought and the gradual alteration of Berlin official attitudes towards Hungary from the end of the Great War to the Nazi occupation of Hungary in 1944. Its primary focus is the analysis of Hungary's changing role in German military and economic strategy towards East-Central Europe, and the impact of international developments on German actions and policy towards Hungary. Romsics demonstrates the underlying differences and occasional similarities of the various German *Mittel-Europa* plans at the beginning of the century, the concept of *Lebensraum*, as well as German domination over the continent during the Second World War – *Pax Germanica*.

The next contribution deals with Soviet Russia's policies towards Lithuania, Latvia and Estonia during the interwar period. Its authors, Oleg Ken and Alexander Rupasov, argue that these three Baltic countries, despite their apparently limited political and economic values, occupied a disproportionally important role in the foreign policy-planning of Moscow. In their detailed analysis, Ken and Rupasov uncover the evolution of Communist Russian elite views on the limits of Baltic States' independence. They demonstrate that in the early interwar years, Moscow searched for the most appropriate political relations with Kaunas, Riga and Tallinn through trade, investments and corruption. However, the Bolsheviks failed to assure the unique Eastern orientation of the Baltic governments and, after a short but dynamic stage of the Litvinov peaceful diplomacy in 1933–35, Moscow suddenly refused any further rapprochement with them. Ken and Rupasov conclude that the USSR succeeded in establishing its complete control over the Baltic republics only with the help of Nazi Germany as a part of a Stalin-Hitler deal on the remapping of Central Europe in the autumn of 1939.

The second part, 'Economy and Diplomacy,' brings our attention to the Central European involvement of the two Great War winners – Great Britain and the United States. Due to their geographic positions, which prioritized ocean communications, but not Europe's heartland, these Anglo-Saxon powers had a rather distanced approach and limited interests in Central Europe. Nevertheless, as the following three papers will indicate, London and Washington exercised a profound influence on the political architecture of the region through diplomatic channels and economic leverage.

Here, the first contribution is offered by Tamás Magyarics, who investigates UK–Hungary relations in the 1920s. Magyarics starts with the assumption that soon after the First World War, Whitehall revised its negative attitude on its vanquished enemy – Hungary. London realised that without Hungary's reconstruction, (Central) Europe's peace and prosperity could not be achieved. Magyarics argues that through investment and financial penetration in Hungary, Britain also wished to balance the French, and later the German, influence in the region. At the same time, this economic expansion was also supposed to strengthen the sterling and help Britain repay the loans it owed to the US. However, the paper concludes that as Britain was no party to the revanchist endeavours of the Magyar governments, the two countries started to drift apart again in the late 1920s.

The next chapter moves us to the eve of World War 2. In it, Sorin Arhire tells the story of fluctuating British relations with Romania, which, in his view, became particularly dynamic in the late 1930s. As Arhire stresses, after Hitler remilitarized the Rhineland in 1936, London significantly increased its interests in Romania. Their rapprochement culminated in April 1939, when London (and Paris) guaranteed the independence of Romania. However, a pro-Western orientation did not offer real protection to Bucharest, which, after the Allies's debacle of 1940, was forced to give up a third of its territory to its neighbours (Russia, Hungary and Bulgaria). Seeking international protection, Bucharest allied with Berlin and even joined its anti-Soviet invasion in June 1941. That, along with the anti-Semitic campaign and persecution of British citizens in Romania, drastically affected the Whitehall mood in 1941: in February 1941, London suspended its diplomatic relations with Bucharest and, in December, it declared war on Romania.

The relationship between the US and Czechoslovakia is the topic of the next contribution. Its author, Artem Zorin asserts that the United States had a special role in the fate of Czechoslovakia. To demonstrate this, Zorin examines the development of US policy between 1918 and 1945, particularly focusing on the American attitude towards the fate of Czechoslovakia. Zorin demonstrates that while Washington maintained friendly relations with Prague; at the same time, it had a cautious and pragmatic position regarding the economic and diplomatic issues of Czechoslovakia. Thus, during the

Prague-Berlin quarrel of 1938–39, the White House decided not to interfere in the conflict, but adhered to the policy of non-recognition of the Nazi occupation of Czech lands. Zorin points out that America provided an important support for the Czechoslovak exiles during World War 2. Nevertheless, at the end of the war, Washington distanced itself from guaranteeing Czechoslovak independence and its incorporation into the Soviet sphere of influence.

The third and final part, 'Propaganda and Perceptions,' seeks to investigate concepts, ideas, motives and values that stood behind Great Power decision-making. The last three contributions scrutinize the conceptual side of international relations, from discursive practices to personal biases. Examining cases from Germany, Russia and the United States, they study the interrelations between individuals, groups and mass convictions.

War propaganda, as a means of social mobilization, is the topic of Ivan Basenko's chapter. He reflects on the Polish question, which was barely presented in imperial Russian press before 1914; and then became one of the major sources for the tsarist anti German campaign. The Polish question was integrated into the official tsarist concept of 'sacred struggle' between 'Germandom' and 'Slavdom.' The hidden message of this propaganda, according to Basenko, was to urge Poles to support Russia against the Central powers and to motivate other imperial subjects to fight for the 'liberation' of Poles. Using prominent daily newspapers of Kiev, the centre of the Southwestern region of Russia, Basenko explains how printed media reflected the Petrograd policy towards Poland and Germany.

Agne Cepinskyte's study examines the 'Baltic dream' of 1920s Germany. More precisely, Cepinskyte investigates Weimar geopolitical understanding of the place of the East Baltic countries (especially, regarding their German minorities), and how these lands were interlinked with Germany. Focusing on speeches and government records of the prominent Weimar statesman Gustav Stresemann, Cepinskyte portrays the hidden layers of the Second *Reich* political thinking. The author underlines that Berlin became particularly interested in the Baltic-Germans not least because they would potentially help Germany build a bridge to economic markets in the East. The main argument here is that the early interwar diplomacy of cooperation was at odds with the interests of the increasingly active conservative circles in the *Reich*. Thus, Cepinskyte believes that Weimar foreign policy makers had to balance between friendly relations with the Baltic States, and the accusation of betrayal of the Baltic-Germans.

The concluding chapter is written by Halina Parafianowicz, who evaluates the personal impact of US President Herbert C. Hoover (1929–33) on the relations between the US and Poland. An emblematic leader, glorified by his role in American relief for post-war East-Central Europe, Hoover enjoyed the image of being a distinctive friend of Poland. According to Parafianowicz, the early ears of his presidency witnessed the symbolic strengthening of Polish-American relations. Nevertheless, Parafianowicz accurately points out that Hoover's Polonophilia was not as strong as Warsaw wanted it to be. In fact, Poland occupied a marginal place in US diplomacy under Hoover, who was preoccupied with the devastating effects of the Great Depression on the US as well as Europe. This led to the decline of bilateral economic relations. Under Hoover, the Washington-Warsaw political atmosphere was seriously damaged because of the propagation in official American circles of the idea to revise the German-Polish border in favour of Berlin.

Part One

Geopolitics and Security

1

Hungary's Place in German South-East European Policy, 1919–1944

IGNÁC ROMSICS

German ideas about *Mittel Europa*, and as a part of this, German political thought towards South-East Europe has evolved for over 200 years. During the European reconstruction after the Napoleonic Wars, the 39 German principalities – including Prussia, Bavaria and the four Free Cities – played second fiddle to other events, or were the subject of decisions made in London, Vienna and St Petersburg. Then, the major issue for German politics was to end geographical disintegration, and create economic and political unity. However, in this period, ideas emerged envisaging national unity beyond geographical limits determined by linguistic dividing lines, and linking it to the idea of a broader Central European economic union. Johann Gottlieb Fichte (1762–1814) envisioned a unified German state as a national state limiting its external trade to a minimum (*Der geschlossene Handelsstaat* Tübingen, 1800). But his followers, such as Friedrich List (1789–1846) thought in much broader geographical terms. List was convinced that the future was in the creation of greater economic units, and if the German states wanted to become a Great Power, their customs union (formed in 1834) would also have to unite their trade policy. Then the Germans would have to form a political confederation with Belgium, Switzerland and Denmark and, finally – together with Vienna and Budapest – they would have to occupy the position of the declining Ottoman Empire on the Balkans, strengthening their influence to the Mediterranean and the Black Sea. Ottoman rule – as he wrote not soon before his death – 'would have to be succeeded by a German-Hungarian Eastern Empire, whose frontiers would have been washing by the Black Sea and the Adriatic Sea, and which would be dominated by German and Magyar spirit.' Apart from the theoretical framework of *Mittel-Europa*, more practical ideas, such as the Berlin-Baghdad railway, could also be linked to List.[1]

From then, the Mittel-Europa idea persisted in German political thought; it became a realistic political program after German economic unity in 1871, and not least because of the new German state's political and military power especially during the 1890s. As such, it appeared as the complimentary element of German imperialism and colonial policy, and – according to some opinions – as an alternative of this, it united certain political and economic alternatives. The various plans that emerged between 1890 and 1914 can be organized into four main categories.

The export oriented industries, banks and industrial managers aimed for a multi-national customs area, which as a core included a German-Austrian-Hungarian bloc, but included the Balkans, the Benelux states as well as France and Scandinavia. This plan neither aimed to reduce international trade, vital for Germany, nor to politically repress the member states of the German customs union, and did not threaten their sovereignty or planned territorial annexation. One of the most well-known concepts is that of Frederich Naumann, protestant theologian and social-reformer, whose book *Mitteleurope* was published in German in 1915, and in Hungarian in 1916. Supported by the big land owners and the All-German Union (*Alldeutcher Verband*), these ideas, characterised by different *völkisch* and racial-biological theories, primarily aimed to subjugate the Central European region. And at the same time, in this framework, the *Mitteleuropa* concepts implied the inclusion of Polish and Russian territories in the East and Northern French and Belgian territories in the West (*Weltpolitik versus Lebensraum*). Regardless of the significant differences in these concepts, there are certain similarities: the expansion of the 'Small German' base of the 1871 empire towards the Atlantic Ocean in the West, and towards the Black Sea in the Southeast. This German dominated neo-mercantilist region was also supposed to guarantee the security of the region, as a fourth world power, against Britain, Russia and the United States in a future global crisis.[2]

The imperial political leadership favoured the liberal-imperialistic version of the *Mitteleuropa* idea until 1917. However, in 1914, German chancellor

---

1   William Henderson, *Friedrich List*, Reutlingen, 1989, 121–34. Compare to: Juda Pentman, *Die Zollunionsidee und ihre Wandlungen im Rahmen der Wirtschaftspolitischen Ideen und der Wirtschaftspolitik des 19. Jahrhunderts bis zur Gemenwart*, Jena: G. Fischer, 1917.

2   Henry Cord Meyer, *Mittel Europe in German Thought and Action 1815–1945*. The Hague: International Scolars forum, 1955; Fritz Fischer, *Krieg der Illusionen*. Düsseldorf: Droste, 1969; and one of the new theoretical reviews: Woodruff D. Smith, *The Ideological Origins of Nazi Imperialism*. New York-Oxford: Oxford UP, 1986.

Theobald von Betthman-Hollweg (1909–17) still claimed: 'A common Central European economic union is achievable, through custom union agreements, which would include France, Belgium, Holland, Denmark, Austria-Hungary, Poland, potentially Italy, Sweden and Norway. This union – without common constitutional union, with the nominal freedom of states, although under German leadership – has to guarantee Germany's economic rule over Central Europe.'[3] After Russia's withdrawal from the war in 1917, government circles, enjoying the full support of the military high command, also started to think along the lines of annexationist ideas, which would have reduced Russia to the frontiers it had under Peter the Great (1682–1725) at the beginning of the 18th century. Thus, they aimed to settle an important part of the detached Russian, Ukrainian, Polish and Baltic territories with Germans.

After the Peace Treaty of Brest-Litovsk between the Central Powers and Soviet Russia, for a brief period in the spring and summer of 1918, it seemed that the German political-economic bloc was achieved in the East. The Spa Agreement, signed between Austria-Hungary and Germany on 12 May 1918, provisioned a close economic, political and military union between the two states eventually leading to a customs union; Serbia and Romania were under German and Austro-Hungarian occupation; Bulgaria and Turkey, as well as the newly created states of Ukraine and Finland also belonged to the German alliance system.[4]

As a result of military defeat and the Versailles peace treaty, Germany not only lost its colonies and European acquisitions, but also temporarily lost its Great Power status, which it acquired between 1866 and 1871. However, the potential for Germany's future ascendancy remained. With large American loans, the German economy had already recovered by the 1920s, regained its Great Power status in the continent by the early 1930s, and by the mid-1930s, it aspired to become a world power.

We are concentrating on one aspect of this ascendancy and eventual fall – Germany's policy toward South-East Europe, more precisely, towards Hungary. Instead of analysing economic relations, conditions of the German minorities and the Nazi military leadership, which have been studied extensively, our focus here is the development of German South-East European policy, its relations to *Mitteleuropa* ideas, its integration into foreign policy, and the reaction of target countries, especially Hungary.

---

3   Fritz Fischer, *Griff nach der Weltmacht*. Düsseldorf, 1984, 94.
4   Fischer, Griff nach der Weltmacht, 94; Gyula Tokody, Az Össznémet Szövetség (Alldeutscher Verband) és közép-európai tervei 1890–1918. Budapest: Akadémiai, 1959, 79–95.

1919/1923-1929: The policy of Stresemann

Until its collapse, Austria-Hungary occupied a special role in German federation plans. Due to its German character, its middle-power status, and common foreign political aims, the Monarchy was not only the subject of German strategy, but was also the partner of Berlin. After the redrawing of the frontiers of the region after 1918, this situation had also changed. Austrian independence was considered by the German leadership as a temporality, and they were convinced that Austria would eventually become the part of Germany. On the other hand, Hungary – significantly weakened from all points of view – became one of the South-East European 'medium and small states' which were industrially under-developed and irreconcilably hostile towards each other, which the 1929 report of the German Foreign Ministry considered 'as a whole ... balkanised.' Reflecting on this idea, the notion of *Südeuropa* became deeply entrenched in Germany. It included primarily Hungary, Romania, Yugoslavia and Bulgaria, as well as on an ad hoc basis Albania and Greece. On the other hand, the term *Balkan-Donauraum* also did not disappear completely, but perhaps the difference between the two became even more blurred.[5]

German political interest towards the region – for the reason that the countries still complemented each other economically – did not diminish compared to the pre-war era, but actually increased. Paradoxically, the conditions were all there. The strengthening of ties and links, broken at Versailles, now had better opportunities in the long-run as a result of the atomization of the region, the break-up of the Habsburg Monarchy and the permanent weakening of Russia. The only question remaining was when and how Germany will be able to reverse French, and to a lesser extent British and Italian, influence in the region. The foreign policy of the Weimar Republic between 1923 and 1929, under the leadership of Gustav Stresemann, had two strategic aims: reestablishment and strengthening of economic and trade links, and the support of German minorities.

It was mainly the processing industry and the diplomatic core – socialized in the milieu of *Mitteleuropa* ideas – that supported the restoration of these economic ties. One viewpoint from 1926 claimed: '... because [these countries] have very under-developed, or, like Austria and Czechoslovakia, one-sided industries ... countries in the middle and lower Danube are the natural markets of the German industry.' 'It is expected that as a result of the

---

5   *Die politische Lage in Südosteuropa*, 28 August 1929 // Archiv des Auswärtigen Amtes, Bonn (hereafter, AA). Politische Abteilung II. Generell. Pol. 4. Balkan. Bd. 3.; Hans-Paul Höpfner, *Deutsche Südosteuropapolitik in der Weimarer Republik*. Frankfurt, Bern: Peter Lang, 1983, 94–5.

intensification of their agriculture and the further exploitation of the raw materials, the buying potentials of these countries will increase. [...] Our aim is to create appropriate conditions for the German economy here through treaties with these countries.'6

Accordingly, already in the beginning of the 1920s, Germany signed commercial treaties with Yugoslavia, Bulgaria and Hungary on the mutual basis of the most favoured nation clause. Germany's share of the foreign trade of these countries had already multiplied between 1920 and 1923. Because of certain prolonged disputes regarding the 1917–18 German occupation of Romania, Berlin signed such a treaty with Bucharest only in 1928. Regardless, German-Romanian trade had already intensified in 1921–22, and Romania's most important trading partner from 1923 was Germany. At the same time, Germany was only the third most important trading partner for Hungary and Yugoslavia.[7]

This hierarchy was not accidental. Abundant in certain raw materials, Romania and Yugoslavia – regardless of their political allegiance to the French alliance system – became the important trading partners of Germany in South-East Europe. On the other hand, Hungary and Bulgaria primarily became important as markets and agricultural producers and played a less important role in German thought. It was noted that '… [T]he opportunities for the German economy in Romania are greater than in any other countries in East-Central Europe'; and also in Yugoslavia, 'as the strongest and most promising Balkan countries,' explained a Foreign Ministry note.[8]

Berlin traditionally considered the German minorities, descendants and German-speaking population in the region as the integral part of the German nation. In order to preserve their identity, and through this, in order for them to be utilized as a stepping stone for the *Reich*'s influence, Berlin continuously supported the German diasporas. Except for Bulgaria, where they lived in only very small numbers, there were significant German minorities in all three South-East European countries: 500,000 (3.6% of the population) in Yugoslavia, 750,000 (4.2%) in Romania and 550,000 (7%) in Hungary. The Weimar Republic considered these 2 million ethnic Germans the natural supporters, and tools, of Germany's South-East European economic, cultural and political endeavours. Their role in German foreign policy was summed up in the aforementioned 1926 memorandum: 'Hundreds of thousands belong to

---

6   *Akten zur deutschen auswärtigen Politik* (hereafter, *ADAP*), Serie B. Bd. III, Göttingen: Vandenhoeck und Ruprecht, 1968, 353.
7   Höpfner, Deutsche Südosteuropapolitik, 112–302.
8   Höpfner, *Deutsche Südosteuropapolitik*, 116; *Freytag* (Bucharest), 20 Nov. 1925 // AA, Politische Abteilung II. Generell. Pol. 4. Balkan. Bd. 2.

the German minorities in Hungary, Yugoslavia and Romania. Their survival and strengthening, for very practical purposes, is our primary aim. Their role in the united German nation is to serve as economic, political and cultural links between the German Reich and those other countries where they live.'[9] Supporting German language instruction among the Saxons in Transylvania, Stresemann stressed: 'regardless of the greatest efforts of the Saxons in Transylvania, today we have to count the collapse of the German school system there. If we do not intervene, we would surely lose this cultural base in South-East Europe. The result of this would not only be the collapse of our cultural expansion politics in South-East Europe, but a very significant economic impairment to the German nation as a whole. The Saxons in Transylvania constitute such a core of Germandom there, which has primary significance towards our economic policy in Romania, Yugoslavia and Bulgaria.'[10]

The German foreign political aim to strengthen German minorities cannot be signified in trade relations only. However, from the available fragmentary evidence, it can be argued that the funds provided by Berlin for the moral and political support of German schools, press and churches, as well as the several economic and cultural associations, and education of the minority elite (scholarships) all played a significant role. This was the case regardless of the fact that, compared to the German minorities living in Belgium, Denmark, Poland, Czechoslovakia and the Baltic region (*Grenzdeutsche*), South-East Europe (*Auslandsdeutsche* or *Volksdeutsche*) always lacked priority in official policy.[11]

Until 1929, German foreign policy kept its distance from meddling in the politics of the region, and the antagonisms of the states in South-East Europe. 'The policy of Germany in the Balkans is determined by restraint and neutrality, and in case our policy becomes active, it would promote the preservation of peace' – argued reports on the region each year.[12] Or, as Stresemann claimed in 1926: 'With good prospects in the Balkans, we are now following a policy of restrain. We will follow this policy, unless certain power reshuffles occur. Our aim is to maintain good relations with all countries in the Balkans.'[13]

9 *ADAP*, Serie B. Bd. III, 353.
10 *ADAP*, Serie B. Bd. VII, Göttingen : Vandenhoeck und Ruprecht, 1974, 48–9.
11 Höpfner, *Deutsche Südosteuropapolitik*, 303–42; Lóránt Tilkovsky, 'Németország és a magyar nemzetiségpolitika, 1921–1924,' *Századok*, 1 (1978), 3–48; Lóránt Tilkovsky, 'Németország és a magyar nemzetiségpolitika, 1924–1929,' *Történelmi Szemle*, 1 (1980), 52–90.
12 *Die politische Lage in Südosteuropa*, 27 August 1927 // AA, Politische Abteilung II. Generell. Pol. 4. Balkan. Bd. 2.
13 Höpfner, *Deutsche Südosteuropapolitik*, 119.

This intentional restrain, which contradicts policy towards South-East Europe during and before the war, can be explained with Stresemann's policy (sketched in 1919, but becoming official only in 1923) that primarily aimed for peace with the Western powers and the recognition of Germany's Western frontiers. Also it pursued the final settlement of German reparations, restoration of German sovereignty in the Saar and the Rhineland, the peaceful revision of the Eastern frontiers, and the *Anschluss*. A more active German policy in the region would have eventually clashed with French Danubian and Balkan strategy, and would have compromised current German reconciliatory tendencies. Paris, at least in words, showed a certain leniency towards the unification of Danzig and Germany, and the elimination of the Polish Corridor, which cut Prussia into two. However, nobody expected it to concede to the idea of a German sphere of influence stretching from the North Sea to the Black Sea.[14]

The Hungarian public and the political elite did not understand Stresemann's foreign policy, his South-East European strategy, and the role he envisaged for Budapest as an independent polity without Vienna. When the Hungarians understood, they adopted an offended stance. Their elite, which were socialized in the final decades of the Habsburg Monarchy, felt that Hungary's small power status was only temporary, and remained captive of notions about a Hungarian Empire. Budapest attempted to deal with the German leadership as an equal partner or, at least, in accordance with *primus inter pares* principle (with which, it also perceived its neighbours). Hungary considered it evident that because of century-long cultural connections, the sharing of fate against the 'sea of Slavs' and military comradeship in the Great War, Germany would help Hungary, and would effectively support Budapest's revisionist ambitions. It necessarily had to realise this was a pipedream.

First, mandated by Hungary's Prime Minister István Bethlen (1921–31), Prince Lajos Windischgrätz visited Stresemann in 1923 with the idea of German-Hungarian cooperation. Windischgrätz summarized the viewpoint of Stresemann as follows: 'No, my dear prince, a blind and a deaf cannot achieve much together; foreign political cooperation has not many benefits.'[15] Bethlen met a similar reception in 1925. 'A too close cooperation with Hungary is not advisable, as it would burden Germany with the problem of Hungarian wishes for the recovery of territories acquired by Czechoslovakia,

---

14   For French lenience, see: *ADAP*, Serie B. Bd. VII. 483–4; for German foreign policy in general: Andreas Hillgruber, *Die gescheiterte Grossmarcht. Eine Skizze des Deutschen Reiches 1871–1945*. Düsseldorf : Dorte, 1980, 63–71.
15   Ludwig Windischgratz, *Helden und Halunken*, Wien-München-Zürich: W. Frick-Verlag, 1965, 165.

Romania, Yugoslavia and Austria.'[16]

Gaining momentum after the 1927 Treaty of Eternal Friendship signed with Italy, Hungary renewed its diplomatic efforts for achieving a political collaboration with Germany in 1927–28, and also for the creation of a German-Italian-Austro-Hungarian revisionist bloc. However, the German attitude remained cool. Stresemann instructed his Envoy in Budapest to act like he did not know about the Hungarian proposition. 'Joining the Italian-Hungarian cooperation is out of the question, as it would negatively affect our relationship with France and Yugoslavia' – he explained.[17]

The continued rejection of Hungarian overtures did not mean that Germany was not aware of the ethnographic injustices of the Trianon Peace of 1920, and would not consider certain elements of Hungarian revisionist aims justified. In one of his conversations with the Czechoslovak Foreign Minister Edvard Beneš (1918–35), German Under-Secretary of State for Foreign Affairs Carl von Schubert (1924–30) clearly referred to this. Of Beneš's accusations, he declared: '... truly, just like for most of their history, the Hungarians are restless. On the other hand, I have to state that this restlessness is justified. It was the gravest mistake to cut deep into Hungarian ethnic space.'[18] Similarly, in 1928 Schubert told Kálmán Kánya (the Hungarian Minister in Berlin), who persistently argued for revision and the similar fate of Germany and Hungary, that: 'The Hungarians, to a certain extent, have to be patient with us. It is completely clear that one State could help another State, like one person helps another, if it is healthy and has fully recovered its strength.'[19] In the context of Germany's strategy, it should have been understood in Hungary that until Germany's minimal demands (the final settlement of reparations, the withdrawal of occupational forces from the Rhineland, the resolution of the problem of Danzig and the Polish Corridor) are met, Germany's hands are tied and it cannot endorse Hungarian revisionist claims.

Apart from revisionism, and differences in opinions about political collaboration, there were other problems in the German-Hungarian relationship. One of these was the collaboration of the German (Bavarian) and Hungarian far-right in the early 1920s which was tolerated and to a certain extent supported by the Hungarian political leadership. The more democratic and more careful German leadership disapproved of this. In 1922,

---

16   *ADAP*, Serie B. Bd. III, 354.
17   *ADAP*, Serie B. Bd. VII, 159–60.
18   *ADAP*, Serie B. Bd. IX (1), Göttingen : Vandenhoeck und Ruprecht, 1976, Schubert, 22 May 1928.
19   ADAP, Serie B. Bd. VIII, Göttingen: Vandenhoeck und Ruprecht, 1976, 197–8.

Germany protested against Hungary hiding the leaders of the Kapp coup (1920) and the killers of Matthias Erzberger, and recalled its Budapest Envoy Franz Egon Fürstenberg who was too lenient towards Bethlen.[20]

In the second part of the 1920s, the main issue in the bilateral relations was the question of German schools in Hungary. The Bethlen government attempted to solve this problem in 1923 by organizing three types of schools. In type A, the language of instruction for all subjects was German, type B schools were bilingual, while in type C schools, German was taught as a foreign language. In theory, this system would have been satisfactory to all. But, the government never funded type A and B schools to the extent it did type C ones. Accordingly, the number of type A schools reduced from 49 to 33 between 1924 and 1927, type Bs from 73 to 55, while type Cs increased from 169 to 265. Bethlen also criticized the privileges German youth from Hungary enjoyed against other Hungarians in German state scholarships. He was also suspicious towards the extensive traveling of German youth to Hungary, and their growing networks there. He did not consider this as a naturally developed relationship between German minorities and the German mother country, but as tools and an attempt of pan-German advance into Hungary. In the 1920s, Bethlen often referred to the dangers of a consequently German advance into Hungary.[21]

The promotion of a German-Hungarian revisionist collaboration, and criticism towards revisionist-expansionist Germany were apparently in contrast to each other. On the level of rhetoric, this could be reconciled by overemphasizing the role of Hungarians in South-East Europe and with rosy viewpoints about German-Hungarian collaboration, but these two were irreconcilable.

Apart from these, there were also other issues troubling German-Hungarian relations in the second half of the 1920s: the critical voices of the German left-wing press towards the anti-democratic social structure and policies of the Hungarian government; the question of Burgenland; and the trade balance which became more and more favourable for Germany, but more and more un-favourable for Hungary. The most important of these was the latter. Between 1922 and 1929, the volume of German industrial imports into Hungary significantly exceeded Hungarian exports to Germany. The primary

---

20 AA. Politische Abteilung II. Ungarn. Pol. 2. Bd. I, compare to: Bruno Thoss: *Der Ludendorff-Kreis 1919–1923. München als Zentrum der mitteleuropäischen Gegenrevolution zwischen Revolution und Hitler-Putsch*. München: Stadtarchiv, 1978.
21 For school policy, see Tilkovsky, 'Németország és a magyar nemzetiségpolitika, 1924–1929', 76–7; for the declarations of Bethlen: *ADAP*, Serie B. Bd. XIV. Göttingen: Vandenhoeck und Ruprecht, 1980, 235–8 and *Gróf Bethlen István beszédei és írásai*, II, Budapest: Genius, 1933, 123.

reasons for this were very strict German sanitary regulations, and strongly protectionist German agrarian policy and the 1925 custom tariffs. By 1927, the Hungarian export of cattle was severely diminished, and other meat exports were also significantly reduced. Thus, from 1925 onward, the Hungarian government constantly lobbied for the revision of the 1920 commercial treaty, and the signing of a mutually beneficial new trade agreement. But, because Germany was satisfied with the situation, and also had no interest in improving political relations with Hungary, Berlin seemed to constantly postpone such decisions. Preparatory talks remained in preliminary stages until 1930.[22]

The problem surrounding Burgenland was that Hungary never gave up hope to recover this territory, transferred to Austria in 1921, which was mainly inhabited by Germans. The Hungarian press often published articles about righteous Hungarian claims towards Austria, and Bethlen and his Foreign Ministers also made such comments. The Hungarian political elite hoped that if Hungary acknowledged the *Anschluss*, Germany would return Burgenland. But, German political leadership considered the territory – with Austria – as part of Greater Germany. Paul Löbe, the Reichstag President, declared in his speech at Kismarton in 1928 that not only the 6 million Austrians, but also the 60 million Germans stood for this province. Stresemann, when the Austrian Chancellor notified him about the Hungarian claims, exclaimed in outrage: 'I never promised Burgenland to the Hungarians, and I am ready to declare this publically.' However, in order to avoid further deterioration of their relationship, both parties refrained from openly raising the issue.[23]

Because of German ambivalence towards Hungarian revisionist foreign policy, by the end of the 1920s, the Berlin-Budapest 'friendly' relationship cooled. The initial friendship towards Germany, both in the Hungarian press and the public, was replaced by disappointment. The head of the Hungarian Telegraph Agency, Miklós Kozma noted in his diaries in November 1928: 'For two years public opinion has noted Germany abandoning its traditional friendship towards Hungary;' moreover, he added, 'there is such [a] difference between the *Erfüllungspolitik* ('policy of fulfilment') and Hungarian policy, that the Hungarian public, whose perceptions are based on German-Hungarian comradeships, cannot understand it.'[24]

German diplomats delegated to the region, in particular German Minister in Budapest Hans Schoen (1926–33), had also perceived this change of tone. In

---

22 Fejes Judit, *Magyar-német kapcsolatok 1928–1932*. Budapest: Akadémiai, 1981, 26–55.
23 *ADAP*, Serie B. Bd. III. 212 and 218–20, also Bd. X. 341–4.
24 Adatgyűjtemény. 12 November 1928 and Berlini út, 18–27 Nov. 1928 // Magyar

their reports in 1929, they kept repeating 'the Hungarian government is dissatisfied with the German government,' 'Hungary cannot expect anything from Germany,' and thus 'Hungary gradually distanced itself from Germany and slowly became our enemy.'

In order to strengthen these notions, Bethlen exaggerated French overtures to Hungary aimed at political cooperation. In front of German diplomats, Bethlen pretended that he was very interested in this French policy. As a result of these, Hans Schoen recommended the extension of German-Hungarian trade and the invitation of Bethlen to Berlin.[25] The recommendations of Schoen and others were not without effect. However, until the death of Stresemann in October 1929, and even under the great coalition cabinet of Hermann Müller (1928–30), which also included the Social Democrats, German policy towards Hungary did not change until such as time when the foreign ministerial post was replaced by the conservative Heinrich Brüning (March 1930). As a foreign policy report noted in August 1929: 'The German *Reich* cannot provide any assistance for Hungary to fulfil its foreign political goals, which are often non-compatible with German aims.'[26]

1929–32: Rethinking *Mitteleuropa* policy and the first attempts to realise this concept

In late 1929-early 1930, German foreign policy changed, signalled by the changes of officials: Hermann Müller was replaced as the head of the government by Brüning, Stresemann was replaced by Julius Curtius (1929–31) then later by Konstantin von Neurath (1932–38), Secretary of State for Foreign Affairs Carl von Schubert was also replaced by Bernhardt von Bülow (1930–36). The difference in political thought was that while Stresemann aimed to achieve his goals in cooperation with the French within the framework of the Versailles treaty, Brüning and Curtius aimed for revision with contesting the international status quo. As a result of these changes, German policy shifted towards an anti-French course. Regarding South-East Europe, this shift was manifested in the changing nature of German policy; after that, economic policy became more and more a political instrument. Thus, political ambivalence and neutrality had stopped. The slogan, as German historian Dirk Stegman highlighted, once again became German dominated *Mitteleuropa*. Accordingly, German policy returned to pre-war multi-nation

---

Országos Levéltár (hereafter, MOL), K 429 Kozma Miklós iratai, 2. Csomó.
25   Koester, 18 July 1929; Zechlin, 4 August 1929; Curtius, 12 January 1930 // AA, Politische Abteilung II. Ungarn Pol. 2. Bd. 3.
26   *Die politische Lage in Südeuropa*, 28 August 1929 // AA, Generell. Pol. 4 Balkan Bd. 3.

based principles. Apart from the liberal economic thought of the 1920s, autarchy once again became acceptable, and not only in the circles and clubs of the intelligentsia, such as the '*Tat*,' the club of Hans Zehrer and Ferdinand Fried, but among the influential industrial and financial elites also. The CEO of one of the most important heavy industry associations, the *Langmanverein*, Max Schlenker was convinced that the priority of German policy should be to integrate the ten small '*mittel*' states towards the Black Sea with Germany in a customs union. This would create an economic space, he argued, which would surpass the population of the United States, and would rival France's current political and military hegemony. A. Heinrichbauer, a major coal industry figure, demanded the same. German policy, he noted, should aim to culturally and economically integrate these ten small countries into the German sphere with economic incentives. A little later in 1931, Carl Duisburg, another influential industrialist, argued for 'a closed economic sphere stretching from Bordeaux to Sofia,' because, as he wrote, only this could give the economic background to 'Europe, which it needs for retaining its role in the World.'[27]

In the government and the diplomatic core, several ambassadors, Under-Secretary of State for Foreign Affairs Bülow, and primarily, the Minister for the Economy Hermann Dietrich belonged to Germany's more active and offensive South-East European policy group. Summarising different influences coming from the economy and the diplomatic core, Bülow wrote in his memorandum to Brünning in August 1930: 'More likely than in any other part of Europe, the affairs of South-East Europe are in a ductile and fluid state. German policy has to take the initiative, as Germany's future lies in that region.'[28]

Regional economic difficulties, which the Great Depression further exacerbated, helped these German aims. South-East European stability in the 1920s was based on Western financial aid. Germany, also needing financial subvention, missed out on that opportunity. Germany acquired a key position in this equation when it became a market for South-East European export, which these countries needed to pay back Western loans. During the crisis, when demand decreased worldwide, the German market became vital for South-East Europe. Germany thus acquired an economic weapon, something it did not possess in the 1920s. German intentions and the internal

---

27   Dirk Stegman, 'Mitteleuropa 1925–1934: Zum Problem der Kontinuitat deutscher Aussenhandelpolitik von Stresemann bis Hitler,'in: *Industrielle Gesellschaft und politisches System*. Bonn: Verlag Neue Gesellschaft, 1978, 203–21; Roswitha Berndt, 'Wirtschaftliche Mitteleuropaplane des deutschen Imperialismus 1926–1931,' in: *Grundfragen der Deutschen Aussenpolitik seit 1871*. Darmstadt: Wissenschaftliche Buchgesellschaft, 1975, 305–34.
28   Hans Jurgen Schroeder, 'Deutsches Sudosteuropapolitik 1929–1936,' *Geschichte und Gesellschaft* 1(1976), 10–3.

problems of South-East Europe – as the historian György Ránki pointed out three decades ago – coincided.[29]

The first sign of the change of German intentions in South-East Europe was the surprise declaration of the German-Austrian customs union in March 1931. Concurrently, trade relations with South-East European countries were reviewed and reorganized. Accepting complaints coming from the region, and overcoming the resistance of the German agrarians, Germany signed trade agreements with Hungary on 27 June 1931, and on 18 July 1931 with Romania. These provided advantages for live animal export from both countries to Germany. Hungary and Romania returned the favour by providing custom preferences and reductions for German industrial imports. These ended the principle of 'greatest preference,' and free unrestricted trade, and pointed towards the autarchic trading policy of the *Third Reich*.[30]

In 1931, this German trade offensive met the rigid resistance of the victor powers of the Great War. Germany did not only have to step back on the customs union with Austria, but could not even ratify the preferential treaties. Thus, between 1930 and 1932, there was still a gulf between German ambitions in South-East Europe and political realities. Briand's plan in 1930, just like the one of Tardieu in 1932, for a regional political and economic cooperation under French leadership and with the exclusion of Germany failed – just like the British plan for a Danubian customs union. The German position, which now openly confronted the French, had the elements that 'the economic union of the Danubian states without Germany is the union of these states against Germany,' and that 'the prerequisite of a just and stable European status quo is the formation of a German sphere of influence.'[31]

The tool of any German defence against French and British plans was the instrumentalisation of the antagonism of the Central and South-East European states in the region. As well as the argument that the breaking of these ties was not in the interests of these countries either. In this respect, it based this policy on Sofia in the Balkans, and on Budapest in the Danubian basin. This however, meant that the role of Hungary in German foreign policy had to be reviewed.

The first sign of this re-evaluation was the invitation of Bethlen to Berlin in

---

29 Ránki György, 'Hitel vagy piac,' in: *Mozgásterek, kényszerpályák*, Budapest: Magvető, 1983, 341–82.
30 Schroeder, *Deutsches Sudosteuropapolitik*, 15–6. For the German-Hungarian treaty, see: Fejes, *Magyar-német kapcsolatok*, 121–37.
31 Ránki György, *Gazdaság és külpolitika*. Budapest: Magvető, 1981, 112–220 (117).

November 1930. Since the war, he was the first statesman from the region to enjoy the hospitality of the German government. His reception was tellingly cordial. The press, which previously struck a critical tone about him and his political system, now presented the territorial losses of Trianon and the achievements of his consolidating efforts, and referring to the centuries old special relationship it noted that both states belonged to the same camp in European politics. The same tone described the comments of German politicians. For example, in the toast of Chancellor Brünning, phrases such as 'comradeship' and 'German-Hungarian eternal friendship' dominated to such an extent that Bethlen could have said it.

What was more important than diplomatic niceties was that at this time the foreign policy of both countries were discussed to a great extent. The basis for Curtius was – and this was the declaration of the new foreign political doctrine – that in the most important questions, such as revisionism and disarmament, German policy went parallel with that of Hungary. Although he added that Germany did not contemplate the creation of a new alliance system, but hoped that in time, cooperation between Hungary and Germany would be closer.[32]

The first sign of a German-Hungarian rapprochement was the signing of the 1931 commercial treaty, which did not come into force. In this same period numerous ministerial telegrams and internal documents dealt with the current and future role of Hungary in Germany's South-East European policy. In these, Hungary appeared as the natural ally and instrument of German penetration. As the head of the department, Gerhardt Köpke, instructed the German ministers in Budapest and Belgrade in January 1931: 'Weakening the French alliance system in East-Central Europe is our mutual aim with Hungary; thus, we wish success for Hungary's aim to weaken the Little Entente.' Schoen replied to the circular telegram: 'It seems to me also that we have to consider Poland and the Little Entente as the integral parts of the French alliance system, whose weakening is in our interest. This is the reason why we have to welcome and support the strengthening of Hungary.'[33]

Of course, German and Hungarian interests did not fully coincide. As Curtius mentioned during his negotiations with Bethlen, Poland, who was Hungary's friend, was the primary target of German revisionism. Morever, Hungarian

---

32   Bundesarchiv, Koblenz R 43. I/157. 13–14 and 36–54. For the reaction of the German press: Zentrales Staatsarchiv, Potsdam. 61 Re. Pressarchiv Nr. 491. B. 9234., 88–105. A summary of the meeting has been published in: *Iratok az ellenforradalmi rendszer történetéhez*. Volume 4. Budapest: Kossuth, 1967, 450–6.
33   *ADAP*, Serie B. Bd. XVI. 464–5. The correspondence was analysed in detail by Fejes, *Magyar-német kapcsolatok*, 98–100.

revisionist aims in Romania and Yugoslavia were not in Germany's interest. And finally, in the question of Burgenland, a collision was dormant between Hungary and Germany. Thus, long term German and Hungarian interests only coincided in Czechoslovakia. For this reason, the leaders of the *Auswärtiges Amt* (Ministry of Foreign Affairs) rejected the November 1932 recommendation of its Envoy in Budapest that the Hungarians should be notified that their aims for natural frontiers would be supported. Instead, on 1 December 1932, the policy towards Hungary was summed up as:

> The importance of Hungary in German foreign policy is that it is our natural ally in the two most big political questions, which have importance for Germany's recovery, namely disarmament and the revision of frontiers. [...] Regarding frontier revision, the specific aims of these two countries are different, but the common aim is to initiate the revision at any point in the frontiers. The differences in the specific aim have the consequence that the two countries cannot actively support each other.[34]

The increased political significance of Hungary coincided with the increase of its economic weight. The aim to transform bilateral trade relations to a regional economic cooperation meant that geographical positions became more important, especially Hungary's central geographical situation on the continent. With this tendency, although still only in the sphere of planning, Budapest regained its role as a link between the Central European centre and the Balkans. The aforementioned December 1932 report noted:

> Our special economic interests in Hungary exists because Hungary is situated in the heart of South-East Europe, in the part of Europe, which due to its location we believe would become the market of our industry. Moreover, Hungary is directly adjacent to Austria and lays in the line of the trajectory of our natural economic expansion, and that any combination of economic collaboration depends on its collaboration. Thus, it is our crucial aim to deepen our economic relations with Hungary.

The new policy of Germany towards Hungary was received amicably and with satisfaction by the leadership in Budapest. 'The ice has been broken in Germany. French dominance is over, it is over that German-Hungarian friendship will be looked upon as a nuisance' – wrote Miklós Kozma, reflecting

---

34   Notizen, 26 November 1932 and Aktenvermerk, 1 December 1932 // AA, Politische Abteilung II. Ungarn. Pol. 2 Bd. 4.

on Bethlen's invitation to Berlin and his friendly reception in Berlin, in his diaries. The public, as well as Kozma, believed that German-French antagonism would be soon replaced by a German-Italian rapprochement, which would have automatically meant that Hungary would have gained more importance and that the subject of revision would become active again.[35]

1933–1937: Organising the economy of South-East Europe

According to traditional viewpoints, Adolf Hitler's accession to power divides the history of Germany between 1919 and 1944 into two eras: the one of the Weimar Republic and the other of Nazi Germany. More recently, German and international historiographies contest this distinct periodisation. They point out that the two eras are much more interlinked than the earlier German post-war historiography admitted, largely preoccupied with the identity crisis of Germany and which called Nazism an error (*Betriebsunfall*). These new historiographies also point out that Nazi Germany also has its own distinctly separate eras.

Regarding our topic of the development of German policy towards South-East Europe, the questioning of this periodisation is perfectly valid. Nazi South-East European policy continued without the interruption of the Danubian and Balkan policy of the late Weimar Republic. South-East Europe was just as important for the Nazis as for the industrialists and foreign political leaders of the Weimar Republic between 1929 and 1932. Otto Wilhelm Wagener, the head of the economic office of the National Socialist German Worker's Party (NSDAP) noted on 23 November 1931: 'If the living space of the people was not enough, National socialism would not be afraid to acquire territory with force. [...] Germany has to form a strong economic body with the Balkans, Scandinavia and perhaps even with England. The psychological and material reserves of this autarchic organisation will guarantee it advantage over other autarchies.' Werner Deitz, the 'great economic sphere' expert of the party was thinking along the same lines. The primary aim of Nationalist Socialist Germany – he noted before the Nazi accession to power – should be to penetrate Central and East-Central Europe as a whole, including South-East Europe, and to economically link the national economies here to the German political and economic sphere.[36] Hitler himself – in the spirit of *Mein Kampf*, as well as the so-called Second Book – summarized his foreign political aims

---

35 Adatgyűjtemény, 10–13 December 1930 // MOL, K 429. Kozma Miklós iratai, 3. csomó.
36 Bernd-Jürgen Wendt, "Mitteleuropa' – Zur Kontinuität der duetschen Raumpolitik im zwanzigsten Jahrhundert,' in: Wolfgang Bachofer and Holger Fischer (eds.), *Ungarn, Deutschland. Studien zu Sprache, Kultur, Geographie und Geschichte*. München: Trofenik, 1983. 299–304, (quotations on page 318).

to the chiefs of staff of the *Wehrmacht* immediately after his accession to power as: 'uncompromising Germanisation, finding new export opportunities and new leaving space in the East.'[37]

The ideas of the traditional (industrial and diplomatic) and National Socialist elites about *Mitteleuropa* and South-East Europe had not only similarities, but also had dissimilarities. For the elites of the industry, the bank sector and the Foreign Ministry acquiring *Mitteleuropa* was a peaceful economic goal that would have respected national sovereignty in the region. In this respect, this can be considered as the continuation of pre-war liberal imperialist aims. But, the Nazi's *Mitteleuropa* concept was permeated with racial and hegemonic ideas, which considered acquiring the territories of inferior people not only as a necessity but the duty of the superior Germanic race. Clearly, such plans were similar to the pan-German ideologies of the early 20th century.

In the final years of the 1930s, and particularly during WWII, these differences became more prominent and clear for everyone. However, immediately after the accession to power of the Nazis in 1933, the similarities were more prominent. Practically, the same people conducted the late Weimar (between 1930 and 1932) and the early Nazi foreign policy. Also, until the end of the 1930s the foreign policy tools did not change (political pressure through economic means, and the instrumentalisation of German national minorities). The new policy of the Nazis was summarized at the 7 April cabinet meeting: 'We have to attempt helping Yugoslavia and Romania economically, firstly in order to achieve political influence there, as well as to secure these countries as export markets. At the moment, it is very difficult, for the same reasons as in the case of Hungary. But we have to give it a try, and if necessary, export reductions have to be provided for their export oriented economies.'[38]

Breaking the hegemony of the German agrarians, Hitler took the side of the industrialists and the Foreign Ministry. Thus, Germany concluded bilateral economic treaties with the countries of the region between 1933 and 1935. These treaties expanded the 1931 preferential agreements, which now provided barter trade for the agricultural products and raw materials of the South-East European region to Germany, as well as opened these markets for German industrial products. These treaties were beneficial for South-East Europe, as they now allowed the regional countries to come out of the recession and for their economies to grow. The treaties were also beneficial for Germany, as it, in a matter of years, became dominant both as an exporter and an importer. In 1932, the German economy was only responsible for 10% to 25% of the export and import of the region. In 1938–1939 this was 40% to

---

37   Hillgruber, *Die gescheiterte Grossmarcht*, 77.
38   Ránki, *Gazdaság és külpolitika*, 235–6.

55%, and in the case of Bulgaria 65% to 70%. However, the proportion of German imports from Hungary, Bulgaria, Romania and Yugoslavia was still below 10% in 1938, and only grew beyond 10% after 1939. With this, Germany acquired an effective weapon, which could have injured the countries of South-East Europe, without allowing them to respond effectively.[39]

Like previously, German ethnic minorities also played a key role in Nazi South-East European policy. Instead of the social and state organisation, which Hitler deemed too bureaucratic and ineffective, Nazi leadership created a new central organisation, the *Volksdeutsche Mittelstelle* (Coordination Centre for Ethnic Germans), with Joachim von Ribbentrop, the future Foreign Minister, as head. Moving beyond the traditional policy of the protection of minorities, the new organisation envisaged the ethnic Germans to become the 5th column of Nazi Germany. Apart from using it for intelligence purposes, it was utilized to popularize Nazi ideology, as well as for political pressure. These were discouraged not only by Hungarian authorities but other countries of the region as well, and often led to a cooling of the relationship with the Third Reich.[40]

The instrumentalisation of economic policy and ethnic German minorities for Germany's penetration was coupled with the strengthening of scientific and cultural ties. In the capitals of the region, German cultural institutions and German language schools were founded, funds for Humboldt and other scholarships were increased and academic exchanges became more regular. Cultural, artistic and scientific cooperation became particularly significant in the Hungarian and Bulgarian context, while Romania's and Yugoslavia's traditional Francophile orientations held back expansion to some extent. Evidently, the aim of German cultural diplomacy was to prepare the region culturally and linguistically, and to use the German language in the long run as a *lingua franca*.[41]

The Hungarian leadership of the 1930s welcomed the strengthening of economic and cultural ties, and after the accession of Hitler to power it hoped that political cooperation would also be expanded. They hoped that Germany, just like Italy, would also support Hungarian revisionist ambitions, the creation of a 'strong Hungary in its traditional historical area, the Carpathian basin.' In

---

39   Ránki, *Gazdaság és külpolitika*, 247–349, and more recently Othmar Nikola Haberl, 'Südoseuropa und das Deutsche Reich vor dem zweiten Weltkrieg,' *Südosteuropa*, 39/9(1990): 514–25.
40   Raymond Poidevin, *Die unruhige Grossmacht*. Freiburg-Würzburg, 1985, 181–91.
41   Mackensen, 15 October 1934 // AA, Politische Abteilung II. Ungarn. Pol. 2. Bd.

his 14 February letter to Hitler in 1934, Hungary's Premier Gyula Gömbös (1932–36) argued that the restoration of historic Greater Hungary is not only in Hungary's interest, but also essential for German imperial policy, because 'only a strong Hungarian state could check the unwarranted ambition of a small nation against Germany and Hungary.'[42] So called 'coffee-house foreign policy-makers,' who were politically less educated, even called for and fantasised about a German-Hungarian empire in these years, and worked on plans, which, if created, would 'even take the breath away of the enemies of Germany and Hungary, and as such would push European policy into a different direction.'[43]

However, the Hungarian leadership and the 'coffee-house foreign policy-makers' soon became disillusioned. If Stresemann and Brüning strictly followed a policy in the interest of Germany, altruistic attitudes were even further from the perceptions of Adolf Hitler. On the basis of the notion that Hungarian (and Bulgarian) revisionism would not weaken but in fact strengthen the cooperation of the Little Entente, the National Socialist leadership, similarly to the Weimar Republic, rejected Hungarian propositions for the creation of a revisionist bloc, and thus the possibilities of a closer German-Hungarian cooperation. Thus, Berlin, both in 1934 and 1936, rejected Hungarian propositions for an anti-Little Entente consultative treaty. 'If we were to agree to the Hungarian proposal' – commented Baron Neurath in 1936 – 'we would strengthen the cooperation of the Western powers and the Little Entente.'[44] Similarly to Bülow, Hitler also recognised the German-Hungarian mutual revisionist interests against Czechoslovakia. In his conferences with Hungarian politicians – such as with Prime Minister Gyula Gömbös in 1933 and 1935, or with the regent Miklós Horthy (1920–44) in 1936 and with Prime Minister Kálmán Darányi (1936–38) in 1937 – the Führer stressed that 'Hungary should concentrate all her efforts against Czechoslovakia, and that 100% revisionist aims are hopeless.' Contrastingly, the Serbian and Romanian leaders were assured that Germany did not 'support Hungarian revisionist ambitions without reservations.'[45] The same opinion is reflected in the comments of other leaders of the Nazi Empire about

---

5., and also, Büro des Staatssekretarärs. R. 29784. 28 April 1939. Anlage 4.
42   György Ránki (et al.), *A Wilhelmstrasse és Magyarország*. Budapest: Kossuth, 1968, 67. For the foreign policy of Gömbos, see: Pál Pritz, *Magyarország külpolitikája Gömbös Gyula miniszterelnöksége idején 1932–1936*. Budapest 1982.
43   Nagy Sándor Zoltán and dr. Horváth Kálmán, Letters to Adolf Hitler, 14 February 1935, 11 October 1934 // AA, Politische Abteilung II. Pol. 2. Ungarn. Bd. 5.
44   Minute by Neurath, 4 May 1936 // AA, Politische Abteilung II. Pol. 2. Ungarn. Bd. 5; Minute by Bülow, 11 January 1934 // AA, Geheimakten. Ungarn. Pol. 2. 2. R. 30513.
45   Andreas Hillgruber, *Deusche Aussenpolitik im Donauraum 1930 bis 1939*. In: *Die Zerstörung Europas*. Frankfurt-Berlin, 1988. 140; Andreas Hillgruber, 'Deutschland

South-East Europe. In the autumn of 1934, at the funeral of the Yugoslav king Alexander I, Hermann Göring declared that Germany was not a revisionist state and would not 'pull chestnuts out of the fire' for Budapest. Evidently, he aimed to reduce Serbian and Romanian suspicions towards German policy. The ideologue of the Nazi party, Alfred Rosenberg, in articles on 15 November 1936, as well as in October 1937 noted that supporting wider revisionist ambitions were not in the interest of Germany. The choice of words made it clear that it was addressed to Budapest, Belgrade and Bucharest.[46]

The Hungarian press always reacted with tension to such articles and comments. German responses to Hungarian protests were initially characterised by a patronizing tone. But as the Hungarian protests became more frequent, German responses became brusquer. 'It is tiring that I have to comment on our relationship with Hungary every other month' – exclaimed Neurath after his interview with Hungarian Minister Döme Sztójay (1936–44) on 15 January 1937.[47]

The seemingly minor dispute between Hungary and Germany in the 1930s regarding the geographical location of Hungary was a sign of bigger and more severe underlying issues. As noted earlier, after 1918, according to German perceptions, Hungary belonged to South-East Europe, and some interpretations even placed it in the Balkans. This notion already existed in Germany in the 1920s and also appeared in textbooks in the 1930s. One of the elementary textbooks in 1932, for example, wrote about Hungary:

> From a one hour train ride to the East of Vienna, this purely German city [is where], the real Balkans starts. Here lays Hungary with it plains and gypsies, fleas and cockroaches. The Hungarian nation is sentimental and melancholic, as well as raw and impulsive. [...] Austria-Hungary was more like a political union of a dual monarchy than an organic one. Deep inside, Hungarians are closer to the peoples of the Balkans than to our beloved compatriot Austrians.[48]

Comments such as these, similar to the one of Göring and Ribbentrop, were

---

und Ungarn, 1933–1944,' *Wehrwissenschaftliche Rundschau*, 1 (1959), 653–4; Martin Broszat, 'Deutschland-Ungarn-Rumanien,' *Historische Zeitschrift*, 206 (1968), 45–52.

46   Broszat, 'Deutschland-Ungarn-Rumanien,' 49–53: in more detail see: Pritz, *Magyarország külpolitikája*, 203–19.

47   Minute by Neurath, 15 January 1937 // AA, Politische Abteilung IV. Pol. 2. Ungarn. Bd. 1.

48   Minute by Schoen, 8 February 1932 // AA, Politische Abteilung II. Ungarn Pol. 2. Bd. 4.

often the subject of Hungarian protests and press reactions. But this was all in vain. From the German perspective, Hungary remained as one of the countries of the Balkans, while according to Hungarian categorization it was East-Central European or at least Northern Danubian. '[T]hey should not speak of Hungary as it belonged to the South-East European region or South-East Europe. Hungary does not consider itself a Balkan nation, and it upsets her if it is categorized as such,' informed Sztójay in the spring of 1934. Later, this became the subject of very serious parliamentary debate in Budapest, and a prominent Member of Parliament Tibor Eckhardt considered it in 1937 to be one of the reasons for the cooling of Hungarian-German relations.[49] Because of the differences in revisionist ambitions, and the different Hungarian and German interpretations of Hungary's role in South-East Europe, by 1936–37, public sympathy towards Germany, similar to the 1920s, decreased and, moreover, in some circles, reached rock bottom. It is increasingly difficult to conduct a pro-German policy, noted Hungary's Foreign Minister Kálmán Kánya (1933–38) to the *Völkischer Beobachter* in January 1937, because 'it became customary to refer to Hungary in Germany as a scapegoat, and to celebrate Romanians as heroes and Yugoslavs as Gods.'[50] Similarly to Bethlen's attempts at a rapprochement with France and Poland in 1928–29, Hungarian diplomacy after 1933 also experimented with black-mailing the *Wilhelmstrasse* in such ways. 'If Germany does not abandon its friendly relations with Yugoslavia, we would form a Danubian alliance with Czechoslovakia and Austria, and as such will block the Danubian region from Berlin,' the Hungarian Envoy to Berlin, Szilárd Masirevich (1933–36), conveyed to the German foreign minister in November 1934. The Hungarian diplomat lost his job as a result of his mischievous comment. However, his superior, Kálmán Kánya, repeated the warnings. 'The German notion that Hungary relies on the *Reich* is completely wrong. If tendencies continue, there is a strong possibility for the complete redirection of Hungarian foreign policy: complete separation from the *Reich* and normalizing relations with Hungary's neighbours. It should not be believed that this is impossible.'[51]

Dissatisfaction with German policy led to attempts at a rapprochement with the Little Entente in 1938. However, neither these nor the earlier Hungarian warnings changed the course of German policy. In Berlin they knew all too well that Hungary would not be able to renounce revision, and that France and the Little Entente would never fulfil these ambitions. To Masirevich's protest, Neurath mockingly replied that 'he agrees to a Hungarian alliance

---

49   Minute by Köpke, 9 March 1934 // AA, Politische Abteilung II. Ungarn Pol. 2. Bd. 5; Minute by Ermannsdorff, 10 September 1937// AA, Politische Abteilung IV. Pol. 2. Ungarn Bd. 2.
50   *A Wilhelmstrasse és Magyarország*, 199.
51   *A Wilhelmstrasse és Magyarország*, 88, 89, compare to 199; Pritz, *Magyarország külpolitikája*, 210–4.

with the 'beloved Czechs.' 'I do not know where Hungary would get support for its revisionist ambitions, if it would not get it from us,' he noted elsewhere.[52]

In the context of the cooling bilateral relationship, Germany did not support the 'separatist' aims of the German national minorities, which were now beyond cultural aims, to the extent they were supported in Czechoslovakia and Poland. Hitler's directive in relation to this was that the Hungarian minority question should not be handled in a way that it would burden the German-Hungarian relationship.[53] Regardless of this, a pan-German imperial propaganda was continued with the same intensity, and the differences between the German ethnic minorities and the Hungarian government escalated. At the end of 1935, the extensive German state subvention of the Swabians in Hungary was revealed, and the Hungarian government arrested German students distributing propaganda material in Swabian villages.[54] However, direct meddling into the internal affairs of Hungary – as well as into the affairs of the three other South-East European states – was not that extensive until 1938. Apart from economic and cultural expansion, the policy of *Deutschtum* manifested only very weakly, and the fascist Hungarian far-right also did not play a significant role. Hitler not only sympathized with Gömbös, but also believed that the following conservative Darányi cabinet was a better solution than the far-right opposition groups around Ferenc Szálasi.[55]

1938–1941: *Pax Germanica*, the creation of German political hegemony

In the mid-1930s a new era started in German foreign policy. Initially, the differences were more apparent in the tools utilised than in the goals. The creation of military alliances against the status quo, violence, the threat of military force and the *ultima ratio*, military action, were not used either between 1930 and 1932 or between 1933 to 1936. However, after 1936, these became the most important tools of German foreign policy. The first sign of change was the reintroduction of conscription in 1935. And then it was continued with the remilitarisation of the Rhineland, the initiations of the first four-year plan – to create the economic foundations of the *Blitzkrieg*, with

---

52   Minute by Neurath, 17 November 1934 // AA, Politische Abteilung II. Ungarn Pol. 2. Bd. 5; Minute by Neurath, 25 November 1936 // AA, Politische Abteilung IV. Ungarn. Bd. 1.
53   *A Wilhelmstrasse és Magyarország*, 90–1.
54   *A Wilhelmstrasse és Magyarország*, 13; compare to: Lóránt Tilkovszky, *Hét évtized a magyarországi németek történetéből 1919–1989*. Budapest: Kossoth, 1989, 73–92.
55   *A Wilhelmstrasse és Magyarország*, 269.

intervention in the Spanish Civil War, and with the Berlin-Roma axis and the Anti-Comintern pact with Japan. Both treaties, signed in November 1936, aimed to overthrow the *status quo* and to create a new world order. This new course, as in 1929 and 1930, coincided with the dismissal of officials both on the top and the middle structures of policy-making. Everybody who did not agree with the new course, or aimed to decelerate change had to leave. The conservative Neurath, who followed the Bismarckian tradition, was replaced with Ribbentrop – Hitler's political advisor – as head of the Foreign Ministry; and Baron Ernst Weizsacker became the new Under-Secretary of State. Economic Minister and Chairman of the *Reich Bank* Hjalmar Schacht, who was an advocate of the liberal-imperialist *Mitteleuropa*, was dismissed in 1937. After changes in the course of policy in 1935–36 and the replacement of officials in 1937–38 it soon became clear that the Nazi *Mitteleuropa* policy was very different from the conservative notions advocated by Curtius, Neurath and Bülow. It also became clear that for Hitler, *Mitteleuropa* was not the goal which would make Germany a world power, but was only a tool in achieving world dominance. Thus, this new course utilised new tools, and was the rethinking of old ambitions.[56]

This new course of German foreign policy was soon felt in policy towards South-East Europe. The shift occurred in 1938 with the *Anschluss* and the destruction of Czechoslovakia. The six war years after 1938 produced varied and radical shifts in German South-East European policy and more radical policies than those of the Weimar era and the mid-1930s. However, the aim to turn the region into the political and economic colony of German policy, and after 1941 the German army, was a common thread in this era. If this could not be achieved with 'peaceful' economic and political means, it was to be accomplished with the army through the occupation of reluctant countries.

Due to the nature of German policy, which aimed to adjust its tactics according to circumstances, plans about Hungary were also less rigid and changed constantly in reaction to circumstances and Hungarian policy. However, different German and Hungarian interpretations of Hungary's role in the region remained constant.

The source of the first minor disagreement was about the new German-Hungarian frontier. Of course, Hungary could not contemplate to protest the *Anschluss* in the spirit of the Italian-Austrian-Hungarian Agreement – signed in the 1930s – as Italy already acknowledged it. However, many felt that Hungary should have had its share of the 'loot.' Officially, through diplomatic channels, remembering earlier German rejections, Hungary did not raise the

---

56   Hillgruber, *Die gescheiterte Grossmarcht*, 78–85 and Wendt, 'Mitteleuropa', 325–9.

issue of Burgenland, but through unofficial means Hitler was notified that Hungary would consider it as a *'noble gesture'* if that strip of territory, or at least part of it, would be returned to Hungary. This provided ample opportunity for the German Under-Secretary of State to educate the Hungarian leadership about the ethnic composition of Burgenland, as well as to point out that 'territories in the South West of Lake Neusiedl (Fertő) are ethnically German,' and that the 'experts consider the circumstances of the 1921 plebiscite very questionable,' and thus it would be time that 'certain Hungarian circles would forget once and for all notions which are out of the question here.' Moreover, 'certain German circles' produced and distributed maps which depicted the Western Transdanubia *Deutsch-West-Ungarn* labelled as 'lost territories' – the Hungarian leadership decided to shelf the problem and never return to it.[57]

In his aim to destroy Czechoslovakia, Hitler hoped Hungary would play the role of agent provocateur. He wanted Hungary to be the sole aggressor, and thus the outbreak of conflict would have provided an opportunity for the German army to intervene. On this occasion, disregarding the ethnic principle, in return he offered Slovakia as a whole to Hungary. Certain circles in Hungary, especially the military, were keen for military action; the political elite – the Regent Horthy, the Prime Minister Béla Imrédy (1938–39) and the Foreign Minister Kánya – wary of the unfavourable international circumstances did not want to assume this role. However, they insisted on territorial claims for the entirety of Slovakia and Ruthenia, which went beyond the ethnic principle. This attitude upset Hitler, who, between the Munich Conference of 29 September 1938 and the First Vienna Award of 2 November 1938, where Southern Slovakia was attached to Hungary, noted maliciously to Hungarian politicians lobbying in Berlin: 'If there were a war, Hungary could have received Slovakia as a whole.' 'Now, Hungary has to adapt to the possibilities.' 'The Slovaks' – he continued his monologue – 'now want to become independent and do not want to unite with Hungary.' Thus, it was impossible and pointless to enforce a plebiscite on the Slovaks – from which Hungary hoped to regain the Northern territories mostly inhabited by Slovaks.[58]

German-Hungarian disputes about the future of Ruthenia continued after the First Vienna Award. After the Hungarian occupation of Southern Slovakia in November 1938, the Hungarian public – as the German Minister in Budapest Otto von Erdmannsdorff (1937–41) also reported – demanded 'Everything Back!,' 'Give Bratislava Back!,' 'Common Hungarian-Polish Border!,' and it

---

57   AA, Politische Abteilung II. Ungarn Pol. 2. Bd. 2 ; *A Wilhelmstrasse és Magyarország*, 265.
58   *A Wilhelmstrasse és Magyarország*, 303–6, compare to: Juhász Gyula: *Magyarország külpolitikája 1919–1945*. Budapest. Kossuth, 1988, 186–95.

was rumoured that if it was only up to Italy, Hungary would have got back much more. Bethlen's usual New Year's Day article in the *Pesti Napló* reacted to this, where he even accused Berlin of betraying Hungarian interests.[59] For such communications, the German diplomacy reacted with increased frustration and anger. 'In Hungary, now they are talking about the great 1000 year old Kingdom of St Stephen. 'However, I' – noted Hitler to the momentary Foreign Minister István Csáky in January 1939 – 'could counter these demands with greater German demands.' It was this same rejection that was reflected in the 2 February 1939 note of Hans Georg von Mackensen (1933–37), a former minister in Budapest: 'Hungary has to realise that its power is inadequate to conduct an imperial policy. Its insistence on Bratislava is not more than, for example, Italy insisting on Bratislava because it was part of the Roman Empire.' Hitler however noted that he does not necessarily insist on the ethnographic principle in the case of Hungary. He also insisted that 'deviation from the ethnic principle in favour of the historical one can only be achieved together, because success can only be guaranteed with the close coordination of actions.'[60]

The 'close coordination of actions' – Hungary's political adjustment to Nazi Germany was readily accommodated by the Béla Imrédy government. In late 1938, it agreed to the legalisation of the *Volksbund*, the National Socialist organisation of ethnic Germans in Hungary, and on 24 February 1939, it joined the Anti-Comintern Pact. At the same time, Budapest promised to leave the League of Nations. It completely abandoned this anti-Nazi Western international organisation on 11 April 1939. As a reward, as well as to share the responsibility, Hitler agreed to the Hungarian occupation of the mostly Ruthenian inhabited Subcarpathian Ruthenia on 15–16 March 1939. This action was a part of a Czechoslovakia destruction operation, which also included the creation of Germany's Protectorate of Bohemia and Moravia and the independent Slovak State.[61]

With the Austrian *Anschluss* in 1938 and the establishment of the Protectorate of Bohemia and Moravia in 1939, the core of the greater-German *Mitteleuropa* was created. As a result, the French security system collapsed; the elbowroom of the states of South-East Europe was now reduced to a minimum. Winston Churchill accurately noted at the end of 1938, that the Danube valley until the Black Sea, now lay open before Hitler; and Ribbentrop

---

59   Report by Ermannsdorff, 12 November 1938 // AA, Politische Abteilung IV. Ungarn Pol. 2. Bd. 2; Count István Bethlen, 'Az új esztendő küszöbén,' Pesti Napló, 1 January 1939.
60   A Wilhelmstrasse és Magyarország, 343–5 and 356.
61   In more detail, see: Lóránt Tilkovszky, *A revízió és nemzetiségpolitika Magyarországon 1938–1941*, Budapest: Akadémiai, 1967; and Juhász, *Magyarország külpolitikája*, 199–214.

in April 1939 claimed that 'South-East Europe is our sphere of influence.'[62] The opportunity to tighten economic relations with the region, and to expand political influence there as far as possible was taken by the Germans.

In the economic sphere, Germany already had a dominating role in most countries of the region since the 1933–36 clearing treaties. Although these treaties created dependency and conserved outdated structures, they were still based on mutual benefits, and did not cause the direct exploitation of the region. However, the 1938–40 treaties did not aim to secure mutual markets, but to totally integrate the national economies into the German dominated greater regional economic sphere. Hitler openly declared this aim in regards to Romania: 'It would be better for Romania to immediately renounce its plans for industrialization. It should direct its agricultural products to the German market. In return, we will supply industrial products.'[63] However, the German government did not need to put much pressure in order to conclude such treaties, because for these countries the German market was essential. Some countries, like Hungary, even asked Germany to sign such treaties. Their dissatisfaction only mounted during WWII when Germany was not able to supply these countries with industrial products anymore, and, in effect, forced a zero percent trade credit on them.[64]

From the political point of view, Berlin's aim in 1938–1941 was adhering Romania and Yugoslavia – as it already did with Hungary and Bulgaria – closer to the German sphere of influence. In order to ensure undisturbed economic cooperation with these countries, Germany still refused to endorse Hungarian and Bulgarian revisionist ambitions, and supported a rapprochement on the basis of the *status quo*. Consequently, in the second part of 1938, Yugoslavia and Romania moved closer to Germany. For example, Romanian King Carol II (1930–40), during his visit to Hitler on 28 November 1938, declared, 'he wanted a closer cooperation with Germany.' However, after the destruction of Czechoslovakia, when Britain and France made a final attempt at blocking German penetration to the region, this process halted and reversed. In March 1939, similarly to Poland, Greece and Turkey, Romania also accepted the Anglo-French guarantee of its independence. Simultaneously, the pro-German Milan Stojadinović cabinet (1935–39) fell in Yugoslavia, and was replaced by the pro-Western and pro-Russian Dragiša Cvetković government (1939–41).[65]

---

62   Broszat, 'Deutschland-Ungarn-Rumanien,' 61; A *Wilhelmstrasse és Magyarország*, 385.
63   Ránki György, *A Harmadik Birodalom árnyékában*. Budapest: Magvető, 1988, 105.
64   Michael Riemenschneider, *Die deutsche Wirtschaftspolitik gegenüber Ungarn 1933–1944*, Frankfurt-Bern-New York-Paris: Peter Lang, 1987, 141–78.
65   Hillgruber, 'Deusche Aussenpolitik,' 142–4; Broszat, 'Deutschland-Ungarn-Ru-

Berlin looked unfavourably on these events. However, until economic cooperation was uninterrupted, and these governments did not attempt to bloc Romanian oil exports to Germany, the *Auswärtiges Amt* had no reason to change its policy towards South-East Europe. Thus, Hungarian and Bulgarian revisionists still did not get a green light. Hitler and Ribbentrop, like nothing happened, still suggested Hungarian-Yugoslav and Hungarian-Romanian rapprochement on the basis of the *status quo*.[66] Distancing their countries from Germany was not only the feature of Romanian and Yugoslav policy during the spring of 1939, but it was also the characteristic of the newly formed Pál Teleki government in Hungary in February 1939. The clearest signs of this were the refusal to participate in the Polish campaign and the refusal to allow German military passages through Hungary in the summer and autumn of 1939, respectively. Hungary followed this policy regardless of strong German military and political pressure. The temptation in this case was Slovakia, what Hitler now called a 'worthless salient.' Hitler also declared that for him 'Slovakia [was] only important militarily' and apart from this, for him 'the fate of Slovaks [was] irrelevant.'[67]

Between the Polish campaign in September 1939 and the Battle of France in May–June 1940, the maximal German aims in South-East Europe were Romanian-Hungarian and Yugoslav-Hungarian rapprochement, the minimal to guarantee peace. The Hungarian elite were receptive to an agreement with Yugoslavia, and did not step up against Romania with arms. However, they declared on every occasion that, 'Hungary had territorial claims on Romania,' 'Which had to be fulfilled before the end of the war.' For the sake of Balkan peace, Hitler rejected such demands until the summer of 1940. However, in the summer of 1940, rather unexpectedly, he changed his mind, and took on the role of arbitrator in the dispute. Paradoxically, the reason for his change of attitude was the same, which rejected dealing with the issue, peace in the Balkans and economic interests.[68]

The problem escalated with the Soviet threats to use force if Romania did not transfer Northern Bukovina and Bessarabia at the end of June 1940. In this situation Budapest wanted to move immediately. It increased Budapest's determination that it could seemingly count on Moscow's support. 'If we are leaving free reign to event, weapons will fire themselves here against Romania' – the German Envoy Erdmannsdorff in Budapest described the mood in Hungary on 2 July. But war would have undoubtedly meant the cessation of

---

manien,' 72–3.
66   *A Wilhelmstrasse és Magyarország*, 386, 418.
67   *A Wilhelmstrasse és Magyarország*, 419. In more detail, see: Manfred Nebelin, *Deutsche Ungarpolitik 1939–1941*, Opladen: Springer, 1989, 9–76.
68   *A Wilhelmstrasse és Magyarország*, 468, 501.

Romanian oil shipments to Germany and the penetration of the Red Army in the Balkans. Hitler could not allow either of these to happen. Romanian oil was as important to him as Swedish iron, and obviously, allowing the Soviet Union to take the initiative was not in his interest.[69]

Bucharest attempted to avert the immediate threat of frontier revision with a radical readjustment of its policy. On the 1st of July it renounced the British guarantee, and signalled that it was ready to follow the German line in its policy. However, pushing events into a different direction now proved impossible. The Second Vienna Award on 30 August 1940, elaborated by the German and Italian Foreign Ministers, created such a compromise between the Hungarian demands and the Romanian offer, which favoured Hungary. Regardless of the problems surrounding this arbitration, its ethnic basis was more justifiable than the Trianon frontiers. However, it cannot be said that ethnic justice was the aim of Hitler here. A few days after the arbitration, he noted to Sztójay: 'Our attitude in this case was not dictated by abstract notions, but by the oil question.' On another occasion he summarized the essence of his Romanian and Hungarian policy: 'keeping several irons in the fire we aimed to direct events according to German interests.'[70]

Hitler's calculation was correct. With the division of Transylvania he acquired a new weapon, which could be used against both countries effectively at any time. Consequently, these two countries embarked on a competition for the goodwill of Berlin, which was unprecedented among the allies of Nazi Germany. It was evident in the autumn of 1940 when, after the signing of the Tripartite Pact between Berlin, Rome and Tokyo; Hungary and Romania were competing with each other, and joined the pact only a few days apart. The same was repeated after the declaration of war against the Soviet Union in the summer of 1941. 'As the ally of Britain, Romania lost everything, now as the ally of the Axis, it will get everything back. This revisionism had started already,' Erdmannsdorff claimed on 18 July 1941, pointing to the pro-German characteristics of Romanian foreign policy.[71]

In autumn of 1940, the primary aim of German policy in South-East Europe was the involvement of Yugoslavia in the Nazi alliance system. The Yugoslav-Hungarian Treaty of Eternal Friendship was signed in this sense on the basis of the *status quo* in December 1940. This treaty, and Yugoslavia's adherence

---

69 A Wilhelmstrasse és Magyarország, 504, 516–7; compare to: Nebelin, Deutsche Ungarpolitik, 77–134.
70 A Wilhelmstrasse és Magyarország, 530; compare to: Nebelin, Deutsche Ungarpolitik, 149; Broszat, 'Deutschland-Ungarn-Rumanien,' 67.
71 Report by Ermannsdorff, 18 July 1941 // AA, Büro des Staatssekretars. Ungarn, R 29787.

to the Tripartite Pact on 25 March 1941, seemed to shelf Hungarian revisionist ambitions in that country indefinitely. But, the turn of events in Belgrade – the coup d'état on 27 March, and the Yugoslav Treaty of Friendship signed with the Soviet Union, pushed German policy towards Yugoslavia, and German perceptions about Hungarian revisionism, onto a different course. The Yugoslav coup, the failures of Italy in the Greek campaign started in October 1940, and the appearance of the British army and navy in the Aegean Sea threatened the rear of the envisioned campaign against the Soviet Union and the Balkans seemed to emerge as the base for a second front. To avoid this, Hitler immediately decided to destroy Yugoslavia, and to support Hungarian revisionist ambitions.

Such a level of understanding towards Hungary, and opinion about the leading role of Hungary in the Danubian region, had not been heard in Berlin until then. Even Hitler himself appraised the Hungarians. During one of his interviews with Sztójay Hitler said:

> He had two friends in the Balkans – Hungary and Bulgaria – and he cannot see why, now after such turn of events, the problems of these countries cannot be solved once and for all, [...] if there was to be a war, Hungary has Germany's support for her ambitions. And, regarding Hungary's ambitions to have an outlet in the Adriatic, Germany supports these wishes. Once and for all, he will cut out the Balkan's tumor. [...] Now, the time has come for making every injustice right. After all, historically, Germany and Hungary always belong together. Both countries face the enormous Slavic wave.[72]

The only reason for these promises, and the repetition of Hungarian arguments in Berlin, was to guarantee Hungarian participation in the war against Yugoslavia. Declining this or German military passage through Hungary – argued the historian Andreas Fritz Hillgruber – would certainly lead to the German invasion of Hungary also.[73] Fearing this, and of course in order to fulfil its territorial ambitions, regardless of London's warnings, Budapest decided to participate in the campaign. With promises to support Bulgarian ambitions for an outlet on the Aegean Sea, Germany was also able to convince Sofia to join the campaign.[74]

After the successful completion of the Marita campaign against Yugoslavia in April 1941, such encouragements to Hungary ended from Berlin. The

---

72   A Wilhelmstrasse és Magyarország, 562–3.
73   Hillgruber, 'Deutschland und Ungarn 1933–1944,' 661.
74   Detlef Vogel, 'Deutschland und Südosteuropa,' in: Wolfgang Michalka (ed.),

importance of Hungary diminished again and Hitler did not keep the promises he made to Hungary. The ethnically very mixed (Hungarian, Romanian, Serb and German) Banat, what he promised to Hungary, but what was also claimed by Romania, remained under German military administration. Hitler wanted to decide its fate only after the war. He also left the question of the Muraköz – north of the Drava – open, in order to ensure the security of the Csáktornya-Ljubljana-Fiume railway, what Hungary claimed on historical precedent. However, Zagreb claimed the territory on the ethnic principle. With this, Hitler also contributed to the escalation of the Hungarian-Croatian relationship, which started as friendly. Adding the Slovak-Hungarian and Romanian-Hungarian antagonisms, the resurgence of the Little Entente under German leadership became a reality. Such initiatives came from Slovakia in the summer of 1941, and gained positive reception both in Bucharest and Zagreb. Although a German veto stopped such initiatives, and as Ribbentrop said 'for the sake of winning the war, "domestic violence" has to cease,' but it remained informally in the politics of these three states towards Hungary. The difference between this alliance and the 1920s to 1930s Little Entente under French leadership was that the latter was a defensive cooperation on the basis of the *status quo*, but this new cooperation within the German alliance system was offensive and aimed to curtail Hungarian territorial gains. To this end, Romania was even inclined to involve Bulgaria in this alliance, and thus openly acknowledging the Bulgarian cession of Southern Dobruja.[75]

With the disintegration of Yugoslavia in April 1941, German hegemony in Europe became complete. Now political hegemony supplemented the already existing economic dominance. Slovakia and Croatia were only independent on paper and were puppet states, their existence completely depended on Hitler. The Serb territories were under German military administration and General Nedić's quisling government. The elbowroom of Bulgaria, Romania and Hungary were reduced to the minimum. Officially, Hungarian sovereignty was spared, but it depended on German interests.

1941–1944: Long term plans and immediate interests

Between the end of the Battle of France in the middle of 1940 and the bogging down of the Wehrmacht offensive at the gates of Moscow by the end of 1941, the departments of the German government worked out detailed plans about the working and structure of the European great economic sphere. As a common characteristic, these plans all considered South-East Europe one unit, and thus divided it not only from *Ostland* – the German

---

Der Zweite Weltkrieg. München-Zürich: Piper, 1989, 536.
75   *A Wilhelmstrasse és Magyarország*, 601, 628, also: Ránki, *A Harmadik Birodalom*, 122.

Lebensraum – but also from the otherwise closely integrated Western and Northern European states, which were closely integrated both politically and economically. The basis of former head of the Economic division, Karl Ritter's plan in the German Foreign Ministry was that economic and political dominance in South-East Europe was a long term interest, thus deepening cooperation in this region was not necessary. 'It would be enough – he noted – to preserve and develop the current level of relations.' The young, 34 year old economic expert of the Ministry of Economy, Gustav Schlotter – with the encouragement of Göring and Walter Funk (Reich Minister of Economics in 1938–45) – worked out a deeper plan for economic cooperation. According to his plans, South-East Europe should integrate to the future Central European German *Mitteleuropa* core with a custom and financial union.[76]

Leading Nazi politician Werner Best, governor of Denmark from 1942, thought about post-war *Mitteleuropa* in terms of the level of political dependency from the ruling German nation. Werner Best divided this region into four groups. The first group, which comprised Hungary, Romania, Bulgaria, as well as Italy and Finland, would have been disposed with complete political and state administration. This administration could have been led by locals, of course 'according to the advice and viewpoints of the governing nation.' The countries of the second group (France, Belgium, the Netherlands, Denmark, and probably Norway, Slovakia and Croatia) would still hold some autonomy in its local administration, but this would have been completely under the direction of 'the governing nation.' Countries in the third group (Estonia, Lithuania and the Czech-Moravian territories) would have local administration, but for countries in the 'fourth importance' (Poland, Latvia, Ukraine and Belorussia), Best envisaged a form of government which did not even have that but a form of colonial administration which would have completely excluded the local population. The 'natives' could have lived their lives in the small localities of the family, neighbours and religion.[77]

The planning of political borders received relatively little attention from peace planners. This is understandable, as under such close cooperation, political frontiers would have been less important than with sovereign countries. However, on occasion – when it involved the problem of German minorities – the question of frontiers was discussed. In the context of Hungary, it was particularly the fate and extent of Transdanubia which was uncertain. Based on the initial plans of the 1930s, the *Volksdeutsche Mittelstelle* – which was

---

[76] Jean Freymond, *Le IIIe Reich et la réorganisation économique de l'Europe 1940–1942. Origines et projets*, Leiden, 1974, 106–42; and Riemenschneider, *Die deutsche Wirtschaftspolitik*, 179–84.

[77] Werner Best, 'Grossraumordnung und Grossraumverwaltung,' *Zeitschrift fur Politik*, 32 (1942), 406–12. It is important to note that countries are not named in this source, thus this categorization is ours.

directed by the leader of the SS – initially envisaged the expulsion of Hungarians from Transdanubia and for it to be colonised and populated by Germans. Later, it aimed to create a strip of German settlements 50–100km wide along the river Danube south of Mohács. In relation to this, in 1940–41, the creation of a separate German province (*Pritz Eugen Gau*) in the Banat, Bačka (Bácska) and Baranya was considered.

The future frontier of the *Reich* and Hungary was another issue. The *Reichsstelle für Raumordnung* (Reich Office for Spatial Planning) in Berlin aimed to extend the *Südmark* to the Balaton-Ljubljana line. Others would have been satisfied with extending the frontier on the basis of ethnicity, with the annexation of Kőszeg, Szombathely, Mosonmagyaróvár and Sopron and their surroundings. The undated memorandum 'Annexation of German Western-Hungary to the German Empire' – originating from Vienna – counted the transfer of 1250 km2 of territory to the *Reich*. Here, out of the 120 thousand inhabitants, 70 thousand were ethnic Germans. The transfer of this territory – argued the memorandum – 'would not be a great sacrifice for Hungary,' but it would guarantee the food supply of Vienna and would make the Southeast frontier of the *Reich* more secure.[78]

Elaborations of long term plans were neglected. Events on the fronts initially made these untimely, and later pointless. The necessity of planning for a prolonged war – instead of a *Blitzkrieg* – shocked Hitler. In early 1942, he stopped any work on developing long-term plans, and gave instructions to subject all efforts to winning the war. With this intent, a new phase in German South-East European policy was initiated – the complete exploitation of the region.

It is well known that Hitler and the military leadership, during the preparation of the Barbarossa operation against the Soviet Union, only counted on the participation of Romania and Finland from his allies. The swift Hungarian, Slovak and Croatian participation thus was not the result of some kind of immense German pressure, but can be explained with the rivalry of these states for German favours.

As of late 1941-early 1942, the situation had changed. Hitler demanded maximal efforts from South-East European countries, just like from Germans, and his relationship to these countries was determined by the extent to which they were willing to send their male populations to the Eastern front to fight, and to what extent they were willing to make their resources (food supplies and raw materials) available for the *Reich*. Thus, economic treaties signed in

---

78 Wolfdieter Bihl, '*Zur* nationalsozialistischen Ungarnpolitik 1940/41,' *Österreichische Osthefte*, 11 (1969), 21–4.

the 1930s and in 1939–40 soon became irrelevant. After 1941, the region had to provide interest-free trade loans for the *Reich*.

Weapons and war materials sent in return only covered a small part of this volume. After Hitler's hatred towards the Jews grew to pathological levels, to what extent a particular South-East European country was willing to exterminate (or to help exterminate) its own Jewish population also became crucial in the eyes of Hitler and the Nazis.

Facts and numerous comments from Nazi leaders show that from the perspective of these criteria, Romania's reputation was the highest. After Marshall Antonescu's far-right takeover in Romania in the autumn of 1940, it was he who became Hitler's favourite, and Romania, his most important ally. Among foreign statesmen, he received the highest German decorations, and he had the privilege to meet the Fuhrer and Chancellor more regularly (20 times, while Benito Mussolini only 15 times).[79]

On the other hand, Hungary, which until 1938 was very keen on close cooperation, although with changing intensity, continued to resist German demands. Of course, visions about 'companionship,' 'comradeship' and a German-Hungarian alliance prevailed, and their significance even increased.

Among the Hungarian elite, it was mostly the high command that had such illusory visions. The most radical among them was Henrik Werth, who, in his 14 June 1941 memorandum argued for joining the war immediately: '… we can only hope for further territorial gains if we remain dedicated to the political goals of the Axis; as a reward of this we will certainly be able to completely restore Greater Hungary.'[80] The judgment of Prime Minister László Bárdossy (1941–42) was also clouded. In his parliamentary speech in January 1942, he said it was the historical destiny of Hungary to regain and control the Carpathian basin as a whole, and described Hungary as a strong point of European stability and cooperation, whose intellectual and economic influence was already felt far beyond its borders. Government Member of Parliament Béla Marton talked in the same sense when he noted, 'Hungary's sacrifices on the Eastern front will guarantee it a leading role in Eastern Europe.' Béla Imrédy also argued for every sacrifice for the purpose of total war. Some even dared to claim – such as Count Imre Károlyi – that for the purpose of a successful war, Hungary should become a German protectorate.[81]

---

79 Ránki, *A Harmadik Birodalom*, 64.
80 Dombrády Lóránd, *Hadsereg és politika Magyarországon 1938–1941*. Budapest: Kossuth, 1986, 226.
81 Note by Jagow, 20 January 1943 // AA, Inland II. Geheim. Ungarn. Bd. 4.

However, official Hungarian policy under the premiership of Miklós Kállay (1942–44) was not determined by such fantasies as doubts remained about a final German victory. Similarly to his predecessor Prime Minister Pál Teleki, he preferred, in the long run, an Anglo-Saxon orientation. After the hesitation of 1940–41, from late 1941 to early 1942 this course of policy in Budapest once again became dominant. However, it has to be admitted that in this course – which was advocated mostly by aristocrats – illusions about Hungarian dominance in the region were also prevalent. But, while military and far-right circles aimed to fulfil the restoration of St. Stephen's state by cooperating with Nazi Germany, Horthy and the conservative circles dominating the government wanted the same but without Germany and with a rapprochement with the Anglo-Saxon powers.[82]

The Budapest rejection or reluctant fulfilment of German demands, which asked for the deployment of the entire Hungarian army, the continued increase of food and raw material supplies to Germany and the deportation of the Jews to the North, as well as the secret negotiations with the Anglo-Saxon powers – which German intelligence continuously monitored – caused understandable dissatisfaction in Berlin. In an interview on 20 October 1942, Weizsacker summarized German grievances to Sztójay in five points: 1) Hungary's persistent references to the state of St Stephen; 2) the social system of Hungary was outdated compared to Germany's; 3) 'the handling of the Jewish question, which for Germany, was unacceptable'; 4) compared to Romania, Hungary is reluctant to commit to the fight with its army, and saves it for a potential offensive war against Romania; 5) egotistical handling of the nationality question.[83]

From the context of the image of Hungary in the perception of Nazi leadership in 1942–44, the comments made by Hitler are of particular importance. In these, he separated Hungary from South-East Europe, and adhered it to territories of *Ostland* which were deemed to be colonized. The following statements from the volume of Hitler conferences with foreign statesmen attest to his notions about Hungary: 'The Hungarians are as lazy as the Russians.' 'From their nature they are the people of the steppe.' 'Socially, the sickest country of New Europe is Hungary.' 'The Hungarians are radical nationalists, they assimilate the German minorities with particular swiftness... whom could only be saved if the state would be taken over from the Hungarians.' 'We liberated the Hungarians from the Ottoman rule, and there will not be order until we liberate them again.' 'The last state where the Jews will be still holding out will be Hungary.' 'For him, Hungary's friendliness

---

82   Gyula Juhász (ed.), *Magyar-brit titkos tárgyalások 1943-ban*. Budapest: Kossuth, 1978.
83   AA, Inland II. geheim. Ungarn. Bd. 5. 30 October 1942.

towards the Jews is puzzling.'[84]

On 10 December 1943, a prominent Nazi, Edmund Veesenmayer, summarized German perceptions about Hungary. The future Nazi governor of Hungary notes: 'Hungary proved that it was unable to conduct a national life in the past, and will remain so in the future.' Veesenmayer argued: 'It does not recognise its interests [and] it does not take its share from the common fighting, thus it is imperative that a German governor would be placed alongside, or even better 'on top of the Hungarian government.' This way, the *Reich* can get 'twice or even more supplies from Hungary,' it could 'deal with the Jewish question there,' as well Hungary should take its fair share from the fighting according to its means. Namely: 'The deployment of every Hungarian peasant, worker or soldier would relieve resources of the Führer. Every bleeding Hungarian relieves our bleeding, strengthens our reserves, and helps us to preserve our strength for the tasks of the post-war period.'[85] The only German elite group, which still respected Hungarians, was some of the generals and officers of the Eastern front who had the opportunity to experience the courage of the Hungarian army. However, their voices were unheard, as their reports got stuck at the high command levels.[86]

Regardless of continued pressure from Berlin, the Kállay cabinet's non-compliance policy towards Germany raised the question in Berlin of reversing Hungary's recent (1938–41) territorial gains. If Hungary would withdraw its troops from the Eastern front and decline deploying them in the Balkans, noted Dietrich von Jagow, the German Minister in Budapest (1941–44), this would have been interpreted as 'Hungary declining its territorial ambitions, which would mean that its Trianon frontiers would be restored.'[87] Hitler had the same opinion. He already told Antonescu that 'we would understand very much if Romania, apart from restoring its frontier, would also gain Odessa and a buffer zone.' Moreover, on 23 March 1944, he made the following personal remark to the *Conducator*: 'Because of the disloyalty of the Hungarian government, and because neither the Hungarian nor the Romanian governments accepted the Second Vienna Award, and because Italy is out of the picture, Germany does not think that it should function as the signatory of the Vienna Award.' It was typical of Hitler's cynicism that earlier he told Hungarian leaders that he would not protest if after the 'Great War' Hungary would 'solve' the Transylvanian question with arms.[88]

---

84 Ránki, *A Harmadik Birodalom*, 93, 97, 141–3; see also: Péter Gosztonyi, 'Hogyan vélekedett Hitler a magyarokról?,' in: *Magyarország a második világháborúban*. München: Herp, 1984, 78–85.
85 *A Wilhelmstrasse és Magyarország*, 743–51.
86 Hillgruber, 'Deutschland und Ungarn, 1933–1944,' 671.
87 *A Wilhelmstrasse és Magyarország*, 733.
88 *A Wilhelmstrasse és Magyarország*, 671–3; Ránki, *A Harmadik Birodalom*, 123,

Parallel to notions about the restoration of the Trianon frontiers, the possibility of the military occupation of Hungary emerged. Such plans were already elaborate by the autumn of 1943. However, this was completed on 19 March 1944, after German intelligence received news about the dropping of British paratroopers to Hungary. With the German occupation, Hungary lost the remainder of its sovereignty, and became a puppet state like Slovakia and Croatia. This nature of affairs was captured by István Bethlen, who, in his memoirs noted that: 'the tragedy of Hungary had just begun. Abandoned by everyone, friends and foes, Hungary sped rapidly towards its annihilation.'[89] But, from the German perspective the conclusion was the following: 'The final result is excellent. The most important German wishes regarding raw materials and their financing had been fulfilled.'[90]

Because of its food supplies and army – contrary to Finland and Bulgaria – but mostly because of its central geographical location, Hitler strongly insisted on retaining Hungary. 'A catastrophe in Hungary would mean the catastrophe of the entire Balkans.'[91]

The geographical position of Hungary, which was a clear advantage in the development of economic relations, now became Hungary's disadvantage in the war, which meant more economic and human casualties. Thus, a clearing of the ruins of the Nazi *Mitteleuropa* could only commence in Budapest and Hungary a few weeks earlier than in Berlin and Germany. Hungarian communists used this circumstance for decades to untruly label Hungary as Hitler's last ally. It appeared first in the manifesto of the Hungarian Communist Party on 30 November 1944, and was adopted by the Hungarian National Liberation Front without change.

Translated by Andras Becker.

130–1.
89   *Bethlen István emlékirata 1944.* Szerk. Ilona Bolza and Ignác Romsics, Budapest: Zrinyi, 1988, 144–5.
90   *A Wilhelmstrasse és Magyarország,* 791.
91   *A Wilhelmstrasse és Magyarország,* 890.

2

Moscow and the Baltic States: Experience of Relationships, 1917–1939

OLEG KEN AND ALEXANDER RUPASOV

After the First World War, the Eastern Baltic region was seen by the European politicians as something that was very far from the mainstream of international affairs. It was seen as 'the edge of diplomacy.'[1] For Moscow, on the contrary, the Baltic region was the starting point of its practical politics and, throughout the entire interwar period, it remained in the sphere of primary concerns.

Nevertheless, scholarship and diplomatic knowledge about the relations between the USSR and the Baltic States rather confirms the first of these assertions. Stereotypes about the marginal nature of the Baltic aspect of Moscow's politics reproduced the essential elements of the thinking of the Soviet political leaders, diplomats and the military men. Experiencing the interwar reality, this approach gave birth to an internal conflict in the Soviet policy towards Estonia, Latvia and Lithuania. This conflict laid between the desirable and the real, between the urge to play a great global role not registering the small states and the actual dependence on them. This conflictive perception strongly affected each stage of the relationships between Moscow and these neighbouring states for two decades. Therefore, the centre of our attention is directed on the shaping and development of the Baltic policy of the USSR. This policy combined general political agenda and economic necessities, great-power calculations and a genuine concern, ignorance and attention to the nuances of the political evolution of each of the Baltic States. The study of this problem facilitates the identification of the sustainable elements in the motives and practical actions of Moscow. It also

---

1   John Hiden and Thomas Lane (eds.), *The Baltic and the Outbreak of the Second World War*. Cambridge: Cambridge UP, 1992, 1 (the statement of a British diplomat D. Gregory).

helps to assess the overall dynamics of the relationship between Soviet Russia and the Baltic States.

The time of unexpectedness: 1917–1920

The first attempts to establish Soviet power in the Baltic provinces of the former Russian Empire took place at the end of 1917. However, these failed endeavours clearly demonstrated that the experience of the world war contributed to the crystallization of opposite political vectors. Although for the Bolsheviks, the Great War was the final proof of the advantages of the international class approach as the only way of humankind's salvation, the political elites of the Baltic States (including the social democrats and socialists) quickly accepted the idea of national self-determination. In a few months, the autonomist aspirations of the Balts were pushed aside by the idea of independent national statehood that in a large degree determined the result of the struggle for this region in 1918–19.

These events in each of the new Baltic States were developing under a similar scenario. After the November revolution of 1918 in Germany, the Red army, relying on the 'pro-Bolshevik' local groups, overthrew the governments in Estonia, Latvia and Lithuania that were created with the help of German occupation authorities. The Bolsheviks established Soviet power in Narva, Riga and Vilnius. By the end of the summer, 1919, despite the lack of significant external assistance (at the same time the Latvian and Estonian units fought against the German 'Baltic division'), the national political and military forces ultimately defeated the supporters of the orientation in Moscow (the capital of Russia and of the International). In addition, in a bloody civil war the Soviet government that struggled for its own existence had no possibilities to change this unexpected outcome in the Baltic region. Already at the beginning of September 1919, the Bolshevik leadership sent proposals to Latvia, Lithuania and Estonia to enter into peace negotiations. For the former Baltic provinces, it was really a gift of fate. While the victorious Western powers left the question about the indivisibility of Russia open, and defeated Germany was not in a hurry to withdraw its troops from the Baltic region, the Soviet government by its offer to start the peace negotiations legitimized the existence of new national states (the Entente powers recognized the independence of Estonia and Latvia only in 1921, and the independence of Lithuania in 1922).

Moscow paid a very 'generous' fee for the readiness of the Baltic States to make peace. The Soviets signed the first peace treaty with Estonia on 2 February 1920. Six months later, the peace treaties were signed with Lithuania (on 11 July) and Latvia (on 12 August). Under these agreements,

Russia recognized the sovereignty of the new states and their boundaries, including the attachment of Jamburg and Izborsk to Estonia, and Pytalovo (Abrene) to Latvia. Occupied by Soviet troops, Vilnius, with its predominantly Polish population, was transferred to the Republic of Lithuania (but, in October 1920, the Vilnius region was occupied by Poland). At the same time, Moscow demonstrated its understanding of the difficulties its new neighbours faced. The decision to transfer the Pytalovo rail junction with its adjacent areas (where Latvians were a minority) to Latvia was motivated by the consideration that otherwise all Latvian railroads would be 'suspended in air,' and the 'people, that have recognized rights for self-determination and for an independent statehood, would actually be deprived of the opportunity [to implement these rights].'[2] The Soviet government finally recognized the new states's rights to repatriation of cultural valuables and to obtain forest concessions and evacuated property.

It is not easy to assess the first steps of Soviet Russia towards the Baltic States. On the one hand, Moscow, in the beginning of the 1920s, paved the way to the 'foreign NEP' (New Economic Policy) and changed the original Bolshevism's attitudes towards the long-term approach of 'peaceful coexistence' with the capitalist world. On the other hand, Moscow's activity was motivated by the need for 'breathing space' before the renewed onslaught on the West. The Baltic States were needed as trade mediators for military materials purchasing and for maintaining the fighting efficiency of the Red Army.[3] In any case, the Soviet leaders were reluctant to abandon their goals to transform the Baltic into the 'sea of Revolution.' Probably, the directive of the Chairman of the Council of People's Commissars, Vladimir Lenin (1917–24) concerning the transfer of Vilnius and its suburbs to the Lithuanian government should be interpreted in this manner. Lenin wrote: 'We consider this not as a renunciation of the Sovietization of Lithuania, but as a delay and as a variant of the form of its Sovietization.'[4] However the Bolshevik prime minister could hardly explain what this formula really meant: the Soviet policy on the Baltic States was just making its only first steps after the signing of the peace treaties in 1920.

On the other side of the border, the national inspiration and the fears experienced in the revolutionary era influenced the formation of new

---

2   Alfred Ioffe, 'Mirnye peregovory mezhdu Rossiei i Litvoi.' 9 May 1920 // Arhiv Vneshney Politiki Rossiisoky Federacii (hereafter, AVP RF). F.151, op. 3, d. 9, l. 60. Moscow, Russia.
3   The main articles of import to Soviet Russia through the Baltic countries in 1920–1921 were the soles of army boots, chemicals, aircrafts (illegally purchased in Estonia) and rifles (provided by Sweden on account of the tsar's orders).
4   Vladimir Lenin, *Neizvestnye dokumenty*. 1891–1922. Moskva: Rosspen, 1999, 358.

worldview attitudes. According to these attitudes, the Eastern Baltic countries, unlike bolshevizing Russia, were the organic component of Western civilization. During the initial stage of the relations between the Baltic States and Soviet Russia (unlike, for example, the Finnish-Soviet contacts), the perception of the border with Russia as coincident with the 'civilization barrier,' just to a small extent affected the consciousness of the Baltic national elites and it was not a primary factor for the subsequent development of their relations with Moscow.[5] The main problem for new States was not to project the emerging identity into the European context, but to provide reliable guarantees of their independence. This, from the very beginning, encouraged these States to unite forces. After the establishment of peaceful relations with Russia, 'the idea of the Baltic bloc got to the stage of organizational and contractual formalisation.' By the middle of September 1919, in order to elaborate a general line of conduct regarding Moscow's peaceful proposals, the first negotiations of the Foreign Ministers of the Baltic States took place in Riga and Tallinn (also, Finland took part in the later meeting). Thus, not the Baltic hostility to the Russian Bolshevism, but the ability of Moscow to understand and take into account their vital interests became the axis of the subsequent relations between the USSR and the Baltic States.

In search for a political course: 1921–1925

During the period of Russia's civil war (1917–21), the Bolsheviks perceived the Baltic States as a battlefield. The victory there, according to the Bolsheviks, could help to create a revolutionary springboard to the West. Despite the conclusion of the peace treaties, such perceptions were only gradually giving way to a more realistic view on the Baltic States. The Sovietization of Georgia in the beginning of 1921 was not considered the completion of the 'first round of wars and revolutions.' With hesitation, the Bolshevik leadership refused the 'idea to seize Bessarabia by the only attack' ('Ilyich [Lenin – *edit.*] was very tempted by this idea') in summer of 1921.[6]

5　　The modern historian begins his essay devoted to foreign policy of the Baltic States with the claim that 'historically they have always been a part of the Western European cultural tradition,' but he acknowledges that the current national identity was 'definitely' born by fifty years of the 'Soviet experience.' See: Romuald J. Misiunas, 'National Identity and Foreign Policy in the Baltic States,' in: *The Legacy of History in Russia and the New Independent States of Eurasia*, edited by S. Frederic Starr. London: M.E. Sharpe, 1994, 93–4. Even in the mid 1930s the statesmen of the Baltic States preferred to use during their joint conferences the Russian language (not French which was generally accepted in contemporary international practice).
6　　*Istochnik* 1 (2001): 58. It is clear therefore the predictions of the beginning of 1921 that 'the next step of the Bolsheviks will be an attempt to strengthen the place of arm on the shores of the Baltic seaside' (Mikhail I. Rostovcev, *Politicheskie stati*. Sankt-Peterburg: S. Petersburg UP, 2002, 178).

The bloody attempt of the Communist coup in Tallinn on 1 December 1924, despite the failure of similar adventures in Bulgaria and Germany a year before (there were more favourable conditions for its success), could be regarded as an example of the persistence of the revolutionary approach. The action of the Estonian Communists relied on the support of Comintern and its Chairman Grigory Zinoviev, who was the actual dictator of Leningrad. However, the lack of coordination with the Soviet secret services during the coup and unexpected retreat of the Red Army units that were previously advanced to the Estonian border, suggest that this coup was rather a 'personal initiative' of Zinoviev, whereas other members of the 'triumvirate' (Jozef Stalin and Lev Kamenev) hardly sympathized with it. The failed 'coup' and the 'white terror' in Estonia that followed weakened the political position of Zinoviev. Probably the highest Soviet circles considered the 'insurgence' in Tallinn primarily linked to the internal struggle for power and did not perceive it as the beginning of a new stage of revolutionary expansion.

On the contrary, defeat in Tallinn was one of the reasons that, in February 1925, the Politburo of the Central Committee of the Russian Communist Party (of Bolsheviks) passed a resolution to stop the 'active intelligence' and 'military and rebel works,' that were guided by the Soviet state bodies in the 'neighbouring states of the USSR' (the resolution also stated that 'more or less normal diplomatic relations' were established with these states).[7] However, already from the beginning of the 1920s, Moscow's attitude towards the Baltic States was essentially determined by the state needs of weakened Russia.

At the end of the civil war, the Soviet economy was lying in ruins. The capital of Moscow's tsardom became the new Russian capital instead of Imperial Petrograd. Two centuries of domination of the Russian Empire over the Baltics were reduced to nothing. In this region, Russia faced problems that were partly similar to those that it faced during the times of Ivan the Terrible (1533–84) and Peter the Great (1682–25). Nevertheless, at the beginning of the 1920, none of the Great Powers tried to fill out the authority vacuum created by the 'Balkanization' of North-Eastern Europe. Thanks to these circumstances, Soviet diplomacy was inclined to perceive the new States not as an external force, opposed to the USSR and similar to the 'real' Western

---

7   Ivan I. Kostyushko, *Materialy 'osoboi papki' Politbyuro TsK RKP(b)-VKP(b) po voprosu sovetsko-polskih otnosheniy. 1923–1944*. Moskva: Institut slavyanovedeniya RAN, 1997, 13–14. Already in summer, 1921, on the initiative of the head of the NKID G.V. Chicherin, the Central Committee of the RCP(b) recommended 'to the Communists of Estonia, Latvia and Lithuania to exercise the greatest diligence in both foreign and domestic policy, taking into account... that currently it is impossible to talk about military aid to them from the RSFSR' (Lenin, *Neizvestnye dokumenty*, 447–9).

states,[8] but as its closest partners and even as a 'permit to the outside world.' It was typical that in 1921–22, the posts of the plenipotentiary representative of Soviet Russia in Tallinn or in Riga were considered quite suitable for the Deputy of the People's Commissariat for the Foreign Policy (Maxim Litvinov) and other member of the Collegium of the People's Commissariat for the Foreign Policy (Adolf Ioffe), respectively.

In February 1922, shortly before the Genoa conference, the Soviet delegation initiated a meeting in Riga with the representatives of the Baltic States. However, when Estonia, Latvia, Finland and Poland signed in 1922 the treaty of the military-political alliance (the 'Warsaw accord'), the functionaries of the People's Commissariat for Foreign Policy (NKID) started to talk about the intrusion of their 'love' towards the Baltic States was becoming 'not only pointless, but even discreditable.'[9] Despite this, Moscow met the challenge of the signing of the 'Warsaw accord' with a proposal to hold a regional disarmament conference (which took place in Moscow in December 1922). After the refusal of Finland and Poland to ratify the Warsaw treaty, Estonia and Latvia signed an agreement of military alliance in November 1923. In parallel, the Latvian government assured Moscow in its firm intention to keep neutrality in the case of the Polish-Soviet armed conflict.[10] From its side, the USSR sent Latvia, Lithuania and Estonia a proposal to conclude a neutrality or even mutual non-aggression pact (Moscow refrained from it before, arguing that the non-aggression pact was an unnecessary excess).[11] The diplomatic correspondence shows that the breakdown of the plans of the consecutive Soviet-Baltic conference was caused not only by the resistance of Warsaw, but also by the internal crisis in the Russian Communist Party that took place at the end of 1923-early 1924.

The basis for political partnership between Moscow and the Balts was accompanied by the development of the economic relations of the USSR with Latvia, partly with Estonia and even with Lithuania (which, being separated from the USSR by the Polish territories, became the hostage of tensions between the USSR and Poland. Also, Kaunas became excluded from the profitable Soviet transit to Germany). Meeting the wishes of these countries to expand trade and economic contacts, Moscow, according to Yakov Ganetsky (Fuerstenberg), a member of the People's Commissariat for Foreign Policy

---

8   Aleksey Chernyh, 'Doklad Ya. S. Ganeckomu.' 20 April 1922 // AVP RF. F. 0135, op. 5, p. 106, d. X, l. 19.
9   Konstantin Yurenev, 'Doklad Ya. S. Ganeckomu.' 7 June 1922 // AVP RF. F. 04, op. 25, p. 172a, d. 51798, l. 67–9.
10   Viktor Kopp, 'Letter to S. A. Aralov' 3 (8) November 1923 // AVP RF. F. 04, op. 25, p. 172a, d. 51798, l. 98.
11   Taking into account the general attention to the German event, this agreement was supposed to give the form of the Protocol on freedom of transit.

and the People's Commissariat of Foreign Trade, was motivated by the desire of economic benefits, and endeavoured to dispel fears that the strengthening of Soviet Russia would mean the 'beginning of the end of any sorts of Latvias.'[12] Trade, primarily transit trade, served as the paramount sphere of interactions between Moscow and the Balts. Mutual interests stimulated extraordinary efforts in the sphere of development of the transport infrastructure. In a short time, the Latvian authorities put in order the port installations of Riga and Ventspils, deepened the waters of the ports, and repaired and built railway bridges and elevators for grain, arriving from Russia.[13] Despite the objections of the Revolutionary Military Council (*Revvoensovet*), Soviet organizations invested funds in the modernization of Tallinn's port. Moreover, plans for analogous investment into the railroads of Lithuania in the interests of timber exports via Memel were nurtured (despite the fact that, since the summer of 1922, there was no trade representative of the USSR in Kaunas).

Soviet diplomats vigorously forged ties with Baltic politicians, officials and journalists. Some of the Director posts in Riga Transit Bank, established in 1923, were offered to the representatives of the Social Democratic party. The year after, when Z. Meyerowitz, one of the most promising politicians of Latvia, became the leader of the Farmers Union, the NKID charged its plenipotentiary representative office (*Polpredstvo*) in Riga 'to try to enter him into our waterways while he is not yet in power.' The achievement of this goal was facilitated by 'the emerging interesting case,' namely 'the ability to drag the Farmers Union into our Cooperative and Transit Bank.'[14] The attempt succeeded and subsequently the Bank saved the enterprises of the Farmers Union with its preferential loans many times. Konstantin Päts, one of the leaders of the Farmers Assemblies and a few times head of the Estonian state, was not ashamed to receive the salary of a legal counsel of the Soviet trade mission ('on trade of petroleum products') during several years. Future prime minister of Lithuania, A. Voldemaras, as far back as 1924 offered his services to the diplomatic mission of the USSR. Apparently, Moscow, through its legations, rendered assistance to different candidates from left-wing radical parties during the parliamentary elections.[15] This perfectly coexisted with cherishing relations with personalities Moscow itself considered fascist or

---

12   Yakov Ganetsky, 'Pismo K.K. Yurenevu'. 15 June 1922 // AVP RF. F. 04, op. 25, p. 172a, d. 51797, l. 52.
13   Zigfrids A. Meierovics, 'Pismo S.I. Aralovu'. 8 August 1923 // AVP RF. F. 150, op. 6, p. 15, d. 18, l. 21.
14   Semen Aralov, 'Pismo K.A. Krzheminskomu'.2 June 1924 // AVP RF. F. 028, p. 1, d. 37, l. 2.
15   Spravka upolnomochennogo NKID pri SNK BSSR. 28 August 1925 // AVP RF. F. 04, op. 25, p. 176, d. 51874, l. 13; B.I. Kantorovich, 'Pismo A.S. Chernyhu'. 31 August 1925 // AVP RF. F. 04, op. 25, p. 176, d. 51874, l. 14.

extreme nationalist.[16]

With the same energy, Soviet diplomacy tried to influence the published media in the Baltic States, including the Russian-language ones. In 1921–22, the Soviet Legation in Latvia subsidized the newspaper *Novyi Put*, whereas the NKID bustled about the permission to sell the newspaper in Estonia and Lithuania, and even searched the advertisers for the newspaper. In 1924–1925, the Soviet mission in Kaunas similarly had a 'special relationship' with a weekly *Vairas*. In addition, the Soviets demonstrated a strong interest in the influential Riga newspaper *Segodnya*. The publications of *Segodnya* caused either flashes of anger or the desire to bribe its editorial board (that most likely was never realized) by the Soviet leaders.

Generally, in relations with the Baltic States, its 'Russian-speaking' politicians and 'provincial' governments, Moscow unconsciously focused on the way of action that was typical of the North American 'dollar diplomacy' of those days.

The initial Soviet assessments of the prospects of coexistence with the Baltic States were overestimated. Already in 1923, Soviet circles started to recognize that the Baltic desire to turn aside from the close arms of a partner was increasing. The new small states put the real guarantees of the preservation of their independence at the forefront, and no assurances from Moscow could stop search in this direction. Despite Russia temporally accepting the arbitration principle, Riga, Tallinn and Kaunas interpreted the Soviet idea of disarmament as a bid for dominant influence in the region, which could be balanced only by the active cooperation, if not with the Great Powers, then with neighbouring Finland and Poland. The USSR faced with the situation, when it was 'impossible' to gain the confidence of the Baltic States, because of 'all our peaceful declarations and reassurances' (that Russia 'will not swallow') could be effective only for the short time.[17] Thus, an idea emerged that it was 'much easier "to put a brindle on" a big government than on the Baltic political pranksters, assured in their impunity.'[18] This way, the peacefulness of the USSR was connected with its inability to recognize the natural concerns of the Baltic States.[19]

---

16   Of course, such 'investments' did not always result in the desired dividends. For example, the leader of the Latvian farmers Karlis Ulmanis, to the dismay of Moscow, 'traveled abroad' spending Soviet gold but shielding it away from the fulfillment of his promises.
17   Yakov Ganetsky, 'Pismo K.K. Yurenevu'. 9 November 1922 // AVP RF. F. 04, op. 25, p. 172a, d. 51797, l. 104.
18   Konstantin Yurenev, 'Doklad Ya.S. Ganetskomu'. November 1922 // AVP RF. F. 04, op. 25, p. 172a, d. 51799, l. 78.
19   The heads of diplomatic and foreign trade departments Ya. Ganetsky sincerely did not understand why the Baltic countries needed naval forces. On the decision of Riga

Therefore, if in the early 1920s the Soviet leaders worried about the external threat to the Baltic States (they predicted the imminent takeover of independent Lithuania by Poland),[20] by the middle of the 1920s, Moscow was concerned with the Baltic States's endeavours to coordinate their activity between themselves as well as their disposition to rely on Helsinki and Warsaw. After the failure of the 'Warsaw accord,' Moscow expected new attempts to create a military-political union (in the form of a Small or a Large Baltic Union under Polish hegemony), that could become an important springboard for the 'big imperialists' – Britain and France. At the beginning of 1925, a regular informational meeting of the military experts from the Baltic States and Poland took place in Riga, but it did not produce serious political or military consequences.[21] This ordinary event became an occasion to review the spontaneously evolving Baltic policy of the USSR. The Politburo, after an analysis by its special commission, decreed that the cooperation of the Baltic States with each other and especially with Poland and Finland is 'fraught with the imminent threat of danger to the USSR.' The economic, diplomatic and intelligence services of the USSR were ordered to prevent such a risk.[22]

The turn in attitude of the USSR towards the Baltic States is partly explained by the changing economic conditions. After the reestablishment of political and trade-economic relations with other European Powers, primarily Britain, France, Germany and Czechoslovakia, the Soviet Union needed either the Balts's commercial mediation or their special services (for example, for secret trade and financial transactions decreased).[23] The commercial port of Leningrad restored its pre-revolutionary turnover and, thus, transit via Latvia ceased to be indispensable for the USSR. Moscow started to regard it as philanthropy, to which Riga should have responded with political concessions. Moreover, the industrial equipment inherited by the Baltic countries was

---

to begin its creation, he responded with the tactless joke: 'I am ready to send to the Latvian government my sincere congratulations on this occasion. Now Latvia will eventually become a great power' (AVP RF. F. 04, op. 25, p. 172a, d. 51799, l. 87).

20   Even at the beginning of 1924, the plenipotentiary minister in Kaunas continued to believe that without Vilnius and without the borders with the USSR, Lithuania 'has no precondition for the independent economic existence' (Ivan Lorents, 'Pismo V.L. Koppu', 4 February 1924 // AVP RF. F. 04, op. 27, p. 183, d. 52017, l. 24).

21   'The Point of view of NKID' is that 'this conference has not decisive importance' (Semen Aralov, 'Pismo A.S. Chernyhu', 14 April 1925 // AVP RF. F. 028, op. 3, p. 6, d. 1, l. 158).

22   Grant M. Adibekov (et al.), *Politbyuro TsK RKP(b)-VKP(b) i Evropa : resheniya "osoboi papki", 1923–1939*. Moskva: Rosspen, 2001, 75–7. Even in the resolution approved by the Politburo they talked not even about possibility, but about the supposed 'fact' of the formation of the Baltic Union.

23   Materials of scripted correspondence between the NKID and its foreign missions (polpredstva), 1920–21 // AVP RF. F. 028, op. 1, d.1, l. 244.

getting old and was incapable of operating (for example, the shipbuilding and ship-repair enterprises of Estonia). That is why it was also losing attractiveness for Soviet customers.[24] In such circumstances, Soviet leaders were ready to reconsider trade relations with the Baltic States mainly from the point of view of providing 'economic pressure' on these States. Taking into account the scale of trade and transit, this stance primarily concerned Latvia.

Finally, new Moscow attitudes towards the Baltic States were formed under the influence of the overture negotiations of the USSR with Poland and Germany. In the autumn of 1924, the NKID held an internal discussion on the possibility of the 'general agreement' with Poland. This would have involved the 'rectification of borders,' including the Lithuanian renunciation of claims for Vilnius, and the creation of a common Soviet-Lithuanian border (not to mention the 'compensation' for the USSR in Eastern Galicia). The real partition of the Baltic region into Soviet and Polish spheres of influence would have been an inevitable consequence of such an agreement.[25] The attractiveness of this 'Polish outline' was restrained by the coldness of Warsaw and by the hot insistence of German diplomacy, which, at the end of 1924, was seducing Moscow with an agreement on the partition of Poland (or, its 'reduction to the ethnographic borders'). Soviet leaders, refusing to negotiate with Germany on that topic, tried to initiate the anti-Polish cooperation of two Great Powers in the Baltic region. As a result, the main direction of Soviet policy, along with putting economic pressure on Latvia, was aimed at keeping the uncompromising position of Lithuania towards Poland. The Soviet objective was to paralyze any efforts to establish a Baltic cooperation in frame of a Large or Small Baltic union. From the beginning of 1925, Germany became the natural partner of the USSR in the Baltic region, whereas Poland became the main enemy.

Competition with Poland: 1926–33

The signing of the Locarno agreements in December 1925 that guaranteed the Western border of Germany, made the international position of Poland and the Baltic States complicated. Simultaneously, it paved the way for a new Moscow foreign policy, and Soviet leaders made some additional adjustments

---

24   In the USSR there were plans to fill the missing industrial potential of Estonia (that was motivated also by the desirability of forming of national proletariat), but under the influence of growth of the anticommunist sentiments, Moscow in 1923 abandoned plans to promote the industrialization of Estonia.

25   Ivan Lorents, 'Doklad V.L. Koppu', 14 August 1924 // AVP RF. F.04, op. 27, p. 184, d. 52021, l. 45–47; Ivan Lorents, 'Dokladnaya zapiska (prilozhenie k dokladu V.L. Koppu ot 31.12.1924)', 30 December 1924 // AVP RF. F.04, op. 27, p. 184, d. 52021, l. 72–82.

to its Baltic policy specifically. Despite its unwillingness to engage in multilateral commitments, in the spring of 1926, the Politburo allowed the NKID to ask Latvia, Lithuania and Estonia about their position regarding the conclusion of a collective (fourfold) pact. This initiative was aimed at attracting Baltic sympathies to Moscow, while, at the same time, detaching them from Poland. Thus, the USSR could appear as the main guarantor of the independence of the Baltic States. However, at the preliminary stage of the negotiations, the undesirable consequences of such a step were already revealed in Moscow. Fearing a dependence on the Soviet Union, Riga and Tallinn were forced to seek the harmonization of their actions with Warsaw and Helsinki. Moreover, they agreed on the basis of the proposed treaty with the USSR in the joint Latvian-Estonian-Finnish memorandum. Thus, Moscow had to limit its policy to more traditional methods of *divide et impera*, that were already outlined in the decision of the Politburo in 1925.

First of all, the Soviets made an attempt to split a single Baltic front by proposing to Latvia a large-scale economic cooperation that took into account the important strategic position of Latvia. In fact, Riga was put into the focus of such states as Britain, France, Poland and Germany, which turned it into one of the centres of intelligence against Soviet Russia. In addition, Moscow hoped to use the contradictions between the Poles and the Latvians. At the same time, Moscow hoped to use the special relationship with the main political forces of that country – the Latvian Social Democratic Party and the Farmers Union.

This attempt had partial success. The Latvian government responded with satisfaction to the proposals for the development of trade and economic ties, and proceeded to the negotiations of the bilateral warranty agreement, which was prepared by the parties in August 1926. From its side, Moscow kept its promise. In November 1927, it signed the trade agreement advantageous to Riga. Later Boris Stomonyakov, a member of the Collegiums of NKID, explained to Stalin the significance of this action: 'Although using this agreement we did not achieve the orientation of Latvia on the USSR, nevertheless by concluding this agreement we undoubtedly have driven a wedge between Latvia and Estonia... and prevented the formation of the Polish-Baltic alliance.'[26] Indeed, the mutual understanding between Moscow and Riga after the signing of an agreement of such importance reached such a level, that it allowed Latvia's Envoy Karlis Ozols to claim: 'both States should be ready to respond by weapon to Poland's invasion of Lithuania. Poland would sit quietly only if it would know that the USSR and Latvia would

---

26   Boris Stomonyakov, 'Zapiska I.V. Stalinu', 14 April 1932 // AVP RF. F. 09, op., 7, p. 55, d. 5, l. 28.

respond to its expansion with armed force.'[27] Since 1926, Moscow noticed that 'the open joint and demonstrative conferences of the Baltic States with Poland ceased.' Moreover, the deterioration of Soviet-Polish relations (especially after the return to power of Jozef Pilsudski in Warsaw in 1926) and 'military alert' of 1927 in the Soviet Union urged Latvia and even Estonia to show a reserved attitude toward Polish advances.

Another direction of Soviet policy after 1925 was oriented towards the cultivation of relations with Lithuania, whereas Germany was also interested in the strengthening of Kaunas's anti-Polish position. Although, while Lithuanian politicians had serious hopes for normalization of relations with Poland, Moscow could achieve little and after paying a considerable political price. On 28 September 1926, after more than a year of delays, the Soviet-Lithuanian Treaty of friendship and neutrality and a secret 'gentleman's agreement,' that provided for exchange of confidential information, were signed. The agreement was accompanied by a note of the People's Commissar Georgy Chicherin (1918–30), which manifested the USSR's support for Lithuanian claims to the Vilnius (Vilna) region. These agreements had 'fatal significance for Polish-Soviet relations.'[28] Baltic neighbours of Lithuania even suggested that the Soviets would soon establish a protectorate over it. However, the time of blooming relations between Moscow and Kaunas was short. The December 1926 coup of *Tautininkas* Party (Union of Lithuanian Nationalist) headed by Antanas Smetona and Augustinas Voldemaras (supported before by the USSR in their struggle against the followers of the Polish-Lithuanian compromise) unexpectedly led to the cessation of political contacts with Moscow until the summer of the following year (the exchange of confidential information was resumed only in 1929). The main conflicts with Lithuania were resolved after the recall of the arrogant Soviet Envoy Sergey Alexandrovsky (who was replaced by Alexander Arosev). Moscow declared its 'interest in the consolidation of the internal situation in Lithuania' and promised to restrain the activity of the Lithuanian Communists (who had to go deep underground under the pressure of repression).[29] The actions of the new Lithuanian authorities disturbed Moscow

---

27   Boris Stomonyakov, 'Zapiska besedy s K. Ozolsom', 2 December 1927 // AVP RF. F. 09, op., 7, p. 55, d. 5, l. 104.

28   Stanislaw Gregorowicz, *Polsko-radzieckie stosunki polityczne w latach 1932–1935*. Wrocław: Polska Akademia Nauk, 1982, 26–7.

29   Boris Stomonyakov, 'Zapiska besedy s Yu. Baltrushaitisom', 13 April 1927 // AVP RF. F. 09, op., 7, p. 55, d. 5, l. 175–6. The leadership of the Polish-Baltic Lender-Secretariat of the IKKI characterized the head of the Lithuanian state as follows: 'Bloody Smetona (a drunkard and speculator) actually turned into Nazi petty monarch with the unlimited rights' ('The current moment and the objectives of the Communist Party of Lithuania', 20 June 1928 // Rossiyskiy Gosudarstvenniy Arhiv Sotsialno-Politicheskoy Istorii (hereafter, RGASPI). F. 495, op. 61, d. 13, l. 402.

only in one, important aspect – the adventurism of Prime Minister Voldemaras (1926–29) could have provoked an armed Lithuanian-Polish conflict which would call for Soviet participation. In the summer of 1928, Soviet diplomacy led Voldemaras to believe that in such a situation, the USSR would stay neutral.

No significant changes occurred in relations between the USSR and Estonia. The development of Soviet-Latvian economic relations fuelled the interest of the Estonian business community. However, as Tallinn oriented its foreign policy primarily on Warsaw, the USSR agreed to conclude the trade agreement with Estonia only in the autumn of 1929. Its entry into force coincided with the beginning of the global economic crisis and with the revision of the general foreign trade priorities of the USSR. Thus, the bilateral trade volume declined sharply. Finally, the use of economic levers for the strengthening of influence in Estonia became impossible for Soviet diplomacy.

Moscow tried to change the balance of forces in the Baltic States, established by the end of 1928, using an unusual peace initiative. Soviet diplomacy belatedly announced the accession to the treaty for renunciation of war as a tool of national policy (the Briand-Kellogg Pact), tried to use it for the demonstration of its role in smoothing the tensions between Lithuania and Poland. At the same time, Moscow did not yield to Warsaw's insistence that the USSR should engage in negotiations with all its Western neighbours. In December 1928, the actual head of NKID, Litvinov proposed Warsaw and Kaunas sign a special Protocol on the early coming into force of the Briand-Kellogg Pact. The 'loyal' Lithuanians, however, informed the Latvians of that plan, whereas the Poles informed the Baltic States. Eventually, Moscow faced such an unwanted 'united front' of Poland and the Baltic States, as it was in 1926–27. Polish diplomacy skilfully cooled Soviet-Latvian relations in spring and summer of 1928. At this moment, Moscow, keeping confidence that Latvia 'remains the state, that in comparison with our Western neighbours mostly does not fit into the program of the creation of the united front against us,'[30] did not pay due attention to the signs of change in the foreign policy sympathies of Karlis Ulmanis, the leader of the largest Latvian party.[31] The Poles, undertaking rapid diplomatic manoeuvres, were successful in getting around Moscow and the result of Litvinov's initiative turned out opposite to what he had hoped for. On 5 February 1929, the USSR, Poland, Estonia,

---

30   Ivan Lorents, 'Doklad S.S. Aleksandrovskomu,' 4 August 1928 // RGASPI. F. 0150, op. 21, p. 41, d. 34, l. 115.
31   Two thousand dollars, paid then to K. Ulmanis were considered as 'just grease' (N.N. Kulyabko, 'Doklad B.S. Stomonyakovu,' 27 May 1928 // RGASPI. F. 0150, op. 21, p. 41, d. 34, l. 26). Ulmanis was trying to blackmail Moscow, demanding to pay the additional amounts and buy one newspaper of the Peasant Union. The Soviet side agreed to pay in exchange for a receipt (Ulmanis gave it), but refused to buy a newspaper.

Latvia and Romania signed the Moscow Protocol (which stipulated the immediate entry into force of the Briand-Kellogg Pact). Lithuania joined only a few months later.

This actual defeat motivated the Kremlin, on the one hand, to provoke the artificial aggravation of relations with Poland, and, on the other, to re-evaluate the results of its ten years of relations with the Baltic States. It became obvious that neither the policy of economic investment ('we have been spending 15 million rubles [per year] in Latvia only. And have not bought Latvia')[32] nor the economic pressure on Estonia brought political benefits. The election of Otto Strandman to the presidency in the summer of 1929 was a prelude to the further strengthening of political contacts between Estonia and Poland. However, Moscow was so tired of the vagaries of Voldemaras that its dismissal in September 1929 and the advent of the politicians that allowed compromise with Warsaw, was not perceived as a serious loss for Soviet diplomacy.

The global economic crisis and the turn of the USSR to rapid industrialization forced Soviet leaders to save monetary resources, whereas manufacturers in the Baltic States were forced to pursue sharply reduced Soviet orders. Therefore, although economic cooperation between the USSR and the Baltic States was minimized, the placing of Soviet order in the Baltic States was turned into an effective political tool. During the negotiations in 1931–32, the Soviets conditioned the prolongation of the trade agreements with Latvia with a list of political conditions (the main condition was the closing of Russian émigré organizations).[33] However, while the Soviet demands were fulfilled, Moscow resigned to sign the promised contract and to increase the transit volumes. At the same time, Soviet economic bodies took additional (and quite successful) efforts to switch export-import flows to the ports of the USSR.

By the beginning of the 1930s, Soviet policy in the Eastern Baltic region came to a standstill. The fatalistic tones, which the leaders of the First Western department of NKID used for describing of existing situation, illustrate it well. In a report concerning the Baltic Union, it was stated that the Baltic States were 'obsessed by the fear of social danger ... of violent Sovietization, which, in their views, the USSR inevitably will attempt to realise.' These officials saw in the alliance of the Balts and the Poles something predetermined by the laws of history: 'As the date of the anti-Soviet war comes closer, more

---

32   Boris Stomonyakov, 'Pometa na doklade I.M. Maiskogo ot 25.4.1932' // RGAS-PI. F. 0135, op. 15, p. 131, d.1, l.52.
33   It is not clear whether this requirement was determinated by the assault towards the non-influential Russian organizations or if it was seen as a demonstration lesson that should be taught to the 'Balts'.

neighbouring States want to rally around Poland.'³⁴ In this situation, the USSR allegedly had no other choice than to await the commencement of cataclysm.

At the same time, the supreme Soviet leadership was inclined to extract internal political dividends from bad relations with the Baltic States. In September 1930, looking for the arguments for the one-and-a-half increase of the wartime army, Stalin put forward a thesis about the need to deploy 'at least 150–160 infantry divisions' that were necessary to ensure the 'defence of Leningrad and of the right-bank of Ukraine.' While Latvia, Estonia, Finland and Poland would not establish an alliance, as Stalin explained to his associate Vyacheslav Molotov, 'they would not fight with the USSR. So, as soon as they would ensure the alliance – they would start a war (and would find a cause).'³⁵ These views were repeated by Soviet propaganda in different variants.

Paradoxically, the USSR found a way out of the impasse in its relations with the Baltic States thanks to Poland. In August 1931, Warsaw actually proposed to renew Polish-Soviet negotiations over the conclusion of a non-aggression pact. The insistence of Stalin, who urged the NKID as well as the members of the Politburo to overcome 'a petit-bourgeois conviction of "anti-Polonism"' and be guided by the 'indigenous interests of the revolution and socialist construction,' together with the pressure of France, that refused to continue negotiations with the Soviets in the case of ignoring the Polish initiative, forced Soviet diplomacy to revise the basis of the attitude of the USSR towards the neighbouring Western States.³⁶ The results were not long in coming: implementing the Warsaw demand, Moscow, simultaneously with the resumption of Soviet-Polish negotiations, made a similar proposal to Riga and Tallinn (as well as to Helsinki and Bucharest).

In February and May 1932, Latvia and Estonia signed the treaties of non-aggression with the USSR. Then, they signed the conventions on conciliation procedure. Thus, their ruling elites were to a large degree satisfied by obtaining legal guarantees of non-aggression, which the USSR previously granted to other states (for example, to Lithuania). Riga and Tallinn saw the conclusion of these treaties as, at least, a temporary abandonment of efforts

---

34   Nikolai Raivid, 'Dokladnaya zapiska M.M. Litvinovu "K voprosu o Baltiyskom soyuze",' 14 January 1932 // AVP RF. F. 05, op. 12, p. 86, d. 68, l. 1,6.
35   L. Kosheleva (edit. et al.), *Perepiska I.V. Stalina s V.M. Molotovym. 1925–1936.* Moskva: Rossiya molodaya, 1995, 209.
36   Oleg N. Ken and Alexander I. Rupasov, *Politbyuro TsK VKP(b) i otnosheniya SSSR s zapadnymi sosednimi gosudarstvami (konec 1920–1930-h gg.). Problemy. Dokumenty. Opyt kommentariya. Ch. 1. 1928–1934.* Sankt-Peterburg: Evropeiski dom, 2000, 248–56, 258–66, 268–72.

to isolate the Baltic States that could be a prelude to their Sovietization. However, the treaties that the USSR concluded with Latvia and Estonia objectively weakened the interest of these states in the military and political cooperation with Poland. That, in turn, encouraged Soviet diplomacy to formulate new tactical tasks.

Towards the protectorate: 1933-39

The shaping of the new Soviet policy in the Baltic States was primarily determined by pan-European processes, which were intensified by the hastened corrosion of the Versailles territorial-political system. The growing ambitions of Germany to have a new role in Europe and the desire of Britain and France to transfer these ambitions through a peaceful and controlled revision of the Versailles system (that was reflected in the negotiation on the pact of four Western Powers in spring-summer 1933) posed an immediate threat to all East-Central European States. In April 1933, Latvia, worried by the establishment of the National Socialist regime in Germany, proposed to convene a conference of the Baltic States with the participation of the USSR. Several weeks later Lithuania put forward the idea to all Baltic States to sign a Protocol to define aggression (this definition was contained in Soviet proposals at the Conference on disarmament in February 1933).

Soviet diplomacy, taking advantage of these initiatives (and of the similar wishes of Turkey, Czechoslovakia and Romania), took the first decisive step towards participation in the pan-European security system. In early July 1933, a series of Conventions for the definition of aggression (with participation of Baltic States) were signed in London. Lithuania, dissatisfied with the participation of Poland in the London conventions, concluded a separate agreement with the USSR a few days later.

The Soviet-Baltic rapprochement in spring-summer 1933 was developing in the context of Moscow's research into anti-German cooperation with Poland. In July 1933, the personal representative of Stalin, Karel Radek, the chief of the Bureau of International Information of the Central Committee of the Communist party of the Soviet Union, made an unprecedented visit to Poland. During the discussions with representatives of Pilsudski, both sides announced their intentions to withdraw from the competition and to coordinate their activities in the Baltic region. Radek even offered the Poles the opportunity to 'take Lithuania' as payment for possible concessions on other questions. He promised that the Soviet Union would react to such a step with full understanding. This offer was a kind of provocation. The Polish government cautiously reacted to the offers of the Kremlin that, in fact, outlined the division of the Baltic region on the Polish and Soviet spheres of influence.

The Soviet offers to Poland that concerned the Baltic States, were partly motivated by the desire to prevent the normalization of Polish-German relations. After autumn 1933, relations between Poland and Germany entered into a more constructive phase: they started a discussion about a non-aggression agreement. This did not go unnoticed in Moscow. At the same time, the Soviets observed the strengthening of the German influence in Latvia and Estonia. The prospect of the Polish-German reconciliation caused fear in the Baltic States and motivated them to seek the parallel normalization of relations with the new Germany. Germanophobia began to compete with traditional public fears of Soviet expansion.

The NKID sought innovative approaches because, as Stomonyakov wrote, 'currently you can never be sure in anything and, right now more than ever, bias regarding political concepts can only hurt the correct assessment of a situation and of good decision making.'[37] In this situation, the People's Commissar Litvinov took an initiative, aimed to attract Poland' cooperation for a new Soviet role in the Baltic region. In mid-December, the Soviets proposed that Poland conclude a joint declaration that should express the bilateral interest of both states in the preservation of the independence of Latvia, Lithuania and Estonia. According to Litvinov, the Baltic States should not know about the Soviet-Polish Declaration until the approval of its content. Therefore, Polish diplomacy (not without reasons) regarded the proposal of the USSR as aimed at the establishment of a common protectorate over the Baltic States. Despite the persuasions of Litvinov, Warsaw requested the opinion of the Baltic States themselves. That resulted in the leakage of information (historians still have no agreement about its circumstances) and the inevitable discredit of the Soviet initiative.

At the same time, at the end of December 1933, the Kremlin authorized the Soviet-French negotiations on the conclusion within the League of Nations of 'regional' agreements on mutual protection from the Germany aggression (involving Belgium, Czechoslovakia, Poland, Lithuania, Latvia, Estonia and Finland). The Soviet position in respect to Latvia, Lithuania and Estonia was explained in the report of M. Litvinov during the session of the Central Executive Committee of the USSR on 29 December 1933: 'We watch not only the phenomena, that represent the external danger of these countries, but also the development of internal political processes, which may contribute to the loss or weakening of their independence.'[38]

---

37 Boris S. Stomonyakov, 'Pismo S.I. Brodovskomu,' 27 December 1933 // AVP RF. F. 0150, op.28, p.60, d.2, l.151.

38 *Dokumenty vneshnei politiki SSSR* (herafter, *DVP SSSR*). T. 16, 789. In

Thereupon, on 17 January 1934, the Politburo adopted the detailed resolution about the Baltic region, which included the implementation of a series of political, economic and 'socio-cultural' activities regarding each of the Baltic countries. The Soviet leadership staked mostly on international-political factors, demonstrating extraordinary moderation in financing the orders in the Baltic States (moreover, Moscow refused to sign any long-term economic agreements).[39] The cooperation with Poland was not mentioned in the resolution; regardless of the outcome of the Polish-Soviet consultations, Moscow was determined to exploit new opportunities to strengthen itself in the Baltic region.

The Polish–German agreement on the non-use of force in bilateral relations (signed on 26 January 1934) finally buried the idea of a joint Soviet–Polish declaration. However, it caused serious anxiety for Lithuania and Latvia, which both feared the prospect of remaining alone. Moscow responded to the changed situation with a series of successful political actions in the spring of 1934. First, Soviet diplomats offered to make, with Germany, a common statement about the respect for sovereignty and non-interference into the internal affairs of the Baltic States. Berlin's refusal only enforced the image of the USSR as the only defender of the independence of the Baltic States. This issue also became the theme of the Soviet-French negotiations on regional agreement (the 'Eastern Locarno') in April¬–May 1934. There, Litvinov tried to obtain Paris's guarantee for the Baltic States in case of a German attack. In June, the French government finally rejected the opportunity to expand their commitments to the Baltic States. Thus, these activities by Moscow should had convinced Baltic politicians and public opinion that, due to the position of Warsaw, Berlin and Paris, their hopes to preserve independence should be connected mainly with Soviet patronage.

Second, on the initiative of the USSR, the duration of its bilateral non-aggression pacts with Lithuania, Latvia and Estonia was prolonged for ten years (until 1945).[40] The appropriate protocols were signed in early April,

---

April 1933, at a closed conference of the Latvian Social-Democrats, where the Estonian socialists were invited, A. Bushevic, promising to initiate the armed uprising of workers against those who would push his state on the path of a violation of neutrality, expressed the hope that the Soviet Union might reject its still 'indifferent' Baltic policy and intervene in the affairs of Latvia. The plenipotentiary minister Alexey Svidersky did his best to clear the transcript from such 'distortions' of the Soviet intentions (Magnus Ilmjärv, *Hääletu alistumine: Eesti, Läti ja Leedu välispoliitilise orientatsiooni kujunemine ja iseseivuse kaotus: 1920. aastate kekspaigast anneksioonini*. Tallinn: Argo, 2004, 216).

39   Ken and Rupasov, *Politbjuro*, 414–24.
40   It is interesting that Moscow refused to accept the Latvian wish to extend the non-aggression pact forever, because 'the documents, signed forever used to lose its value due to the fact that the mind becomes accustomed to them' (L.E. Berezov, 'Zapis

before a similar Soviet-Polish action. The willingness of the Baltic States to accept the Soviet offer gave Moscow the confidence that 'during the roll-call of the states interested in the preservation and strengthening of peace,' they 'will also always respond "yes sir!" ... in unison with the Soviet government.'[41]

The era of Polish dominance in the Baltic region in fact came to the end, but the time for active German penetration into the region had not yet come. A 'window of opportunity' was opening in front of Moscow who hastened to use it. Soviet diplomats demonstrated outstanding ingenuity – in small[42] initiatives and in great ones too – including the rejection of the late 1920s-early 1930s axiom of the inadmissibility of any forms of integration of Latvia, Lithuania and Estonia. Keeping 'the maximum prudence,' Soviet diplomacy embarked on a path of encouragement and even the coordination of these processes. It even invited the heads of the military ministries of all Baltic States to Moscow.

Domestic politics in the Baltic States slowed the Soviet-Baltic rapprochement although it did not particularly alarm Moscow. Soviet circles reacted to the long-awaited state coup in Estonia by Konstantin Päts on 12 March 1934 almost with empathy (moreover K. Päts beforehand inquired about the attitude of Moscow concerning such perspective). Also, the Soviets, demonstrating loyalty to the Lithuanian authorities, notified President Antanas Smetona (1926–40) of the preparation of the military takeover (which, taking place in early June, failed). The putsch, carried out by Karlis Ulmanis on 15 May in Latvia, partly worried the Soviet diplomats that were involved in the development of domestic politics.[43] Of course, they worried not only about the dictatorial aspirations of an old acquaintance, but about his pro-German sympathies, which were now improper. Generally Moscow succeeded in fulfilling its promise to carefully 'watch over domestic political processes.'

At the same time, Moscow expressed concerns that, despite the favourable international context, there was almost no positive dynamics in the relations between the USSR and the Baltic States (the relations 'stand still and... they are weak or almost absolutely not influenced by such facts as the existence of a non-aggression treaty, the rise of German aggressiveness, the

---

besedy s latviyskim poslannikom Alfredsom Bilmanisom,' 22 March 1934 // AVP RF. F. 0150, op. 30, p. 62, d. 6. L. 26).

41   DVP SSSR. T.17, 234 (the authors italics).

42   One of the original friendly proposals was, for example, to grant the Latvian army 'on the basis of reciprocity of some accommodation for sick officers in the sanatoriums of the southern coast of the Crimea and the Black Sea coast' (I.M. Mortyshin, 'Doklad L.E. Berezovu,' 10 November 1934 // AFPRF. F. 0150, op. 30, p. 62, d. 9, l. 18).

43   Contemporary Latvian researchers could not yet establish with sufficient certainty, whether the representatives of Soviet mission in Riga helped K. Ulmanis or his political opponents.

strengthening of the international position of the USSR and our admission into the League of Nations').[44] When the series of political upheavals stopped by the middle of summer, the heads of the Baltic diplomatic agencies received an invitation to Moscow. The first official visits to Moscow of the Foreign Ministers of Estonia and Lithuania took place in July and August of 1934.

The talks between the Soviet and Lithuanian Foreign Ministers Maxim Litvinov and Stasys Lozoraitis on Lithuania's role in the Baltic Union were particularly confident: the difficult international situation of Kaunas highlighted its dependence on the Soviet Union,[45] whereas tensions with Poland and Germany since the early 1930s guaranteed that the future Baltic Union will not become an instrument of Polish or German politics. The treaty of conciliation and cooperation between Latvia, Lithuania and Estonia, signed in Geneva on 12 September 1934, was the result of the dedicated efforts of Moscow. Formally, this treaty was opened for the accession of third states. However, the demand of consensus actually eliminated the extension of the Baltic Entente (as the new formation became called). That allowed Soviet leaders to make an unprecedented step: in February 1935, they completely removed their objections to the conclusion of a military alliance between Lithuania, Latvia and Estonia.[46]

In parallel, the USSR temporally succeeded in improving its relations with Latvia. Ulmanis's government was trying to provide a more independent policy on the assumption that, in this situation, the major powers would fail to agree behind the backs of the Baltic States.[47] This tactic was interpreted in Moscow precisely as blackmail, based on exaggerated beliefs about the USSR's interest in relations with Latvia. Soviet diplomats considered that 'Latvians...became too spoilt with our policy of rapprochement,' they do not understand the 'generous attitude towards them and interpret it as a sign of weakness.' The means aimed to 'correct' Riga's behaviour (the restriction of the Soviet orders, the publications in British press about the anti-Semitism of

---

44   I.M. Mortyshin, 'Doklad B.S. Stomonyakovu,' 21 October 1934 // AFPRF. F. 0150, op. 30, p. 62, d. 3, l. 31.

45   Before the Lithuanian Foreign Minister, Stasys Lozoraitis (1934–38) came to Moscow, the Politburo approved military supplies to Lithuania and agreed to sell cavalry swords, etc. (Protocol No 11 of the Politbyuro TsK VKP (b) meeting ("special") on 5 August 1934 // RGASPI. F. 17, op. 162, p. 49, d. 16, l41). However, the subsequent negotiations brought no results.

46   B.S. Stomonyakov, 'Pismo M.A. Karskomu,' 26 February 1935 // AVP RF. F. 0151, op. 26, p. 49, d. 2, l. 15.

47   Aivars Stranga, 'Russian and Polish Policies in the Baltic States from 1933 to 1935,' in: *The Baltic States at Historical Crossroads. Political, Economic and Legal Problems in the Context of International Cooperation on the Doorstep of the 21st century*, edited by Talavs Judins. Riga: Latvian Academy of Sciences, 1998, 433.

the Latvian government)[48] testified to the inability of Moscow to rearrange the partnership. For the USSR, the tactic of a reciprocal blackmail of Ulmanis was risky. Nevertheless, Soviet pressure and the sudden belief of Ulmanis in the threat of a Soviet-Polish-German détente refreshed the Sovietophilia in Riga. In December 1934, the chief of staff of the Latvian army, General Mārtiņš Hartman (Hartmann) began to inquire about the opportunities of buying planes and tanks in the USSR.[49] Simultaneously, the Ministry of Internal Affairs closed some of the Russian émigré organizations (e.g. the Fraternal society of the former Russian servicemen, etc.). In this context, Moscow typically reduced the staff of its diplomatic missions in the Baltic States in late 1934 – the first half of 1935 (probably, Moscow believed that the time came not only to cat down its expenses for corruption of politicians, but also the salaries of the diplomats). The NKID believed that it could already look through K. Ulmanis and Vilhelms Munters ('these two slyboots') and it cared less about Lithuanian politicians.

The Baltic States loyally responded to the wishes of the USSR expressed during the Soviet–French campaign for the foundation of a regional system of collective security. Therefore, Soviet diplomacy calmly perceived the attempts of Tallinn to play an active role in negotiations on Eastern Locarno as well as the demarches of Estonia, Latvia and Lithuania in favour of providing security in East-Central Europe. While the USSR signed the treaties of mutual assistance with France and Czechoslovakia in May 1935, the desire to establish a common regional system of security evaporated. Although the idea of the Eastern Pact (then the pact of non-aggression and consultation) – involving the participation of the Baltic States, Germany and Poland – remained on the agenda of international negotiations until the spring of 1936.

At the conference of the Foreign Ministers of Latvia, Lithuania and Estonia in May 1935, the interest of these states in the system of collective security was confirmed. Actually, this conference indicated the drift of the political circles of the Baltic States towards the conclusion of agreements of mutual assistance with the Soviet Union. In June, Riga informed allied Estonia about its desire to conclude a Soviet-Latvian treaty, similar to the Soviet-Czechoslovak and the Franco-Soviet one.[50] After signing the Anglo–German naval agreement in mid-June that annulled the restrictions on the building of the German Navy and strengthened the international position of the *Reich*, the Baltic States

---

48   The calculation was based on the consideration that some of the oil, a key product of the Latvian exports to Britain, was bought by the 'Jewish' firms.
49   S.I. Brodovsky, 'Doklad B.S. Stomonyakovu,' 12 December 1934 // AVP RF. F. 0150, op. 30, p. 62, d. 3, l. 5.
50   Tallinn negatively responded to these shifts in Latvian politics. However, Moscow also received information about the differences among the Estonian leadership (A.M. Ustinov, 'Dnevnik,' 30 July 1935 // AVP RF. F. 0154, op. 28, p. 40, d. 6, l. 118.

desire to rely on the USSR increased.

On 10 July, Latvia transmitted a proposal to conclude a bilateral mutual assistance pact to the Soviets. However, there was no answer.[51] The reasons for the unwillingness of the Soviet leaders to extend a system of mutual assistance pacts on the Baltic States was revealed by Stomonyakov, the Deputy of the People's Commissar of Foreign Affairs. Responding to the initiative of the Soviet representative in Lithuania to propose the Soviet-Baltic mutual assistance treaty,[52] Stomonyakov explained that, 'such a Pact, giving us materially nothing, or almost nothing, would one-sidedly tie our hands to the commitment to provide material aid in case of an attack on them by Germany or Poland. When such an attack happens, we could, if we would deem favourable, assist them with our help.'

The desire of Moscow to retain a free hand in the policy towards the Baltic States inevitably led to a weakening of its newfound influence. First, the lack of international guarantees pushed all Baltic States to develop contacts with Germany, the only force able to counterbalance the Soviet influence in the region. This trend gained momentum in 1936. Especially clearly, it manifested itself in Estonia, where public opinion was previously marked by anti-German sentiment. For example, the government of Tallinn refused to support Riga in limiting the travels of the 'Hitler youth' to the Baltic States.[53] Second, Soviet policy created the impression that Moscow pursued the goal to expulse from the Baltic States all forces that could prevent their absorption by the Soviet Union. The American Ambassador to Moscow, William Bullitt, compared the mood in the Baltic missions in Moscow to the expectations that prevailed at Athens and Thebes in the time of Philip of Macedon. 'Yes, said the commander of the Estonian army to the Soviet minister, the USSR is not going to encroach the independence of Estonia. However, he continued, the Soviet Union would broaden due to the 'natural course of things.'[54] Similar

---

51   Stranga, 'Stranga, 'Russian and Polish Policies', 435–6.
52   The plenipotentiary minister M. Karskyi believed that a proposal to conclude pacts of the mutual assistance would not be accepted by Latvia and Estonia, but the fact that the Soviet initiative itself would cause a positive public response.
53   The growing interest of Estonians in Russia should be fairy noted. In accordance with the data of the plenipotentiary representation by the spring 1936, the wish to learn Russian among the students in Tartu reached such a scale that in this small town more than a hundred people earn money by giving private Russian language lessons.
54   A.M. Ustinov, 'Zapis besedy s J. Laidonerom', 25 Avril 1936 // AVP RF. F. 0154, op. 29, p. 42, d. 8, l. 66. After the coup in Estonia in 1934, the Commander in Chief Johan Laidoner and the Chief of the General Staff Nikolai Reek supported idea of the revision of the 'pessimistic' defensive doctrine and for giving it 'activity' (the transfer of military actions onto the territory of the USSR, etc.). This change was associated with the deepening of military cooperation with Germany (Jari Leskinen, *Vaiettu Suomen silta: Suomen*

considerations motivated Estonia to refuse a unilateral Soviet guarantee. According to Heinrich Laretei, the Vice-Minister for Foreign Affairs, this guarantee would be a precondition for the exclusive dependence of Estonia on the USSR.[55] As a result, Soviet-Estonian relations, that were never especially warm, steadily worsened.

However, the main attention of Moscow was still focused on Kaunas. The Soviet diplomats feared that the catastrophic situation with the Lithuanian economy created the favourable atmosphere for the activity 'of the German and Polish agents' and the overthrow of the A. Smetona's Sovietophile regime (indeed, Lithuanian authorities consistently sought to sign the agreement on mutual assistance with the Soviet Union). After the replacement of the leadership of the Estonian Foreign Ministry and the appointment of the pro-German oriented Friedrich Akel to the post of Minister in the early summer of 1936, it became apparent that Lithuania had to forget about the development of cooperation within the Baltic Entente. Thus, Kaunas openly raised the question of a bilateral treaty with the Soviet Union and renewed requests for the sale of weapons and military equipment (the detailed draft of the agreement was officially turned over to the Soviet trade representative in Lithuania in September). At the same time, the interest in the development of contacts with the Soviet Union also intensified in the Defence Ministry of Latvia.

In 1936 and 1937, the Soviet and Baltic top militaries exchanged official visits. First, the Chiefs of General Staffs of Latvia, Lithuania and Estonia went to Moscow (they visited the May-Day parade in 1936). After, in the late winter of 1937, Marshal Alexander Egorov, the Chief of the Soviet General Staff, made a return trip to the Baltic States. The nature of this unprecedented visit for the relations between the USSR and the neighbouring states remained largely unclear. Marshal Egorov was forbidden to discuss military supplies from the USSR to Latvia and Lithuania (though the NKID hoped this directive might be subsequently revised). The presidents of Latvia and Lithuania abstained from the meeting with the Marshal. General Johan Laidoner recommended to the participants of the 23 February 1937 parade in Tallinn [23 February was celebrated as the Red Army Day in the USSR], organized in honour of the arrival of Egorov, to march not as soldiers, but as free citizens.[56] However, Moscow appreciated the information that after the visit of Egorov Latvia's

---

ja Viron sotilaallinen yhteistoiminta Neuvostoliiton varalta vuosina 1930–1939. Helsinki: Finish Historical Society, 1997). Estonia was the only Baltic State that preferred not to seek military materials from the USSR, but chose to buy them in Germany and Sweden.
55   Ustinov, 'Dnevnik. Beseda s H. Lareteem,' 15 May 1935 // AVP RF. F. 0154, op. 29, p. 42, d. 8, l. 93–4.
56   V.H. Gallienne to E. Monson (Riga), 1 January 1937 // Public Record Office (herafter, PRO). FO/371/21106/N1517.

Minister of War, General Jānis Balodis, 'became a clear Sovietophile.' In a speech to the graduates of the Higher Military School in May, 1937, Balodis claimed that despite the system in the USSR being different, which Latvia did not accept, in the situation of a war, Latvia should go along with the Soviet Union.[57]

The content of the negotiations between Egorov and Baltic political and military leaders, or, at least, its context, was undoubtedly determined by two factors: on the one hand, by a growing popularity of the ideas of international neutrality in the Baltic States and, on the other, by the discussions in Moscow about the role of the Baltic States in its military-political planning. Soviet military experts, at least since the early 1930s, regarded the neutrality of the Baltic States in the case of war as an unpleasant circumstance that might complicate the use of their territories by the Red Army. The Defence Sector of the Soviet State Planning Committee, analysing scenarios of future war, believed that 'the Estonian army would closely coordinate its actions with activity of the Finnish and Swedish armies and would participate in joint actions against Leningrad, and Latvia would try to 'force Lithuania to join the Polish-Latvian coalition using the armed influence.' From the point of view of the Soviet offensive strategy, it would be 'much worse, if they (the Baltic States) in the beginning of the war would declare neutrality. Thus, in accordance with the concrete political situation either at the beginning or during the war, we should perform on them the same operation,' that Germany performed in 1914. Therefore, regardless of the position the Baltic States would take at the beginning of the military conflict, 'Estonia, Lithuania and Latvia should be quickly defeated and Sovietized.'[58]

The Soviet strategic plan for the war in the West that operated in the first half of the 1930s put the defeat of the Polish state as its main goal under the assumption that 'Finland, Estonia and Latvia, most probably, would remain neutral, at least for the first period of the war…, that Poland will not have time to occupy Lithuania before our Western front will start its offensive.' The transformation of Germany ('allied to Poland') into the 'main organiser of the anti-Soviet intervention' led Mikhail Tukhachevsky, the Deputy of the People's Commissar for Defence, to the conclusion that 'Lithuania can be easily occupied by German-Polish forces during the first days of war,' and then 'Germany, by threatening Riga, could influence the position of Latvia and get the aviation base for regular raids on Leningrad and Kronstadt.'[59] In the

---

57   S.I. Brodovski, 'Dnevnik' 21 May 1937 // AVP RF. F. 0150, op. 34, p. 71, d. 6, l. 46.
58   N. Snitko, 'Doklad 'O haraktere buduschey voinu i zadachah oborony,' 4 Avril 1930 // Rossiyskiy gosudrastvennyj arhiv ekonomiki. F. 4372, op. 91, d. 91, l. 29–11.
59   M. N. Tuhachevski, 'Doklad K.E. Voroshilovy,' 25 February 1935 // Rossiyskiy gosudrastvennyji voennyi arhiv ekonomiki. F. 33987, op. 3, d. 400, l 226–7.

beginning of 1936, Stalin and Molotov began to publicly speak about the 'borders on credit' – meaning the possible German use of the Baltic territory for aggression against the Soviet Union.[60] On the other hand, Soviet militaries had no scruples to explain that in a case of war they did not intend to respect the sovereignty of the Baltic States.[61] The governing body of the Red Army (probably in 1936 or at the beginning of 1937) elaborated a plan for the 'repetition of Belgium,' but 'the government' refused to confirm it.[62]

Reflecting on these trends, Soviet diplomacy reacted extremely negatively and sentiments for Baltic States' proclamation of constant neutrality intensified in 1936–37. Thus, talking with Kaarel Eenpalu (Einbund), the influential companion of K. Päts, the Soviet Polpred (ambassador) in Tallin Alexey Ustinov said: 'Inaction... during our tense era of the struggle for peace is actually a blow to the system of the collective security and is equal to the support of aggressor, whereas the "neutrality" is therefore such inaction in favour of the aggressor.'

The demand of Moscow for the Baltic States to make a public choice in favour of Germany's foes as well as its reluctance to assume any obligations of protection of the Baltic States's sovereignty – as well as the deepening of the détente with Lithuania and Latvia – indicated a growing crisis in Soviet foreign policy and in the relations between the Kremlin and military leaders. The unleashing of 'the great terror' in the autumn of 1936, partly determined by these general political contradictions, also affected Soviet Baltic policy. On the other hand, the disgust caused in the Baltic States by news about state red terror, destroyed illusions about the goals of the Kremlin and about its reliability as a partner.[63] Wide ostentatious gestures (in June 1937, the Latvian Foreign Minister Vilhelms Munters was honoured to meet Stalin) could not change this situation. It was obvious that Moscow was unable (or unwilling) to assist the Baltic States in obtaining effective international guarantees, or to assume clear political commitments. The Baltic Entente,

---

60   *DVP SSSR*. T. 19, 106–7.
61   Skaife, military attaché to Lord Chilston, Moscow, 23 April 1936 // PRO. FO/371/20349/N2290.
62   '1937. Pokazaniya marshala Tuhachevskogo', *Voenno-istoricheski zhurnal* 8 (1991): 48.
63   In the summer of 1937, the Soviet plenipotentiary minister in Estonia reported about the unprecedented 'unbridled campaign against the Soviet Union' that was unfolding after news about the suicide of the high-ranking Soviet military official Yan Gamarnik, and was assuming the 'hyperbolic dimensions after the publication of the prosecutor's decision about the upcoming trial over Tukhachevskyi etc. on 11 June. The thesis that 'no one now will have desire to contact such an insolvent partner, as the USSR' was noted particularly (A.M. Ustinov, 'Doklad M.M. Litvinovu,' 18 June 1937//AVP RF. F. 0154, op. 30, p. 44, d. 13, l. 24–5.

whose belated establishment promised the strengthening of the position of the Baltic States in their cooperation with the Soviet Union, was perceived (from the end of 1937) as a burden even by such enthusiasts of the Baltic cooperation as K. Ulmanis. The USSR was losing political initiative in the region, which it undoubtedly possessed in 1933–34. The dynamic and multifaceted policy of Germany was weaning the competition for the dominant influence in the region. This situation was aggravated by the killings of the eminent Soviet diplomats, who for fifteen years were involved in the formation and conduction of Soviet foreign policy in the Baltic region.[64]

Following Estonia, Latvia also began to incline to extend cooperation with the Germans. Soviet diplomats often called this tactic the policy of 'equilibrium' between Germany and the Soviet Union – 'one iota to the right, one iota to the left.'[65] In practice, for instance, it prevented President Ulmanis from responding to the newly arrived Soviet polpred to Riga, I. Zotov, who, during the presentation of his credentials in December 1937, expressed desires to develop contacts between military ministries.

The political closeness of the USSR and Lithuania also quickly betrayed the past. In March 1938, using the international crisis following the Anschluss of Austria, the Polish government delivered an ultimatum to Lithuania. Warsaw demanded the restoration of full diplomatic and consular relationships, what actually meant Lithuania's refusal to retain its claims on Vilnius and its surroundings. Previously, the support of these pretensions had always been regarded by Moscow as corresponding to its own interests regardless of any problems which witnessed the history of the Soviet-Lithuanian relations. In March 1938, Soviet diplomacy was slow to intervene in the Polish-Lithuanian conflict. When further ignoring it became impossible, Moscow confined itself by a 'weak move' in relation to Poland and advised the Lithuanian government to 'yield to the violence' (the 'international community,' as Litvinov declared to the Envoy, Jurgis Baltrushaitis 'would not understand the Lithuanian refusal').

In total, the influence of Moscow on the outcome of the Polish-Lithuanian conflict was very small and mostly manifested in the promotion of Poland

---

64   During 1936–38, there were four heads of the 1st Western department of NKID. In addition, the Deputy people's Commissar (previously a member of the Board of NKID), who since 1926 supervised the Baltic direction, B. S. Lomonaco, was arrested after a suicide attempt in the summer of 1938. He was executed in 1941. Lomonaco's fate was shared by polpreds in Latvia (Brodovsky) and in Lithuania (Karskyi). Sabine Dullin, *Des hommes d influences: Les ambassadeurs de Staline en Europe 1930–1939*. Paris : Payot, 2001, 334–7.
65   I.S. Zotov, 'Dnevnik,' 3 December 1937//AVP RF. F. 0150, op. 34, p. 71, d. 6, l23.

rather than in protecting the interests of its client.⁶⁶ Not surprisingly, the USSR's influence reduced in Lithuania after its capitulation. As the new Soviet Envoy stated in August 1938, the wide horizons were opened 'before Germany in Lithuania. It dominates there in the full sense of the word.' The polpred could not offer any leverage measures on Kaunas, except commercial ones. However, the competition with the Germans or the British in this sphere had obviously been meaningless (only five percent of Lithuanian exports went to the USSR).⁶⁷ When in March 1939, Germany demanded Klaipeda (Memel), Kaunas did not think about the appeal to the USSR. From the main political partner of the Soviet Union, Lithuania rapidly turned into the weakest link of Soviet policy in this region (this evolution explains why Moscow consented to place Lithuania into the German sphere of influence in August 1939).

The Soviet positions, in comparison with 1933–1934, were severely weakened, and the fear of the Baltic States being absorbed by Germany was the USSR's only trump card. Moscow could no longer think about the restoration of Soviet influence in the Baltic States, or say anything about its dominance without the consent of the other Powers. Its main efforts at the end of 1938 through mid-1939 were focused on the 'big politics.' During these months, the diplomatic moves of the Soviet Union regarding the Baltic region were repeating the actions which were envisaged five years ago, but the accents were placed differently. The main focus was placed not on the appeal to Poland to cooperate in the protection of the Baltic States's independence,⁶⁸ but on the inclusion of the Baltic theme into the agenda of negotiations with Western Powers.

After the British gave their guarantees to Poland and Romania, Moscow decided to talk to the Balts in a firm tone. On 28 March 1939, Commissar Litvinov, referring to rumours about the German-Estonian treaty on the passage of German troops through the territory of Estonia, handed the Estonian Envoy a note. It expressed the inadmissibility for the USSR of German predominance in the Baltic region (the same note was sent to the government of Latvia). The Commissar's speech sounded like an unequivocal request for the exclusive interests of the Soviet Union in the territory of these

---

66   Sergey Z. Sluch, 'Gitler, Stalin i genezis chetvertogo razdela Polshi,' in: Vostochnaya Evropa mezhdu Gitlerom i Stalinym. 1939–1941. Moskva: Indrik, 1999, 93–96.
67   'Stenogramma soveschaniya u zamnarkomata t. Potemkina,' 14 August 1938// AVP RF. F. 05, op. 18, p. 146, d. 111, l. 33–9. These changes led to a sharp decline of Russian language teaching in Lithuania, the preference was given to English and French languages.
68   A new proposal about this problem was passed using military channels, but not diplomatic ones (Sluch, 'Gitler, Stalin i genesis, 135, 161).

two States: 'Any agreement, "voluntary" or imprisoned under external pressure, which would bring a diminution or limitation of the independence and autonomy of the Republic of Estonia, and which would assume the political, economic or otherwise domination of a third state, would grant it any exclusive rights and privileges...would be recognized by the Soviet government as intolerable and incompatible with the assumptions and the spirit' of the peace treaty and the non-aggression treaty.[69]

The persistent attempts of the Baltic States to find a protector in London or Paris were unsuccessful. The Western Powers did not want to charge them with new heavy obligations. In April and May, the Soviets handed Britain and France two proposals to provide a joint guarantee of the Baltic States. After those unsuccessful moves, the new head of the Commissariat for Foreign Affairs, Vyacheslav Molotov (1939–49) made known the reaction of the Western powers in his public speech: Britain and France 'do not say anything about their assistance to the three states on the North-Western border of the USSR, which may be unable to defend its neutrality in case of an attack by aggressors.'[70]

Latvia and Estonia, disappointed with the policy of neutrality as a way to protect their independence (despite the fact that the Baltic Entente announced its commitment to neutrality during its conference in February 1939), signed the non-aggression pacts with Germany on 7 June. Thus, Moscow faced a dilemma of how to preserve its position in the region. There were only two possibilities – to wage war on Germany or to make an agreement with it. At the same time, Berlin felt that a compromise with the USSR could be achieved in the area of the 'solution of the Baltic problem.' On behalf of the Germans, the head of Italy's Foreign Ministry hinted to the Soviet *chargé d'affaires* that the possibility of providing the joint Soviet-German 'guarantees' to the Baltic States existed.[71] So, Moscow received a proposal to recall its own similar initiative, done in March 1934. However, this time, the proposal could not satisfy the USSR without the inclusion of the 'real' content in these guarantees.

On the other hand, Soviet negotiations with Britain and France opened considerable scope for freedom of action in the Baltic States for the USSR. During these negotiations, the Soviets referred to the need for action against

---

69   Küllo Arjakas (ed.), *Ot pakta Molotova-Ribbentropa do dogovora o bazah: Dokumenty i materialy.* Tallinn: Perioodika, 1990, 17.

70   *SSSR v borbe za mir nakanune vtoroi mirovoi voiny (sentyabr 1938 – avgust 1939): Dokumenty i materialy.* Moskva: Politizdat, 1971, 428.

71   Ingibor Fleischhauer, *Pakt: Gitler, Stalin i iniciativa germanskoi diplomatii. 1938–1939.* Perevod s nemeckogo. Moskva : Progress, 1991, 143.

'an indirect aggression.'[72] The breadth of its interpretation, proposed by the USSR, alarmed Western partners. In August 1939, Moscow suggested that Britain and France should demand a temporary occupation of several ports and islands in the Baltic Sea. At the same time, the Soviet Baltic fleet 'in order to protect the independent Baltic States' should be based on Åland, Moonsund, in Hanko, Haapsalu, Pärnu, Heinaste and Libau together with the united squadron.[73] Actually, the Soviets proposed a joint protectorate of the three powers.

Yet, Germany could offer something more. The Kremlin, which was intolerant of any attempts of the Baltic States to keep neutrality 'during our tense era for the struggle for peace,' agreed to take the position of benevolent neutrality favouring the aggressor in the emerging world war. The Soviet-German secret protocol, signed on 23 August 1939 by Molotov and Ribbentrop, contained the radical and extremely beneficial to the USSR decision:

> In the event of a territorial and political rearrangement in the areas belonging to the Baltic States (Finland, Estonia, Latvia and Lithuania), the northern boundary of Lithuania shall represent the boundary of the spheres of influence of Germany and USSR.

After signing the Molotov-Ribbentrop pact, Moscow asked Latvia and Estonia to open negotiations on a trade agreement, which these states tried to conclude in vain during the previous decade. The Soviet-Estonian negotiations ended within a few days and the Estonian Minister of Foreign Affairs received an invitation to visit the Soviet Union in order to sign the trade agreement. However, during the meeting with Molotov on 24 September, he heard the shocking demand to conclude with the USSR a military alliance or a treaty on mutual assistance, which would give to the USSR rights to have the Navy and Air Force strongholds and bases on the Estonian territory. For the moment, Moscow also refused to finalize the trade agreements with Tallinn. On 25 September, the German Ambassador in Moscow was informed that 'the Soviet Union will immediately proceed to the solution of the Baltic States problem.'[74] Three days later, a new secret Protocol was signed in Moscow

---

72 'The phrase 'indirect aggression' refers to the action upon which any of the listed States [of the Baltic region] agrees under the threat of the use of force by another power or without such a threat and which causes the use of the territory and forces of this state for aggression against it or against one of the causes the loss by the state of independence or violation of its neutrality' (*SSSR v borbe za mir*, 487).

73 *SSSR v borbe za mir*, 575–6.

74 *SSSR–Germaniya. 1939. T.1. Dokumenty i materialy o sovetsko-germanskih otnosheniyah s aprelya po oktyabr 1939*. Vilnius: Mokslas, 1989, 106.

that modified the boundaries of the spheres of influence between the USSR and Germany. The territory of Lithuania, as well as the territories of all other Baltic States, were located within the Soviet sphere of interest. On 28 September, the Soviet-Estonian Treaty of mutual assistance was signed, and soon the USSR signed similar treaties with Latvia (5 October) and Lithuania (10 October).

Additional events were not long in coming. Already in early September, Soviet representatives formulated the 'true desires of the masses of workers' of the Baltic States. The polpred in Riga supposed that these desires were aimed to 'make Latvia a Soviet State and attach it to the USSR as the 12th of the Republic.'[75]

Conclusion

Initially, there were favourable preconditions for the relations of Soviet Russia with the Baltic States (they were perhaps more favourable than the relations of the USSR with its other neighbors along the Western border – Poland, Romania and Finland). Moscow, on the one hand, and Riga, Tallinn and Kaunas, on the other, were objectively interested in the political and economic interaction.

The conditions for the 'divorce' of 1920 did not give reasons for the serious mutual claims (such as, for example, the fate of Ukrainian and Belarusian lands in Soviet relations with Poland, the fate of Bessarabia in relations with Romania or the fate of Eastern Karelia in relations with Finland). The Russian minority did not cause any problems in the bilateral relations. The predominance of anti-Soviet sentiment in the Russian community of the Baltic States protected it from the active intervention of Moscow.[76] The Soviets just occasionally paid attention to the position of the Russians (like during land reform in the Republic of Lithuania and Estonia's resettlement of fishermen from the coast of lake Peipsi and Pihkva to the shore of the Baltic sea, etc.), and the interest in teaching the Russian language was determined only by the desire to facilitate and conduct propaganda. Until 1934, Soviet foreign bodies

---

75   *Ot pakta Molotova-Ribbentropa*, 26.
76   Only in the 1930s the Baltic States started to realise that 'some [Soviet] propagandistic agencies' had pursued 'different policies' than the NKID. For example, these USSR agencies demonstrated an increased interest in some Russian organizations of a fascist trend in Estonia (like '*Young Russia*', which, in accordance with the statement of K. Eenpalu, was conducting the 'increased agitation... in the border zone, supporting the Soviet Russia and praising Stalin's national policy, and encouraging, in a case of war, not to use weapons against the USSR' (A.M. Ustinov, 'Dnevnik,' 3 March 1936// AVP RF. F. 0154, op. 29, p. 42, d. 8, l. 39–40.

avoided arguments about national or racial community. Therefore, for example, they were more interested in the potential use of the Polish minority in Latgale than in the possibility of an appeal to the Russian diaspora. In the early 1930s, Moscow hosted several trains with Jewish families from Lithuania, while it denied return permission to Russian peasants.[77] The inertia of this approach prevailed until 1940. While Moscow advertised the 'reunion' of Ukrainians and Belarusians on the ruins of the Polish State, the 'Russian card' was not played in relations with the Baltic States. On their part, the Baltic States (unlike, for example, Finland) also demonstrated the utmost restraint regarding the protection of Estonian, Latvian and Lithuanian national minorities in the USSR.

Ideological differences and subversive Communist activity had no significant impact on inter-state relations between the USSR and the Baltic States. This circumstance was partly caused by the extremely small memberships of the Baltic Communist parties (which, sometimes, had only dozens of people). Moreover, as Soviet methods of collectivization and industrialization became well-known in the Baltic States (thanks to the permeability of the boundaries), it diminished the attractiveness of the socialist experiment and Moscow was not sure about the appropriateness of expenditures for the pro-Soviet periodicals publication. At the same time, the Russian theatre, painting, literature as well as innovations in Soviet public education elicited great interest in the Baltic States. Thus, in the 1920s-early 1930s, cultural relations were quite intensive.[78]

Finally, the basis for durable inter-state relations was the objective interest of the USSR in the conservation of the zone of independent Baltic States. The very existence of this was a natural buffer that protected the territory of the USSR from the threats of the Great Powers – whether that was Britain in the 1920s or Germany in the 1930s. Similarly, the young Baltic States were acutely aware of the need for regional cooperation as the main protection against manipulation by the major European powers that sought to overcome deep divisions generated by the results of the World War. But these

---

77   Since 1933, Comintern matured the idea of deploying by the Communist party of Estonia of the struggle for the rights of the Russian population of the Pechersk region ('even' right up to secession). The emergence of this idea, however, was determinated not so much by the beginning of the 'nationalization' of foreign policy of the USSR, but many by the traditional Communist rigorism: each section of the Comintern should protect national minorities (for example, Polish section should protect the German minority) up to the collapse of the state.

78   About the activities of the All-Soviet society for cultural relations with foreign countries in the Baltic States see at: Magnus Ilmjärv, *'Juunivalitsuse moodustamisest Leedus, Lätis ja Eestis ning Nõukogude Liidu kultuuridiplomaatiast'*, Acta Historica Tallinnensia 4 (2000): 104–44.

requirements were rarely embodied in joint political action, as it was during the conclusion of the London conventions about the definition of the aggressor in 1933.

Generally, the facilities of coexistence between Russia and the independent Baltic States during the interwar period were lost or reversed. Soviet-Baltic relations were constantly evolving from crisis to crisis. Not forgetting about the impact that political instability had on bilateral relations in the Baltic States, or about the trends of the 'original Patriarchal nationalism,' adventurism and corruption, which affected the part of the national elites, it should be stated that the primary responsibility for their development is certainly on the Soviet side.

From the mid-1920s until late-1930s, the Soviet Union tried vainly to play the Great Power role in the Baltic region. Ridiculing the provincialism, dependence and corruption of the neighbouring small states, Moscow tried to treat them as proverbial 'banana republics' – thereby discrediting their opinions and destroying sincere hopes for mutually beneficial cooperation (this was especially apparent during the Soviet-Latvian negotiations on the extension of the trade agreement in 1931–32). Simultaneously, Soviet leadership failed to use the 'negative capital' – a genuine fear in the Baltic States of resurgent state power and the Communist ideology of new Russia. The use of this fear could have been an important precondition for the establishment of lasting political relations and conditions of compromise. Instead, Moscow preferred to spend its 'negative capital' on the petty bullying of the Balts for the sake of closing small emigrant societies and achieving such little goals.

The Soviets did not understand what they wanted in the Baltic region. A hierarchisation of goals and objectives, and an adequate assessment of their own capabilities and resources was not conducted. In the early-1930s, the Soviet Union was forced to renounce its plans to force the Baltic States to turn away from Poland and negotiate with Moscow one by one, from positions of weakness. The non-aggression pacts opened a short era of Soviet-Baltic détente. However, the emergence of a real military threat not only motivated the Baltic States (especially Latvia and Lithuania) to look for rapprochement with the Soviet Union, but also provoked a desire in Moscow to shy away from taking on any obligation which could hamper its diplomatic manoeuvres. In the mid-1930s, despite the fact that the Soviet Union had an army of one million and the largest number of tanks in the world, it was afraid to 'compromise' itself by selling Lithuania cavalry checkers. As a result, the USSR failed to fulfil the first commandment of a Great Power – to act in accordance with its own interests and support the weaker states that respect those interests. The USSR influence in the Baltic region in the late-1930s was undermined by Soviet policy itself. Nonetheless, the USSR acquired power over a stubborn Estonia, a constructive Latvia and a friendly Lithuania from the hands of Berlin despite its own ruined Baltic policy.

Translated by Raisa Barash

Part Two

Economy and Diplomacy

3

Balancing in Central Europe: Great Britain and Hungary in the 1920s

TAMÁS MAGYARICS

This chapter complements the much longer studies on British-Hungarian bilateral relations in the 1920s by Miklós Lojkó and Gábor Bátonyi. Since the publication of their monographs, a number of scholarly works have been written on various aspects of the bilateral relations between the two countries as well as on some of the major actors in contemporary political life, such as, for example, Pál Teleki by Balázs Ablonczy; while Sir Bryan Cartledge's book about the British perception of the Trianon Peace Treaty of 1920 provides invaluable insights into the thinking of British politicians with reference to Central Europe.[1] Though new archival materials and secondary sources do not warrant a new interpretation of bilateral relations between Great Britain and Hungary in the post-WWI years, they do offer interesting new additions to the diplomatic and political history of the years in which Hungary was looking for a new role in international life, while Great Britain had to re-evaluate its prewar policies based on the Rankean 'pentarchy,' that is, the balance of power in Europe between five Great Powers (Austria-Hungary, France, Great Britain, Germany and Russia). This period also signaled the beginning of British 'retreat' from the affairs of Central Europe, with repercussions that turned out to be extremely tragic for the region and Europe in general.

It is stating the obvious that British foreign policy on the continent was driven

---

1   Miklós Lojkó. *Meddling in Middle Europe. Britain and the 'Lands Between' 1919–1925*. Budapest: CEU Press, 2006; Gábor Bátonyi. *Britain and Central Europe 1918–1933*. Oxford: Clarendon, 1999; Balázs Ablonczy. *Pal Teleki (1879–1941). The life of a controversial Hungarian statesman*. New York: Columbia University Press, 2006; Sir Bryan Cartledge. *The Peace Conference of 1919–1923 and Their Aftermath*, 2009.

to a large degree by balance of power considerations in the 19th century as well as in the early-20th century. Austria-Hungary played a pivotal role in these calculations in London. While the British government deemed the survival of Austria as a Great Power of primary national interest during the 1848–49 Hungarian revolution and war of independence, the Dual Monarchy's alliance with the unified and rising Germany in the last decades of the 19th century changed the British outlook on, and the image of, the Monarchy. It was especially Hungary that started to be viewed increasingly critically, then with outright hostility, by the British government and press alike at around the turn of the century. The various British observers who influenced official circles and the public at large in Great Britain, foremost among them Robert William Seton-Watson, or the Vienna correspondent of *The Times*, Wickham Steed, attacked Hungarian social and political conditions from a liberal point of view.[2] The outbreak of the 'Great War' only, naturally, intensified agitation against Austria-Hungary in Britain, and this time the call for the federalization of the Monarchy and the emancipation of the Slavic peoples living within its borders became stronger by the day as the war dragged on. A key outlet for these ideas became *The New Europe*, a journal established in 1916 with contributors such as Seton-Watson, Wickham Steed, the Leeper brothers (Reginald and Allen), and – among others – Tomáš G. Masaryk, who was later elected the first President of Czechoslovakia in 1918. The periodical ceased to exist in 1920 as it had fulfilled its mission.[3]

For the better part of the war, as Bryan Cartledge argues 'nobody in London desired the destruction of Austria-Hungary,' and 'the British War Cabinet approved the prime minister's view that after the war Austria-Hungary should be in a position to exercise a powerful influence in South-East Europe.'[4] The position of Prime Minister David Lloyd George (1916–22), however, changed in 1918, almost in parallel with that of Woodrow Wilson's, with regard to the Dual Monarchy: now he wished to apply the principle of national self-determination (or 'national aspirations') to such a degree as it was practicable. The shift towards the breakup of Austria-Hungary became more pronounced after Charles Habsburg's failure to secure a separate peace in the spring of 1918. This new thinking was more in harmony with the ideas which had gained ground in the Foreign Office due to, among others, Seton-Watson, Wickham Steed and Allen Leeper, who were to advise the British delegation at the Paris Peace Conference after the conclusion of hostilities in November 1918. They, together with Harold Nicolson, served as experts on Central Europe, and were sitting on the subcommittees deciding the postwar

---

2   Géza Jeszenszky, *Az elveszett presztízs. Magyarország megítélésének megváltozása Nagy-Britanniában (1894-1918)*. Budapest: Magyar Szemle Könyvek, 1994.
3   On the history of *The New Europe* see Harry Hanak, '*The New Europe*, 1916–1920', *The Slavonic and East European Review* 39 (93) 1961: 369–99.
4   Bryan Cartledge, *The Will to Survive*. London: Hurst & Co., 2011, 320.

borders in the region. Nicolson also entertained a very bad opinion of the Hungarians,[5] but he confessed that they were treated unfairly after the war because the parallel sessions of the subcommittees drawing the new borders did not coordinate with each other.[6] Though Prime Minister Lloyd George realised the dangers of the harsh peace terms imposed on Germany, and especially on Hungary, the French and the British Foreign Office were against the re-opening of the questions: both State Secretary Arthur Balfour (1916–19) and his successor Lord Curzon (1919–24) argued that the settlements based on the experts's opinions should stand. Harold Nicolson even credited the British delegation with preventing the Hungarians from being invited to discuss the terms, and cynically added that 'it does not matter much.'[7]

The Paris Peace Conference brought some underlying tensions between Great Britain and France to the surface. Although, on the whole, they agreed that the 'perpetrators' of the war should be punished and, more specifically, Germany's military and industrial capabilities should be crippled to an extent that it should never again try to upset the balance of power in Europe, the French were more vindictive in their demands than the British for geopolitical and historical reasons. Their idea of creating a buffer zone with client states along the eastern borders of Germany (and the western borders of Soviet Russia) meant, by default, that they favoured the successor states in Central Europe to a larger degree than even the British did. The French idea of 'squaring the circle,' that is, to incorporate Hungary into the French zone of influence together with Romania, Czechoslovakia and the Kingdom of Serbs, Croats and Slovenes (later Yugoslavia) was short lived under Prime Minister Alexandre Millerand (1920) and General Secretary of the Foreign Ministry Maurice Paléologue in the first half of 1920. The so-called Millerand-letter ('*lettre d'envoi*') of 6 March 1920, in which the French Prime Minister held out hope to Hungary that her borders might be re-negotiated by the League of Nations, aroused the suspicion and, consequently, the opposition of the British. The French business interests, primarily that of the Scheider–Creuzot complex that sought to acquire assets (such as the Hungarian national

---

5   'My feelings towards Hungary were less detached. I confess that I regarded, and still regard, that Turanian tribe with acute distaste. Like their cousins the Turks, they had destroyed much and created nothing. ... For centuries the Magyars had oppressed their subject nationalities ...' Harold Nicolson, *Peacemaking 1919*. London: Constable & Co., 1945, 27.
6   Nicolson, *Peacemaking 1919*, 104.
7   Cartledge, *The Will to Survive*, 328. It was only David Lloyd George who asked for further details concerning the ethnic Hungarians who got into the 'successor states' after the head of the Hungarian delegation in Paris, Count Albert Apponyi's speech to the Peace Conference on 16 January 1920. For the details of the British approach to the question of Hungary's new borders see, among others, Mária Ormos, *Padovátol Trianonig, 1918–1920*. Budapest: Kossuth, 1983, 376–82.

railway) in Hungary, provoked the same reaction. London did not want to see unrivalled French economic and political influence in Central and South-East Europe; Paris entertained the thought of creating 'a confederacy of Danubian states with Hungary as the axis of a pro-French Central Europe.'[8] As for Hungary, the country was in dire need of any help after losing about two-thirds of its former territory and a similar proportion of its population as a result of the Treaty of Trianon (signed on 4 June 1920). Besides the territorial and population loss, the areas lost to the so-called successor states included some of the richest in minerals, and industrial and communication infrastructures were seriously disrupted too. Therefore, the Hungarian Minister in Vienna, Dr. Gusztáv Gratz (1919–21) pointed out to the British High Commissioner Francis Oswald Lindley (1919–20) with all justification in early July 1920 that 'in view of our situation [he cannot be surprised] if we feel compelled to accept a friendly offer of France. ... [W]e feel that Great Britain has no sufficient interests in Hungary to support us ... [O]ur experts who visited London came back with the impression that the only British interest is in the Danube river ...'[9]

The truth is that Great Britain did have economic and political interests in Central and South-East Europe. In fact, London played the leading role among the Great Powers (France, Great Britain, Italy and the United States) which were constituting the Allied Military Commission after the suppression of the Communist dictatorship in Hungary in August 1919. The British had a clear objective of pushing for the establishment of a stable government, and putting Admiral Miklós Horthy at the head of the country. The British interest was primarily of an economic nature. The short-lived Communist dictatorship in Budapest from 21 March to 1 August 1919 displayed the pivotal role of Hungary in economic and trade relations in Central Europe. Strategic interests dictated that the region be stabilised and consolidated. A relatively prosperous chain of countries in Central Europe had the potential to resist a renewed German economic and political expansion into the region (on paper), as well as to provide a *cordon sanitaire* along the western borders of Soviet Russia, and to prevent Bolshevism from spreading into Western Europe. Regarding economic opportunities, the countries in the region offered exceptionally lucrative opportunities for foreign investments as each one of them was short of capital to build or rebuilt their economies. More specifically, the emerging British interest towards the Danube, which practically had been under the control of the British under Admiral Sir Ernest T. Troubridge, could also be attributed to their endeavour to gain a secure trading route for shipping oil from the Romanian oil fields. The British suspected that the

---

8   Lojkó, *Meddling in Middle Europe*, 25.
9   Françis Deák and Dezső Újváry (eds.), *Papers and Documents Relating to Foreign Relations of Hungary*. Volume 1, Budapest: Royal Hungarian Ministry for Foreign Affairs, 1939, 437–39.

French would like to gain control over the Danube from the Black Sea as far as the German section of the river, and then to connect it with the Rhine. Budapest and Vienna would have had to play the role of processing the raw materials imported from the East. This clash of interests ultimately resulted in a French withdrawal from the dispute over the control of shipping on the Danube.

The French decision should be put into a broader context: Paris did not wish to confront the British over this relatively marginal question because of certain security considerations. The French hope that the United States – either on a bilateral or a multilateral framework – would provide security guarantees against a potentially resurgent Germany, had been dashed with the defeat of Woodrow Wilson's liberal internationalist vision by the US Congress and the public. Neither of them was ready at this point to assume a global role in security issues, so the Western European members of the former Entente were left to their own devices. The only meaningful supporter of French security concerns regarding Germany was Great Britain. Therefore, the French government concluded that the Danube and, for that matter, Hungary, was not worth risking British 'goodwill,' and decided to abandon plans of promoting economic interests in face of British opposition there. Moreover, the driving force, urging a more active French policy towards Hungary at the Quai d'Orsay, Maurice Paléologue, resigned late September 1920 and was succeeded by Philippe Barthelot (1920–33), who was not very well disposed towards Hungary.

The British, on the other hand, were instrumental in shaping political life and consolidating political power in Hungary. Sir George Clerk, a British diplomat who was sent to Budapest by the Peace Conference in October 1919 to oversee the creation of a new government, supported those political forces, namely the aristocrats and the groups around Admiral Miklós Horthy, who had been shunned earlier by, among others, the French. He and London favoured Admiral Horthy as the future head of Hungary because he was regarded to be a 'safe pair of hands' who would be able to bring the rather turbulent conditions in the country under control. Sir George also insisted that formal recognition of the new government be extended only if it would respect democratic civil rights.[10] He also put forward a plan for the treatment of Hungary (and Austria) in the future: he recommended lifting reparations payments so that the two countries' economies could be put on a firm footing, and he suggested that a Central High Commission be set up to arbitrate

---

10   The British government did not really engage in a thorough investigation into the situation in this respect; it accepted, one suspects, out of Realpolitik considerations, the assurances by Sir Thomas B. Hohler, the High Commissioner of the British mission in Budapest in that there was no terror any longer.

questions related to 'interethnic conflicts and revisionist claims.'[11]

Besides the formation of the government, there was one more domestic political question the following year (1920), in which London exerted relatively strong pressure on Budapest: the Peace Treaty of Trianon between Hungary and the Allied Powers. There was widespread, one may even say, universal opposition in Hungary to the treaty imposed on the country, but any prospect of 'peaceful coexistence' with the neighbours (which was Hungary's vested interest given the latter's military superiority) depended on the acceptance of the treaty as it was. The Allied High Commission, in which the British were playing a leading role, handed a strongly worded joint *démarche* to the Hungarian government urging Budapest to reconcile itself with the treaty containing extremely harsh conditions, which it did on 13 November 1920. London took a very firm position on the question of a potential return of King Charles IV or, for that matter, any Habsburg ruler to the throne of Hungary. The question first came to a head in November 1920 when Archduke Joseph Habsburg suggested that power be handed to him because the government was not stable enough. The Deputy of the British High Commissioner in Budapest, Wilfried Athelston-Johnson, informed the Habsburg Archduke that 'His Majesty's government cannot even consider the possibility of his candidacy.'[12] When Archduke Joseph protested that King Constantine I of Greece (1913–17, 20–22) had been allowed to return to power, High Commissioner Thomas Hohler (1920–21) called his attention to the fact that Greece was not surrounded by the countries of the so-called Little Entente (Czechoslovakia, the Kingdom of the Serbs, Croats and Slovenes, and Romania). Moreover, the British diplomat was worried that the return of a Habsburg ruler might provoke a civil war in Hungary as well. Then, in March 1921, Charles IV himself tried to reclaim his throne. The last Emperor of Austria and King of Hungary got in contact, through Prince Sixtus of Parma, who had already tried to mediate between the Austrians and the French in 1918, with Prime Minister Aristide Briand (though the French politician later denied the contact).[13] The topic was the return of Charles IV to Hungary where he enjoyed fairly substantial support among the so-called loyalists. The British got wind of the impending attempt of the restoration of Habsburg-rule in Hungary. They were also more than sceptical that Charles IV really thought that he had any chance of getting his throne back, while, on the other one,

---

11 Lojkó, *Meddling in Middle Europe*, 22.
12 Elek Karsai (ed.), *Számjeltávirat valamennyi magyar királyi követségnek*. Budapest: Táncsics, 1969, 140.
13 According to Colonel Edward Lisle Strutt, who was regarded a confidant of Charles IV, Aristide Briand stated that if the Emperor returned to Hungary and declared himself King of Hungary, and it would seem to be a fait accompli, neither France nor Great Britian would oppose it in any way. Karsai, *Számjeltávirat valamennyi magyar királyi követségnek*, 168.

they warned the Hungarians against entertaining any such idea.[14] The early British warning was motivated largely by the concern that the neighbouring states might take (military) action against Hungary. Despite the advice to the contrary, Charles IV decided to return and arrived in Western Hungary on 27 March 1921. He got into negotiations with Governor Horthy, who managed to persuade him to leave and thus to prevent a potential political turmoil in the country. Charles IV finally left for Switzerland on 5 April.

However, the king did not give up hope to return, and Charles IV made another attempt in October that same year. This time the British intervention in Hungary proved to be stronger than it was six months before. Britain, France and Italy repeated what they declared in their joint note of 3 April 1920: they unequivocally stated their determined opposition to any restoration of a Habsburg-rule in Hungary. High Commissioner Hohler even threatened Prime Minister István Bethlen (1921–31) with refraining from putting pressure on the capitals of the Little Entente countries so that they would practice restraint.[15] In fact, as Hungarian Foreign Minister Miklós Bánffy (1921–22) reported to the Cabinet, the representatives of Czechoslovakia, Romania and the Kingdom of the Serbs, Croats and Slovenes visited him after the British-French-Italian *démarche* had been delivered. These diplomats told Bánffy in no uncertain terms that their countries would take all measures necessary to maintain peace in Central Europe in case the Hungarian government was not able to do what was required of it. To exert even more pressure, High Commissioner Hohler, in the company of his colleagues, paid a visit to Governor Horthy, and they reiterated the warning which they had given to Foreign Minister Bánffy earlier. In reality, Great Britain also put pressure on the Czechs and the Yugoslavs to stop their war preparations. Otherwise, the British warned them, London would break off diplomatic relations with both of them. Hohler then held a conference with Prime Minister Bethlen and Foreign Minister Bánffy on 5 November, where the British High Commissioner emphasized that the main reason why the Great Powers were opposed to the return of Charles IV was that they feared that it would lead to a war in the region which they would like to avoid at any cost.[16] The Great Powers at this point found it important to request from the Hungarian government that the House of Habsburg be dethroned – in order to prevent the recurrent attempts by the members of the royal family to regain their rule in Hungary; these attempts clearly undermined the political stability of Hungary and the region alike. Steps were also taken to defuse the current crisis. Meanwhile, a

---

14   Hungarian Envoy in Vienna, Szilárd Masirevich reported that Colonel Strutt of the British Legation strongly recommended in mid-March 1921 that the Hungarian government not get involved in any scheme of this nature. Miklós Horthy, *Emlékirataim*. Budapest: Európa, 1992, 151.
15   Horthy, *Emlékirataim*, 155.
16   Karsai, *Számjeltávirat valamennyi magyar királyi követségnek*, 247.

Cabinet meeting was held in London on 26 October in which Foreign Secretary Lord Curzon gave an account of the events in Hungary, and the members present agreed that Charles IV should be removed from Hungary as he was 'in the centre of plots.' Several ideas were floated as to the potential venues of his exile, including Italy (discarded because of the vicinity of the Kingdom of the Serbs, Croats and Slovenes), Malta (ruled out because the Prince of Wales was just visiting the island), and finally they decided that they would ask Spain to provide a place of retirement for the former Habsburg ruler on an island belonging to Madrid. After all, Charles IV left Hungary for good on 31 October, and was carried to the island of Madeira on board the HMS Cardiff; he died shortly thereafter on 1 April 1922 in the Spanish flu epidemic that claimed the lives of millions of people after the Great War.

While the Bethlen-government and Governor Horthy were able to count on British support in their efforts to stave off the attempts by the Charles IV to regain his throne (technically speaking he had only relinquished, in a declaration issued at Eckartsau on 13 November 1919, 'every participation in the administration of the State' so long as the 'vis maior' blocking his rule existed), London proved to be insensitive to Hungarian demands for self-determination with regard to Western Hungary/Burgenland. At the same time, the British Foreign Office informed Budapest that it would not block a referendum which was to decide the future territorial affiliation of the disputed land. Former Prime Minister, Pál Teleki visited the French and British capitals in spring and summer 1921 to gain support for the Hungarian position. Teleki was fairly persuasive in private talks with, among others, former Prime Minister Henry Asquith, Lord Beaverbrook, and a few members of the House of Lords. Nevertheless, he ran into troubles in the Foreign Office. He made some critical remarks about the indifference, even ignorance, of the complicated ethnic issues in Central Europe, as well as the provisions regarding the minorities in the peace treaties, which did not go particularly well with, among others, Alexander Cadogan. In fact, Cadogan believed that Hungary could not postpone the transfer of Western Hungary to Austria any more.[17] He also regretted that the dispute prevented better relations between Austria and Hungary. The question was finally settled on 13 October 1921 after intensive talks in Venice; a referendum was held in and around Sopron (Ödenburg). A decisive majority then decided in favour of Hungary on 14–16 December 1921.

---

17   Ablonczy, *Teleki Pál*, 211–2. Count Teleki was later appointed a member of the so-called Mosul-commission. Great Britain wanted to keep the vilayet inside Iraq, while Teleki came to the conclusion that it was only the religious affiliations that should decide the fate of any territory in the Middle East. London, understably, became quite dissatisfied and disappointed with his activities, though Teleki later asked the Hungarian Envoy to London, Iván Rubido-Zichy to inform the Foreign Office that he would be willing to take the British interests into account as much as possible.

The single most important issue in British-Hungarian relations was the economic and financial stabilisation of Hungary. They reflected British priorities in the region: stable economies with substantial British economic and financial presence and, through it, influence over local governments. The broader objective can be said to have been – with a modern expression – a 'double containment' of the potential German and French interests in Central and South-East Europe. London did not wish to be politically or strategically tied down in these 'faraway lands' (borrowing Neville Chamberlain's memorable comment on Czechoslovakia during the Sudeten crisis in the late 1930s). Great Britain's policies towards these countries were motivated by another factor: British debts to the United States. As a number of countries were required to pay reparations after the war, foremost among them Germany, but also Hungary, it was in the interest of London to enable these countries to make payments so that Britain would also be able to make good on its financial obligations to the US. In general, one may conclude that similar ideas motivated the US when it tried to create a situation in the defeated countries, especially in Germany through the Dawes Plan, the Young Plan and, finally, the Hoover Moratorium in which they were able to fulfil their reparations obligations. As we will see later, it was predominantly British and American banking institutions that underwrote the League of Nations loans in the 1920s.

The competition for Hungarian business and financial assets between Great Britain and France started right after the conclusion of the war. The French wished to acquire the Hungarian state railways (*MÁV*) together with the *Hitelbank* (Credit Bank), which controlled about 230 companies in the country. The Governor of the *Hitelbank*, Adolf Ullmann (1895–1925), favoured the British, while Great Britain protested in a diplomatic note dated 4 June 1920 against the acquisition of the *MÁV* by the Schneider-Creuzot complex. The high hopes created in Hungary by the Millerand 'letter d'envoi' had a financial connotation as well: Finance Minister Loránd Hegedűs (1920–21) wished to base the new Hungarian currency on the French franc. It is perhaps unnecessary to remark here that the idea was torpedoed by London. Meanwhile, British banking interests had gained a foothold in Hungary by establishing the *Angol-Magyar Bank* (English-Hungarian Bank) in late spring 1920. The predecessor of the *Angol-Magyar Bank*, the *Magyar Bank* (Hungarian Bank) and the *Kereskedelmi Rt.* (Commercial Joint Stock Company) had been called into being in 1896 in order to guarantee commercial links between Hungary and the Balkans. It had established affiliates in Romania, Greece, Bulgaria and Turkey; thus, it fitted perfectly into the British strategy in the region. The *Angol-Magyar Bank* had two British partners: the Imperial and Foreign Corporation and the Marconi Group, which acquired 250,000 shares. The transaction was facilitated by Alfred Stead, who was an expert on the Danube-shipping issues. (At the same time, a British group acquired a share in the Austrian *Donau-Dampschiffgesellschaft* and the *Süddeutsche Dampschiffgesellshaft*. The underlying objective was clear: to control the shipping routes from the Balkans and the Romanian oil fields.) The Governor of the *Angol-Magyar Bank*, Simon Krausz, attempted to arrange a loan of 10 million pounds, but the British rejected the request with the explanation that they would not extend any loan to Hungary until the Treaty of Trianon was signed and ratified by the appropriate Hungarian authorities. Budapest made another attempt at getting a British loan in 1921 through another banker, Gyula Walder. However, the British were still reluctant to comply with the request referring to the uncertain political situation created by the repeated attempts of Charles IV to return to Hungary. The third Hungarian request came from Hungarian banks which wanted to stabilise the Hungarian currency (*korona*) with a two or three million pound sterling loan. This time the request was turned down because of the obscure situation regarding reparations payments.[18]

The situation changed in 1922: the two sides started to move closer to each other. The Hungarian chargé in Paris reported that he had met the British Under-Secretary for Foreign Affairs Sir Eyre Crowe (1920–25) in London, and that he enquired whether Hungarian companies or the government would not like to get a loan from Great Britain. Eyre's offer was not, of course, without self-interest: British banks and industrial units were seeking investment opportunities, and the loan thus received was to be spent in Britain.[19] On the other hand, the Hungarian Finance Minister Tibor Kállay (1921–24) made an exploratory tour in Paris, London and Rome concerning a bigger loan. The Hungarian government hired Sir William Goode[20] in January 1923 to facilitate business and financial contacts in London. The breakthrough came with Tibor Kállay and Prime Minister István Bethlen's visit to London on 7–10 May 1923. They met the most important British politicians from Prime Minister Bonar Law (1922–23) to Foreign Secretary Lord Curzon, as well as the Governor of the Bank of England Montagu Norman (1920–44), who was to play a crucial role in the League of Nations loan, which ultimately set Hungarian finances on a firm footing. The two Hungarian politicians also had talks with other prominent members of the financial world, including Anthony de Rothschild and Lionel de Rothschild. The shifting British position was indicated by the fact that the government disregarded the protests by R. W. Seton-Watson and the former Hungarian President, Mihály Károlyi, who lived in Britain at that time in exile, against the visit of Kállay and Bethlen. Moreover, it seems likely that Montagu

---

18 Tamás Magyarics, 'Nagy-Britannia Közép-Európa politikája 1918-tól napjainkig', Part I, *Pro Minoritate* (Summer 2002), 16–7.
19 Karsai, *Számjeltávirat valamennyi magyar királyi követségnek*, 271.
20 Sir William Goode was the Head of the Austrian Reparations Committee; after being hired by the Hungarian government, he was serving for 20 years as Hungary's financial advisor in London.

Norman's suggestion of depoliticisation of the financial reconstruction of Europe prevailed over the ideologically more committed voices in Britain (the Foreign Office and Sir Otto E. Niemeyer at the Treasury) – and over the French approach as well. Again, self-interest did play a role in Norman's strategy: the regeneration of European trade would be bound to strengthen the sterling too. However, his vision of 'an economic federation' of countries along the Danube without customs barriers did not materialise because of political and ethnic tensions in Central Europe.[21]

The British advised the Hungarians that they should approach the League of Nations – with British support. (It happened on 4 May 1923.) The financial talks did not go smoothly. First, London had to convince the French, the Italians and the members of the Little Entente that an external load extended to Hungary was vital for the political stability of Central Europe. The countries mentioned worried first and foremost that Hungary would give preference to the repayment of the future loan to the reparations payments. When Prime Minister Bethlen threatened resignation because the talks seemed to be stalling, the British cautioned the opponents against obstruction. Thus, they let the Czechs know that they would receive the second tranche of the loan issued to them by the Baring banking house only if they accepted the British plan for the reconstruction of Hungary and cooperated with the efforts to put Hungary on a firm economic footing. The pressure resulted in a softening of the positions of the Little Entente: they were willing to disconnect the reparations payments from the loan at the conference held in Sinaia, Romania on 28–30 July 1923.

The 'magic formula' was finally worked out by Sir Arthur Salter, the Head of the League of Nations Financial Committee with Montagu Norman. The reparations payments were disconnected from the loans of some 10 to 12 million pounds. Moreover, a political protocol was attached to the financial provisions which stated that 'largely due to British influence, it did not rule out Hungary's moral right to seek territorial revision by peaceful means.'[22] Then in December 1923, Hungary pledged to pay 200 million golden crown (*korona*) within 20 years as reparations. However, the realisation of the League of Nations reconstruction loan ran into difficulties. As the reparations continued, which Montagu Norman opposed, the Bank of England declared that it could not support the deal under the existing conditions. After all, the Rothschild banking house in London subscribed four million pounds sterling, another four million was subscribed by Speyer & Co. of New York, while the rest (two million) was subscribed by Swedish, Swiss and Czech banks.[23]

---

21 Lojkó, *Meddling in Middle Europe*, 64–5.
22 Lojkó, *Meddling in Middle Europe*, 99.
23 György Barcza, *Diplomataemlékeim 1911–1945*. Volume 1. Budapest: Európa, 1994, 188.

A Boston financier, Jeremiah Smith, was picked by the British and the Americans to administer and control the spending of the loan and to oversee the policies aimed at enhancing the state revenues. The National Bank of Hungary began its operation on 24 June 1924; out of the seven major shareholders, two – the Anglo-Austrian Bank and the Midland Bank – were British, while the largest shareholder was the National City Bank of New York. In fact, the League of Nations was perhaps more important from the political point of view than from an economic one; only about 25% of the loan was spent 'on meeting arrears or current account deficits of the budget.'[24] Its real benefit for Hungary was the improvement of Hungary's international image after the war, the Communist dictatorship, and the backlash following the 'red terror.' One of the culminating points of the loan program was the introduction of a new currency, the *pengő*, on 1 January 1927.

Great Britain and Hungary began drifting away from each other in the latter half of the 1920s. Despite Montagu Norman's hopes, Hungary decoupled the *pengő* from the pound-based system. More importantly, though, Budapest was not willing to commit itself to an 'eastern Locarno.' Foreign Secretary Austen Chamberlain (1924–29) tried to persuade Prime Minister István Bethlen to conclude agreements with Hungary's neighbours similar to the Locarno Treaty, which had been signed by the Germans and the French, and the Germans and the Belgians. These two treaties guaranteed the borders between Germany and its two western neighbours. The Hungarian Premier promised to initiate negotiations with Hungary's neighbors, and talks were indeed held between Hungary and Yugoslavia to discuss an agreement which would guarantee the borders between them. Meanwhile, however, Hungarian-Italian relations gained importance: for Hungary, the revisionist Italy seemed to offer better and real opportunities to achieve the redress of, at least, some of the injustices of the Treaty of Trianon. It is true that the 'eternal friendship' treaty signed by Prime Minister Bethlen and Benito Mussolini in Rome on 5 April 1927 did not contain too many specifics, but it signalled a definite turning point in the foreign policy orientation of Hungary towards the countries which – in the long run – wanted to change the status quo in Europe.

At this moment Great Britain got involved in a somewhat bizarre incident with Hungary. Harold Rothermere, the owner of the *Daily Mail* published an article in his newspaper on 21 June 1927 under the title 'Hungary's Place in the Sun.' He argued that the dissolution of the Austro-Hungarian Monarchy had been a mistake, and that the new – in part artificial – borders which did not take ethnic boundaries and the right of national determination into account, endangered peace in Europe. He concluded that the revision of the borders would be beneficial not only for Hungary, but also for the so-called successor

---

24 Lojkó, *Meddling in Middle Europe*, 130.

states in Central Europe because a source of serious friction would be removed. He suggested that economic and financial pressure should be exerted by Britain and the US on the Little Entente countries to accept the redrawing of the borders. As Harold Rothermere enjoyed quite good and intimate relations with a number of people in the British government and the Parliament, some suspected that the British government was behind him, and the article was a sort of trial balloon to gauge reactions to the suggestion. The impression was reinforced by the fact that the Foreign Office did not comment in writing for some time. A war of words erupted between Harold Rothermere and especially the Czechs over the treatment of the Hungarian minority in Czechoslovakia. Prague, and the other capitals in the Little Entente countries suspected that Budapest was behind the British press magnate's actions, and accused the Bethlen government of trying to achieve the revision of the Treaty of Trianon 'through the back door.' They were also suspicious of British motives: London repeatedly sided with Hungary in its various disputes with neighbouring countries. There was the case of the Hungarian landholders of Transylvanian origins over properties that had been confiscated without compensation by the Romanian government after 1919 if the landholders had opted for Hungarian citizenship, and the scandal over a transport of weapons spare parts of World War vintage (the shipment, which was sent from Italy to Hungary, was discovered by Austrian customs officers at the Hungarian border town of Szentgotthárd in January 1928 – Hungary's neighbours lodged strongly worded protests and accused Budapest of preparing for a war against them to regain her lost territories). In the case of the former, the British, in principle, recognised that the Hungarians had a strong case against the Romanian authorities' practices, while in the latter, London was instrumental in referring the case to a League of Nations commission, effectively burying the question in the ensuing investigation (which was carried out only by experts who were conducting a rather perfunctory investigation).

However, the Rothermere case was getting evermore awkward for Great Britain, and there was a danger that the somewhat farcical events would have serious consequences. One of them was the threat by the members of the Little Entente to introduce a boycott of trade relations with Britain. London had predominantly economic interests in Central Europe, and its political interests dictated the existence of stable governments in the region which, moreover, would not cause any disturbances that might involve Britain or, for that matter, the Great Powers. The Legation of Hungary was informed in London on Foreign Secretary Austen Chamberlain's direct order that Budapest could not count on the goodwill of the British if it tried 'to fish in troubled waters.'[25]

---

25   Magda Ádám, *A Kisantant és Európa*. Budapest: Akadémiai, 1989, 248.

The events were getting a new twist at this point. The *Daily Mail* published a letter by Gordon Ross, a former member of the Hungarian-Czechoslovak Border Committee on 20 July 1927, in which the British delegate referred to A. Millerand's *'letter d'envoi.'* The authenticity of the letter was challenged by the former Secretary General of the French Foreign Ministry, Maurice Paléologue; his position was shared by a number of Hungarian politicians, including Count Albert Apponyi, as well as the British government. Despite the refutations, the question of the postwar borders of Hungary got into the limelight again; David Lloyd George, who had already expressed his reservations about the justness and the wisdom of the Treaty of Trianon, joined forces with the pro-Hungary 'lobby' in Britain (a few members of the House of Lords and one or two Members of Parliament). They claimed that the borders were not final and adjustments might be imagined to redress some justifiable grievances. The British government swung into action to prevent further escalation. Prime Minister Ramsay MacDonald (1929–35), in an interview given to the Czech newspaper, stated unambiguously that his country 'was not interested in Rothermere's campaign at all,' and that Rothermere should not be taken seriously. The same message was delivered to the Hungarian government through the British Envoy in Budapest. On the other hand, influential politicians in Hungary believed mistakenly that Lord Rothermere was 'a decisive factor' in British political life. They even believed that he would support David Lloyd George at the next general election, which would be won by the former Liberal Party prime minister.[26] The issue was gradually fading away, though as a tragicomic episode, some people in Hungary raised the possibility of crowning Lord Rothermere or his son, Esmond Harmsworth. The Rothermere issue ultimately did not improve Hungary's standing in the eyes of serious political elements in Britain, and it stoked the suspicion in London that even the otherwise prudent Bethlen government was prone to yield to the widespread revisionist spirit in Hungary at the expense of a more realistic foreign policy.

---

26   Gyula Gömbös's letter to Count István Bethlen, March 1929. Bethlen István, *Titkos iratai*. Budapest: Kossuth, 1972, 338–9.

4

British Policy towards Romania, 1936–41

SORIN ARHIRE

Throughout the entire nineteenth century, the peoples of Central Europe were shown no significant official interest by the British; although the latter knew of the existence of the Hungarians, Poles and Romanians, their general attitude was that of gracious ignorance.[1] For many centuries, the British showed greater interest and concern for matters related to the peoples of Transvaal, Honduras and New Zealand than to the Romanians, although the latter were both geographically closer and more numerous.[2] This relatively low interest was the consequence of the fact that Great Britain had no major economic interests in this part of the European continent; at the same time, it was also the consequence of the priorities of British foreign policy which very tenaciously pursued the maintenance of the European balance of power, even when this meant sacrificing the national ideals of the peoples of East-Central Europe. Moreover, because of their insularity, the British had formed their own way of thinking, which made no difference between concepts of 'close' and 'far.' As it is very edifyingly described by Peter Calvocoressi: 'Geographers might talk of the 'Far' East and measure the distance to India in thousands of miles, but to many an Englishman, Delhi and Singapore and Hong Kong were psychologically no further away than Calais; they were often more familiar, and they were, of course, more British.'[3] Therefore it is not at all by chance that when he wrote his famous *Dracula*, Bram Stoker placed the

---

1   Vladimir Tismăneanu, *Reinventarea politicului. Europa Răsăriteană de la Stalin la Havel*. Translated by Alexandru Vlad. Jassy: Polirom Publishing House, 1997, 32.
2   David Britton Funderburk, *Politica Marii Britanii față de România 1938–1940. Studiu asupra strategiei economice și politice*. Translated by Ion Stanciu. Bucharest: Scientific and Encyclopaedic Publishing House, 1983, 21.
3   Peter Calvocoressi, *World Politics since 1945*. London, New York, Boston, etc.: Pearson Longman, 2009, 183.

action in the Eastern end of Transylvania,[4] since for the inhabitants of the British Isles this was Europe's last civilised province, 'the end of the world' beyond which nothingness started.[5]

One may undoubtedly say that while negotiating the 1919 and 1920 peace treaties, which followed the First World War, direct contacts between British and Romanian politicians were more numerous than ever before. The question of new frontiers dominated their diplomatic relations. Founded in 1918, Greater Romania constantly faced the revisionist attitude of the states which had lost their territories to Bucharest's benefit. Throughout the interwar years, Soviet Russia was claiming Bessarabia in the East, Bulgaria was asking for the South Dobruja in the South and at the western borders, Hungary had not given up to getting Transylvania back. By signing the Paris Peace Treaties of 1919–20, London recognised Romanian borders with Poland, Hungary and Bulgaria but the problem of the Eastern frontier remained open. Firstly, Britain and other Allied powers were eager to support Romania in the Bessarabian dispute. On 28 October 1920, they signed a special protocol recognising Bessarabia to be a part of Romania. Although ratified by the British only two years later, the Bessarabian protocol never entered into force due to the fact that Japan did not ratify it.

For almost the entire interwar period, more precisely until 1938, Great Britain did not have a clearly outlined political or economic strategy towards Romania. Most British actions concerning the Romanian space were based on some general principles such as the maintenance of peace, of the *status quo* established following the Paris Peace Conference or of the influence exercised by the League of Nations. Romania did not have an official alliance

---

4   Jan Palmowski, *Dicționar Oxford de istorie universală contemporană. De la 1900 până azi*. Translated by Simona Ceaușu. Bucharest: ALL Publishing House, 2005, vol. II, 460; Irina Livezeanu, *Cultural Politics in Greater Romania: Regionalism, Nation Building & Ethnic Struggle, 1918–1930*. Ithaca and London: Cornell University Press, 1995, 132–4.

5   The historiography of Romanian-British relations has no study which comprises all aspects of their interwar bilateral relations. Historians focus primarily on the study of the development of political, economic and cultural ties between Britain and Romania. In general, Anglo-Saxon historiography was concerned with the analysis of British foreign policy in a wider context describing the attitude of the Foreign Office and the London-based government towards the great European and world powers with few papers dedicated exclusively to Romania. There are also publications dedicated to the analysis of British foreign policy in the era the Second World War, such as Elizabeth Barker's *British Policy in South-East Europe in the Second World War*, which dedicates two chapters to Romania, or Paul D. Quinlan's *British and American Policies towards Romania 1938-1947*. The book of American historian David Britton Funderburk (*British Policy toward Romania: A Study in Economic and Political Strategy*, 1983) is one of the few works dealing exclusively with the Romanian-British relationship in the late 1930s.

with Britain but due to the fact that the latter's support was very important for the League of Nations, it ensured a good relationship between the two countries. However, for almost the entire period between the two wars, Romania played a minor role for the officials in London globally, much less important than other regional countries, like Greece, Turkey or Cyprus, where British interests were strong, but also traditional.

Romania was situated at the periphery of British sea routes, which linked Britain with the Near East and India, but close to the Bosporus and the Dardanelles which gave it major importance in case of war. British public opinion but also the large majority of politicians thought Romania was a far-off East-Central European country where one could get to after a three days journey by rail or a 14-hour flight, as there was no direct route.[6]

The description made by Sir Sacheverell Sitwell who visited Romania in 1937 left no doubt about the little knowledge the British had about the Southeastern state:

> At the first mention of going to Romania, a great many persons, including myself, take down their atlas and open the map. No one would bother to do this over more familiar countries. For Romania, there can be no question, is among the lesser known lands of Europe. [...] It is far away. If you embarked on the train, determined, for some obscure reason, to continue in it upon the longest journey possible in Europe, the probability is that you would step out, four days later, upon the platform of Constanța, on the Black Sea [...]. It is a matter of principle. Most persons are satisfied that Europe ends at the Dniester and the Black Sea. So that Romania is at the far end of Europe.[7]

Fallen under the dominance of a Great Power, Romania could have become a threat to British interests in the Mediterranean. At the same time, since the Prahova Valley was at the time one of the richest oil-fields in Europe, German control over the Romanian territory would have significantly diminished the

---

6   The Orient Express would leave from London each Sunday and Thursday, not from the Victoria Station but from the East Station. As for air travels, there was no direct flight from Great Britain to Romania, but one had to transfer to planes flown by Air France, Lufthansa or Lares. Maurice Pearton, 'British–Romanian Relations during the 20th Century; Some Reflections,' in: *In and Out of Focus: Romania and Britain: Relations and Perspectives from 1930 to the Present*, edited by Dennis Deletant, 8, Bucharest: Cavallioti Publishing House, 2005.

7   Sacheverell Sitwell, *Roumanian Journey*. London: B. T. Batsford Ltd., 1938, 15.

efficiency of a naval blockade, as was in fact proven by the Second World War.

The wave of Britain's interests in Romania was triggered by the German re-militarisation of the Rhineland which started 7 March 1936. This implied the end of all security plans as drawn-up at the end of the First World War and it pushed the British government towards a more conciliatory policy. The reoccupation of the Rhineland also marked its consequences on Romanian diplomacy. On 29 August 1936, Nicolae Titulescu was removed from the head of the Ministry of Foreign Affairs in Bucharest. For four years, he had outlined Romania's foreign policy and clearly oriented it towards France and Britain, while he neglected Germany. The dismissal of Titulescu did not remain unechoed in Britain. The British press showed great interest in the replacement of the Romanian Minister of Foreign Affairs; some newspapers saw it as a major shift in Romania's foreign policy which was no stranger to Germany. Thus, *The Daily Telegraph* stated that the dismissal of Titulescu actually made way to major changes both in Romanian politics and in the general European situation. Moreover, the same newspaper argued that there were enough similarities between the Romanian situation and the coup in Greece by the Germanophile dictator General Ioannis Metaxas (1936–41), and also the preparations made by King Boris III of Bulgaria (1918–43) to bring dictatorship to his country to the benefit of Germany.[8]

British cultural influence and propaganda in Romania

During the nineteenth and early twentieth century, as well as during the interwar period, the cultural influence of Great Britain in Romania was minimal. The British believed that Romania was entirely under the French cultural orbit and thus, there was no point in wasting resources for a cause which was almost lost from the very beginning. Having started with a major handicap compared to France and Germany, the British cultural influence in Romania had been weak all throughout the interwar period. Some sort of revival of this influence became noticeable in 1936 and went on until 1940. Political events had a major influence on the cultural impact of Great Britain in the Romanian society.

France's economic weakness in the mid-1930s, which had major political and military repercussions, triggered a relative decrease of the French presence in Romania. As a result, the British acted in the cultural sector just like they had done in the international theatre, by trying to fill the void left by France's relative withdrawal. Romania was beginning to be a territory increasingly worthy of consideration and Great Britain's efforts, although a bit later. To

---

8   *The Daily Telegraph*, 31 August 1936.

counteract the increasingly significant German cultural influence, the British changed their attitude towards Romania, and allocated larger financial means for the promotion of their own culture.

An important role in British cultural diplomacy was played by the Anglo-Romanian Society. This institution was set up in 1927 at the initiative of a group of English university scholars and intellectuals with the purpose of developing Romanian-British cultural relations. Cultural centres were opened in Cluj, Cernăuți, Galatz and Constanța and on the tenth anniversary of its existence 'The English House' was inaugurated in Bucharest. 'The English House' became the centre of the organization with a library of over two thousand volumes. The existence of this library was all the more valuable as in Romania, there were almost no books in English.[9] As a British journalist noticed during a short visit to Romania, English books were almost entirely absent while the very few that were available were actually published by German publishers and were often exaggeratedly expensive and with significant omissions compared to the originals. Also, important progress was made in spreading the knowledge of English among the Romanian population. In the years between the wars, departments of English language and literature were set up at Jassy, Cluj and Cernăuți universities, and the last one was set up in Bucharest in 1936.[10]

In August 1939, the Foreign Office asked the BBC for the first time to introduce news bulletins in Romanian – this request was first fulfilled as soon as the war started, when a few Romanian speakers from Great Britain were hastily recruited for the job.[11] After the collapse of France and the hasty evacuation of British soldiers from Dunkirk in the summer of 1940, the propaganda messages of the BBC in Romania became more important as they were the only way to counteract the growing influence of the DNB, the official German news agency, which practically controlled all newspapers,

---

9   *Adevărul*, 20 February 1937.
10   At its foundation in 1864, the University of Bucharest could only provide studies in one modern language, which was of course French, with Latin as a classical language. In the 1870s Italian was also introduced, while Slavic languages came in the next decade. The first years of the twentieth century saw the inauguration of a German Studies Department, followed by Spanish and Russian in 1930 and 1934 respectively. As the reader may see, the first English department was only established in 1936, which shows how low the cultural influence of Britain was in Romania. Mihaela Irimia, 'English Studies at the University of Bucharest since the Foundation of the English Department in 1936,' in: *In and Out of Focus: Romania and Britain: Relations and Perspectives from 1930 to the Present*, edited by Dennis Deletant, 15–7, Bucharest: Cavallioti Publishing House, 2005.
11   http://www.bbc.co.uk/romanian/specials/168_bbcro_istorie/index.shtml, accessed 23 July 2018.

radios and news bulletins in Romania.[12] Therefore, on 19 September 1940, there was a request to introduce a second news bulletin and the Romanian broadcasting time reached 4 hours and 40 minutes per week in an attempt to give Romanian listeners the official point of view of the government in London. Britain had been at war for over a year and the BBC was an important part of the war effort, which coded messages to resistance groups in Romania.[13]

The Visit of King Carol II to Great Britain in November 1938

There are important changes that occurred on the international relations in 1938. After the Czechoslovak loss of the Sudetenland to Germany in October, Romanian King Carol II (1930–40) decided to undertake a diplomatic tour to Britain, France and Belgium. In turn, the British too were interested in this visit, as they realised that the *Anschluss* in March 1938 had contributed to the increase of German influence in South-East Europe. Thus, Britain had to act in order to provide the states from this side of Europe another *point d'appui* besides the one provided by Berlin.[14] The Southern Department[15] in the Foreign Office contributed significantly to making this visit happen; as emphasized in a report drawn-up by its officials. If the re-invitation of King Carol had been delayed, Romania's situation in front of Germany would have deteriorated even further – especially since Austria's unification with the *Third Reich* had triggered feelings of fear amongst Romanians rather than a desire to cooperate with the Germans.[16] The official visit of King Carol II to London between 15 and 18 November 1938, as a guest of the British King George VI (1936–52), was prepared to the smallest details.

Carol II held talks both with Prime Minister Neville Chamberlain (1937–40) and with Foreign Secretary, the Viscount Edward Halifax (1938–40) but the results were rather modest. The matter of a British credit granted to Romania for the purchase of war supplies made in Britain remained undecided and in the economic field; although not entirely waiving involvement, the British replied that it seemed natural to them for Germany to hold a dominant position in South-East Europe. Britain continued to be interested in

---

12 Ivor Porter, *Operațiunea 'Autonomous' în România pe vreme de război*. Translated by George G. Potra and Delia Răzdolescu. Bucharest: Humanitas Publishing House, 2008, 66.
13 http://www.bbc.co.uk/romanian/specials/168_bbcro_istorie/index.shtml, accessed 23 July 2018.
14 The National Archives (hereafter, TNA), Foreign Office 371 Romania (hereafter, FO 371) 22445, 180. Kew, UK.
15 According to the organisation of the Foreign Office departments, all matters concerning Romania fell with the competence of the Southern Department.
16 TNA, FO 371 Romania, 180–1.

commercial exchanges with Romania, but for the moment, it settled with the second rank in the foreign trade with this country. The officials in London were also aware that there was a tradition of excellent Romanian-German economic cooperation, which had been interrupted by the First World War. Politically, British officials ensured the king that Europe was not divided into spheres of influence at Munich.[17]

The promotion of the British Legation in Bucharest to the rank of embassy was another wish Carol had. However Whitehall, which had been planning to promote the diplomatic mission in Romania since 1937, now realised that the period following the Munich Conference was not the appropriate time for such a decision. Britain had no desire to pointlessly offend Germany, especially since the freshly instated balance of power already seemed to be very fragile.

In parallel with the talks held by the Romanian king, there were also negotiations between the Romanian Foreign Minister Nicolae Petrescu-Comnen (1938–39) and his British counterpart, Lord Halifax. Within the policy of not economically abandoning Southeastern Europe to Germany, the head of the Foreign Office committed to present to his experts the matter of encircling the *Third Reich*. Halifax's request to drop the prices of Romanian goods at least at the level of international prices as a premise for intensified bilateral exchanges was justified as it was well known that the British could buy wheat and oil from other countries for less money compared to the purchases they could make in Romania.[18] If, however, these purchases were made, they were considered 'unnecessary imports' and their only purpose was to deprive Germany of its important resources.

In the four days of the king's stay in London, there were also mutual gestures of courtesy of the two kings. Carol II made public his decision to donate a piece of land to the Anglo-Romanian Society in Bucharest with the purpose of erecting a building for the future British Institute.[19] George VI in turn awarded his Romanian guest the Order of the Garter, a distinction that the Romanian sovereign had been dreaming of since the spring of 1938. However, this personal achievement did nothing but mitigate to some extent the general lack of success of this official visit to Great Britain.

Organised at a time when major changes occurred in European power relations, the Romanian king's visit to London was a consequence of the

---

17 Andreas Hillgruber, *Hitler, regele Carol şi mareşalul Antonescu. Relaţiile germano-române (1938–1944)*. Translated by Stelian Neagoe. Bucharest: Humanitas Publishing House, 1994, 60.
18 Funderburk, *Politica Marii Britanii*, 83.
19 *Seara*, 25 November 1938.

decision made in Munich. Although there were some rumours saying that the following year King George VI and Queen Elisabeth would be received in Bucharest, which did not happen, the official visit in Great Britain did not yield the expected results. It confirmed that Britain would not provide significant help to Romania against the claims of revisionist states.

The awarding of British guarantees in April 1939

Defying the decisions of the Munich Conference, on 15 March 1939 the German army occupied the rest of the Czech territory that remained after the agreement in the Bavarian capital. The Protectorate of Bohemia and Moravia was created while Slovakia had claimed its independence just a day before, although in reality it was a German satellite. For the British, this was the final straw. Up to that point, Chamberlain had accepted Hitler's claims that Germany had been treated too harshly in Versailles by having been denied the self-determination principle. The ethnic Czech lands' inclusion in the *Reich* was an entirely new development which proved unacceptable for the government in London. Thus, Britain decided to grant independence guarantees to certain East-Central European states, either alone or together with France.[20] As British proposals to conclude general mutual assistance pacts between Great Britain, the Soviet Union, Poland and Romania were rejected (Poland and Romania did not want to challenge Germany), the British government decided to enter into direct contacts with Poland and Romania. The consequences on the Foreign Office policy were very big: 'And so, in its efforts to keep the European peace through a collective security system, the British government was pushed by the Polish and Romanian governments to make decisions which served Polish and Romanian interests. But, whether they also corresponded to the objectives of the British government was debatable.'[21]

In the spring of 1939, when the outbreak of war was becoming increasingly likely, Romania was seen by Chamberlain and also by the Cabinet Committee on Foreign Policy[22] as strategically important both for its oil and for the support it could provide to Poland in the case of a German attack. The Romanian-German economic agreement of 23 March 1939 alarmed London,

---

20   Funderburk, *Politica Marii Britanii*, 94.
21   Hillgruber, *Hitler, regele Carol și mareșalul Antonescu*, 71.
22   The Cabinet Committee on Foreign Policy consisted of Prime Minister Neville Chamberlain, Sir John Simon, Chancellor of Exchequer, Sir Samuel Hoare, Secretary of State for the Home Department, Sir Thomas Inskip, Secretary of State for Dominion Affairs, W. S. Morrison, Chancellor of the Duchy of Lancaster, Viscount Runciman, Lord President of the Council, Viscount Halifax, Secretary of State for Foreign Affairs, Lord Chatfield, Minister for Co-ordination of Defence and Oliver Stanley, President of the Board of Trade. TNA, FO 371 Romania, 23736/1939, 185.

and consequently Britain supported Romania in order to show the Germans that they were not entirely disinterested in East-Central Europe, even though they recognised some sort of economic priority of the *Third Reich* in the region. London's gesture was not necessarily economic, but rather political, which would have constituted the moral support the Romanians needed to hold on to in front of Germany's future economic and political pressures.[23] On 13 April 1939, the British government embarked on an action entirely atypical for its traditional foreign policy by providing guarantees of independence but not of integrity for Romania and Greece after having previously provided them to Poland on 31 March. The guarantees provided to these three countries, but especially to Poland and Romania, were given to intimidate Hitler and make him more moderate, rather than for practical reasons. Most certainly, Chamberlain and his collaborators were aware that it was practically impossible to send British troops to fight for these countries. The British first considered Greece due to the annexation of Albania by Italy. However, the inclusion of Romania in these guarantees resulted from pressures from France, which wished to show proof of Anglo-French unity. By making this decision, in less than one month Britain radically changed its traditional foreign policy towards East-Central Europe.[24]

The granting of these guarantees was a consequence of the failure of the British plan to build in East-Central Europe a system of states united against Germany through mutual assistance treaties. The Romanian government, not wanting to challenge Germany, turned down London's proposals so as to be able to hold onto its ties to the *Reich*. Hence the guarantees given by the British and French to Romania on 13 April were exactly what the Romanian government wanted: a unilateral insurance of the two great democratic powers with regard to Romania's independence; this was because according to the text of these guarantees, the Romanians were not obliged to help Britain and France. The consequences of the Foreign Office policy were among the most significant.

British citizens in Romania in 1940–41

Despite that Romania originally remained neutral in the Second World War, Bucharest-London relations worsened profoundly in 1940, especially during the Romanian national-legionary regime between 14 September 1940 and 23 January 1941. The cooling of relations between the two countries was the result of a continuous process of deterioration of the bilateral relations which

---

23 Funderburk, *Politica Marii Britanii*, 112.
24 Paul D. Quinlan, *Clash over Romania: British and American Policies toward Romania: 1938–1947*. Los Angeles: American Romanian Academy of Arts and Sciences, 1977, 46.

had started a while earlier. The Romanian foreign policy was perceived as hostile due to the hosting of a German Military Mission in Romania, followed further by its accession to the Tripartite Pact in November 1940. The poor bilateral relationships were influenced decisively by two other issues: the withholding by Romanian authorities of British boats from the Danube, and especially the arrest of several British citizens and their subsequent maltreatment by members of the Legionary Movement.

Although the first days of July 1940 witnessed the expulsion of 27 British subjects, along with another hundred that left on the day of proclamation of the national-legionary state of Romania,[25] there were still some British citizens in the Romanian territory, most of them working in the oil sector or in industry. Although, in late September and early October 1940, members of the Legionary Movement kidnapped some British citizens, state police were not involved in these 'arrests.' These British citizens were suspected of preparing the destruction of the oil industry in Prahova Valley, in order to sabotage its oil-export to Germany.[26]

The news about the kidnapping and maltreatment of British subjects reached the diplomats of the British Legation in Bucharest through the Consul Norman Mayers who asked for details from the General Prosecutor of Romania.[27] The British Consul requested that the General Prosecutor let him know whether the competent magistrate had been informed about these illegal arrests because the 48-hour deadline had passed. He also asked to carry out urgent investigations to elucidate the circumstances in which the British citizens were detained, and asked to be informed when he could see the respective detainees.[28]

The day after the intervention of Consul Norman Mayers, the head of the Foreign Office, Lord Halifax, handed over to the head of the Romanian diplomatic mission in London a *note verbale*, which categorically condemned the way British citizens were being treated.[29] The situation had become

---

25 The Romanian Ministry of Foreign Affairs (hereafter, RMFA), fund Anglia (hereafter, Anglia) vol. 41, sheets 5, 8.
26 To see the full statements given by Percy R. Clark, Jock Anderson, Alexander Miller and J. E. Treacy to the British Plenipotentiary Minister in Bucharest, Sir Reginald Hoare, after their release from the hands of the legionaries, see Sorin Arhire, 'Situația cetățenilor britanici în timpul statului național-legionar din România,' *Annales Universitatis Apulensis. Series Historica* 11/I (2007): 363–86.
27 Norman Mayers, 'Letter sent to the General Prosecutor of Romania,' 28 September 1940, sheet 320. RMFA, Anglia vol. 14.
28 Ibid., fund Romania, vol. 131, sheets 381–3.
29 Telegram sent from the Romanian Legation in London to Romania's Ministry of Foreign Affairs, 20 September 1940. Ibid., Anglia, vol. 231, sheet 284.

particularly serious since Romanian Foreign Minister Mihail Sturdza (1940–41) instructed Radu Florescu, the Romanian *chargé d'affaires*, to tell officials in London that the arrested British citizens were being prosecuted for acts of sabotage against the Romanian state.[30] Since the reply did not match the requests expressed by the British side, the breaking of diplomatic relations appeared imminent, as the Romanian diplomat in London declared.[31]

Faced with extremely energetic protests, the *Conducător* (Ruler) of Romania General Ion Antonescu (1940–44) became extremely worried by the prospect that diplomatic ties to Britain might be broken, and by possible air strikes from the Royal Air Force over the Prahova Valley or Bucharest.[32] In consequence, the British citizens arrested by the Legionaries were taken over by state authorities. Later, the Military Tribunal in Bucharest declared them innocent. Finally, the prisoners were free and they left Romania immediately in October 1940.

Resentment towards the way the British citizens were treated continued for quite some time. The British Envoy to Romania, Sir Reginald Hoare (1934–41), insistently requested some sort of 'satisfaction' for the incidents that occurred in September-October 1940.[33] These incidents brought an important contribution to the shift in the Foreign Office policy towards Romania, which resulted in the suppression of the British and Romanian Legations taking place three months later on 15 February 1941.

The breaking of diplomatic relations between Great Britain and Romania in 1941

Romania paid a heavy price for the change of geopolitical balance in Europe after the beginning of the Second World War. In the summer of 1940, Bucharest complied with the Soviet ultimatum to evacuate Bessarabia and the Northern Bukovina, which were immediately annexed by the Soviet Union. In total, the Romanian Kingdom gave to the USSR a surface of 50,762 square kilometres with a population of 3,776,309 inhabitants out of which 53.5%

---

30   Telegram sent by the Plenipotentiary Minister in London to the head of the Romanian diplomacy, 9 October 1940. Ibid., vol. 14, sheet 194.

31   Telegram sent by Radu Florescu to Romania's Minister of Foreign Affairs, 11 October 1940. Ibid., sheet 202.

32   *Stenogramele Ședințelor Consiliului de Miniştri. Guvernarea Ion Antonescu*, vol. 1, Bucharest: The National Archives of Romania, 112. Cabinet Council Reunion from 26 September 1940.

33   Telegram sent by Alexandru Cretzianu, Secretary General of the Ministry of Foreign Affairs to the Minister of Justice, Mihai Antonescu, 11 January 1941. RMFA, Anglia, vol. 14, sheet 497.

were Romanians. At this moment, the Romanian realised that it would not receive any support from the British who were fighting for their own survival in the 'Battle of Britain.' Regarding the impact of France's defeat on British policy towards Romania, it is interesting to mention the viewpoint of American journalist Rosie G. Waldeck, who was in Bucharest at the time.

> To the Romanians, England, the Empire, the Anglo-Saxon way of life, were admirable but something as exotic and far away as the Chinese civilization of the 16th century. In spite of its failings during the previous twenty years, France was the dominating force in Romania and the liberal order ruled only through the medium of France. This was a basic fact not only about the past but also the future. It showed that here no Anglo-Saxon order – any order at all – had to be represented, translated or interpreted by France, Germany or Russia. And this applied not only to Romania, but to the whole of South-East Europe. Nowhere in these parts of the world was England real enough to be accepted as a dominating force. This was why, tonight, after the fall of Paris, the English were already licked in Romania, though they did not acknowledge it. It was not so much that the defeat of France confirmed the notion of the supposed invincibility of the German army, but more that the fall of France robbed the English of their Viceroy in Romania. This Viceroy was France.[34]

Great Britain's reaction to the Soviet annexation of Bessarabia and Northern Bukovina was rather reserved; Philip Broad, a civil servant of the Foreign Office, wrote in a minute that: 'it was almost inevitable that this should happen sooner or later. From our own purely selfish point of view this ... does not greatly change the position. Romania has gone too far towards the Axis Powers for there to be any question of her thinking of appealing to our guarantee.' On 28 June 1940, when Richard Austen Butler, Parliamentary Under-Secretary at the Foreign Office met with the Romanian Minister in London, all he could provide was a statement by which the government in London did not recognise *de jure* that the two provinces belonged to the Soviet state.[35]

A noticeable shift in Great Britain's policy towards Romania would not occur until 1 July 1940 when Romania waived the French-British guarantees in an

---

34 Rosie Goldschmidt Waldeck, *Athene Palace Bucharest: Hitler's 'New Order' Comes to Rumania*. London: Constable, 1943, 37.
35 Elisabeth Barker, *British Policy in South-East Europe in the Second World War*. London, Basingstoke: MacMillan, 1976, 72.

offensive manner. The Foreign Office found out from the press that Romania waived the guarantees without informing them in advance. This made London determined not to reply to Bucharest.[36]

The establishment of the pro-German Romanian government led by General Ion Gigurtu on 4 July 1940 (and with Mihail Manoilescu as Minister for Foreign Affairs), led to an even more striking worsening of relations between Britain and Romania. Romania's withdrawal from the League of Nations on 11 July, the proclamation of the national-legionary state on 14 September, and especially the arrival of a German military mission in Romania, whose role was to protect the oil fields of Prahova Valley and train the Romanian army, convinced the British that Bucharest had permanently moved to the camp of the *Third Reich*. The pro-German orientation of the government of Ion Gigurtu was concluded with the Tripartite Pact and the signature of General Ion Antonescu in Berlin on 23 November 1940.

London, considering that Romania was an occupied country, viewed the further existence of the British Legation in Bucharest as pointless. In the second half of 1940, it no longer fulfilled its role of diplomatic mission, but had become a mere observation point. Under these circumstances, as early as 8 October 1940, Sir Reginald Hoare was given permission to withdraw the British Legation from Bucharest whenever he considered it. Therefore, on 15 February 1941, diplomatic relations between Great Britain and Romania were broken after the blocking of Romania's funds in London.

Romanian emigration to Britain

One of the consequences of the outbreak of war was widespread emigration towards Western Europe because of the Axis conquest of several European countries and the pro-Axis policy shifts of various states. First this targeted France, but when France exited the war, Britain became the centre of emigration. Primarily moving to London but also the rest of Britain, were citizens from Western and Central Europe, and Romania was no exception. The number of Romanian citizens amounted to about 2,000. Some of them had been working at the Romanian Legation and other related institutions, and refused to return home after 15 February 1941 when diplomatic ties between Great Britain and Romania were broken off. There were also other people who had gotten to Britain other ways.[37]

---

36   Quinlan, *Clash over Romania*, 63.
37   Valeriu Florin Dobrinescu and Ion Pătroiu, *Anglia și România între anii 1939–1947*. Bucharest: Didactic and Pedagogic Publishing House RA, 1992, 106.

On 22 June 1941, when Romanian troops, in collaboration with those of the *Wehrmacht*, attacked the Soviet Union, Britain hosted two rival Romanian groups: the Romanian Democratic Committee and the Free Romanian Movement. The first one was led by Victor Cornea, while the second was led by Virgil Viorel Tilea, the former Romanian Plenipotentiary Minister in London. Each of them was aiming to get legal recognition as an official movement from the British government. But as the Free Romanian Movement had only 52 members, including 22 Romanian sailors who had refused to return to Romania in December 1940, and the Romanian Democratic Committee, which was even smaller, British authorities were not keen on recognising either of the two movements because these factions were not representative of Romanian public opinion.[38] Besides their size, the Whitehall had other reasons for not recognising them officially. Both movements were led by people lacking political acumen. Moreover, officials of the Foreign Office were very much aware that the recognition of a movement under the leadership of V. V. Tilea would automatically lead to the deterioration of solidarity with the British cause maintained in Romania by the members of the National Peasant Party led by Iuliu Maniu.[39] What also mattered to the British, after having monitored their activities, was the impression the two groups made. The conclusion they reached was that there was a strong feeling of animosity between Romanians in Great Britain and that 'it is not always safe to take as gospel what a member of one fraction will say about the adherents of another.'[40]

Romania's participation in the German attack on the Soviet Union in June 1941 gave new hopes to the two Romanian groups that they would get their much sought after official recognition. However, the disagreements between them reached maximum levels. Also, Romania's former King Carol II, who abdicated in September 1940, announced from the Mexican capital that he wished to take over the leadership of a Romanian government in exile and to travel to Britain. The Foreign Office, feeling the distance to the former King as well as to the two rival groups, decided on 8 September 1941 to set up a confidential Romanian organisation known as the Romanian Office. Major D. P. Back was appointed to organise this Romanian Office while he also was instructed to perform the duties of a liaison officer between the British government and the newly created organisation. The British were planning to designate the members of this organization and drafted a preliminary list of

---

38 Letter sent by Colonel C. E. Ponsonby to Colonel Scovell, 20 August 1941. The National Archives of Romania, the Central Historic Archives Directorate (hereafter, NARCHAD), Anglia Microfilm Archives (hereafter, AMA), reel 444, frame 503.
39 Report sent by R. A. Butler, Parliamentary Under-Secretary at the Foreign Office, to Brendon Bracken, MP, 24 June 1941. Ibid., frame 77.
40 Letter sent by Colonel Ponsonby to Colonel Scovell, 20 August 1941. Ibid., frame 503.

those who could join the office and also of those individuals who had to be excluded.[41]

The Romanian Office did not have the necessary time to take shape, as on 7 December 1941 Britain declared war on Romania. From this moment, London decided to support the Romanian politician Iuliu Maniu (the leader of the Transylvanian opposition). During 1941, Romanians in England had not managed to agree and put together a united front; at this point, any chance of setting up a Romanian organization to oppose Antonescu's regime had been shattered because in this newly created situation, the British government recommended they stop any political activity.[42] No recognition was possible now but the British government was willing to help the members of the Romanian emigration to participate individually in Britain's war effort, if they so desired.

By the end of 1941, Britain was forced to adopt a firm position towards Romania, Hungary and Finland, whose troops were engaged in German military operations against the USSR. Due to the advance of the Romanian troops on the Soviet territory, the Kremlin had asked the British since early September 1941 to declare war on Romania.[43] But, being convinced that the sympathy of most Romanians went to Great Britain and not to Germany,[44] Churchill was not at all keen on fulfilling this request – he even argued his point of view in a letter sent to Stalin. But the need of solidarity between Great Britain and the Soviet Union plus the fear that Stalin could sign a separate peace agreement with Germany forced Churchill to give in.[45] On 30 November 1941, the British government, through the Legation of the United States in Bucharest, sent to the Romanian government an ultimatum asking them to cease military operations against the USSR by 5 December 1941;

---

41   Document drawn-up by Mr. Leeper for Mr. Murray, 19 September 1941. Ibid., frames 621–5.
42   D. G. Danielopol, *Jurnal londonez*. Jassy: European Institute, 1995, 239.
43   Quinlan, *Clash over Romania*, 71.
44   Probably the British Prime Minister relied, among others, on the statement of Sir Reginald Hoare, former Plenipotentiary Minister in Romania who was saying the following in *The Times* from 18 February 1941 '[...] the Roumanian people almost unanimously hate the Germans and pray for our victory; this is true not only for the French educated higher classes but for the masses [...]'. NARCHAD, AMA, reel 444, frame 402. In exchange, in spite of all the discipline and efforts of the *Wehrmacht*, the Germans did not enjoy too much sympathy in Romania. On the contrary, they were treated with coldness and the Romanians' attitude was in obvious contrast with the warm, friendly atmosphere that they found in Hungary and Bulgaria. Alexandru Cretzianu, *Relapse into Bondage: Political Memoirs of a Romanian Diplomat, 1918–1947*. Jassy, Oxford, Portland: The Centre for Romanian Studies, 1998, 238.
45   Quinlan, *Clash over Romania*, 71–2.

otherwise, the only alternative was to declare a state of war between Britain and Romania.

Marshal Antonescu's reply to the British ultimatum took the form of a justification, counting the acts of violence committed by the Soviets and the loss of Bessarabia and of Northern Bukovina in the summer of 1940. Antonescu argued that Romania was defending itself against Soviet aggression. But he did not reassure London that hostilities would cease as the British had requested.

On 5 December 1941, Churchill approved the declaration of war on Romania, Hungary and Finland. Two days later, this was communicated to the Romanian government. The pressures of the Soviet Union in London proved to be decisive in the British declaration. Soon Churchill confided to Anthony Eden that: 'my opinion about the lack of wisdom of this measure remains unaltered.'[46] Coincidence or not, the British declaration of war on Romania occurred the same day as the Pearl Harbour attack, which led to the globalisation of the conflict through the participation of the United States. Wishing to make the Axis more cohesive, Germany and Italy also declared war on America and on 12 December, in accordance with Article II of the Tripartite Pact, Romania acted similarly.

*Translated by Silvana Vulcan

---

46   Winston S. Churchill, *The Grand Alliance*. Boston: Houghton Mifflin Harcourt, 1950. Apud Ibid.

5

American Policy towards Czechoslovakia, 1918–1945

ARTEM ZORIN

The United States and the struggle for Czecho-Slovak independence

Throughout the 19th century, demographic growth and poverty in the Habsburg Empire forced its Czech, Slovak and Ruthenian populations to migrate – particularly to the United States. By the beginning of the 20th century, approximately one and a half million Czechs and Slovaks lived in the United States. Despite the spread of *Czechoslovakism* (theory of united Czechoslovak nation), they were divided on political, ethnic and religious grounds.

The Czech national movement of the early 20th century fought for federalization of the Dual Monarchy and for Bohemia's historic state rights, equal with Austria and Hungary.[1] The slogan of creating their own state was not popular before World War I. National independence was widely popularized from 1915 by a group of political emigrants, headed by the Czech politician and philosopher Tomáš Garrigue Masaryk. He argued for the need to dissolve Austria-Hungary in order to create a new national state of Czechs and Slovaks. This group established the National Council of the Czech Lands in Paris in order to look for the assistance of the Entente powers and to obtain the support of national communities abroad.[2]

Apart from the obvious importance of the US, Masaryk also connected his

---

1 Victor S. Mamatey and Radomir Luza (eds.), *A History of the Czechoslovak Republic, 1918–1948*. Princeton, New Jersey: Princeton University Press, 1973, 4.
2 *A History of the Czechoslovak Republic*, 14. Victor S. Mamatey, 'The United States and Czechoslovak Independence' in *Czechoslovakia, Crossroads and Crises, 1918–1988*. London: Macmillan, 1989, 65.

hopes with America because of personal reasons. He was married to an American citizen, Charlotte Garrigue, visited the US a few times before the war, and had lectured at the University of Chicago.[3] He also had close ties with wealthy Chicago businessman Charles Crane, a major sponsor of the Wilson's presidential election campaign, a philanthropist and patron of the University of Chicago's Slavic Program. Later, he became father-in-law of Tomáš Masaryk's son Jan. Crane's older son Richard later became the first US Minister to Prague, and another son, John became Masaryk's secretary.[4]

In 1915, Masaryk's supporters in America created the Bohemian National Alliance and in 1917 they founded the Czech-Slav Press Bureau in Washington to streamline propaganda for Czecho-Slovak independence. In June 1917, another leader of the Czecho-Slovak National Council, a Slovak named Milan Rastislav Štefanik, visited the US to meet its politicians and recruit volunteers to fight in Europe. As Masaryk's agents noted, public opinion in America was not well informed about Czecho-Slovak movement for independence, but had traditional sympathies for oppressed nations. Until 1918, the US government did not show much interest in the Czechoslovak issue. First, because of its limited interest in that region; second, because of lack of specialists and information; third, because of its unwillingness to intervene in territorial disputes and conflicts between European nations. President Wilson (1913–21) and his Secretary of State Robert Lansing (1915–20) expressed no desire to support Czechs, fearing the creation of a precedent for other nations (like Poles, Yugoslavs, Irish, etc.). However, Štefanik prompted discussion of the Czechoslovak problem in the American press.[5]

Despite the US declaration of war on Germany in April 1917, and on Austria-Hungary in December 1917, Washington had no particular plans for the post-war settlement in Central Europe and its territorial structure. The State Department had no separate division to deal with this region either. A special research group, the Inquiry, was established under Wilson's friend and adviser Colonel Edward M. House only in September 1917. Consisting mostly of academic experts, it had to make recommendations to the President and the Secretary of State regarding the post-war settlement.[6]

---

3   Tomas G. Masaryk, *The Making of a State: Memories and Observations, 1914–18*. New York: F.A. Stokes Co., 1927, 218-9.
4   Milada Polišenská, *Diplomatické vztahy Československa a USA 1918–1938. 1. Svazek. Ministerstva, legace a diplomaté*. Praha: Nakladatelství Libri, 2012, 36–7.
5   Elizabeth Anne Murphy, *Initiative help: United States-Czechoslovak relations from Versailles to Munich*. A PhD Dissertation theses. Cornell University, 1999, 33; Mamatey, *The United States and Czechoslovak Independence*, 70.
6   James T. Shotwell, *At the Paris Peace Conference*. New York: MacMillan Company, 1937, 3; Murphy, *Initiative help*, 37.

Refusing to enter the Entente, the US was never in favour of secret agreements on territorial questions. Known as a supporter of national self-determination, President Wilson announced that the United States had no intentions for territorial annexation and fought for peace and justice in international relations. But, in practice, Wilson, the State Department and the Inquiry experts were cautious regarding this issue. In the 'Fourteen points,' the president declared in January 1918 that 'The peoples of Austria-Hungary, whose place among the nations we wish to see safeguarded and assured, should be accorded the freest opportunity to autonomous development,' but not to independence. The president, as well as his Entente allies did not want to destroy the empire, believing that it was needed for the maintenance of peace as well as economic and political stability in Central Europe, especially after the revolutionary explosion in Russia.[7] The main goal was to withdraw Vienna from the war. In 1917, the Entente powers began secret negotiations with representatives of new Austro-Hungarian Emperor Charles (1916–18), trying to force him to conclude a separate peace. Only in April 1918, when his unwillingness to break with Germany became evident, allies turned towards the policy of the empire's internal destabilization through the support of national movements.

By that time, the Czecho-Slovak Council created an important base for strengthening its influence. In 1917, the Russian Provisional government concluded an agreement with Masaryk about the organization of an autonomous Czechoslovak army of volunteers, POWs and deserters which was established for fighting the Central Powers. Two other legions were created in Italy and France.[8] But after the Russian October Revolution of 1917, and the Brest-Litovsk peace treaty between the Bolshevik government and the Central Powers in March 1918, using Czecho-Slovak troops against Germany on the Eastern Front became impossible. The French suggested transporting the Legion to the Western Front through Siberia and America. Stretching from Europe to the Far East along the Trans-Siberian Railway, Czechoslovak Legionaries were embroiled in the Russian civil war. They had become the main organized military force in this conflict and a trump card in the policy of the Czechoslovak National Council. These events became prerequisites for a gradual change in US policy towards Czechoslovak movement.[9]

Masaryk, after staying in Russia in 1917 for negotiations over the Legion,

---

7   *Papers Relating to the Foreign Relations of the United States* (hereafter, FRUS), 1918. Supplement 1, The World War. Volume 1. Washington: US Government Printing Office, 1933, 12–7; *Arhiv polkovnika Hauza*. Kniga 4. Moskva, 1944, 151–3.
8   *A History of the Czechoslovak Republic*, 18. Murphy, 40.
9   Harry Hanak 'France, Britain, Italy and the Independence of Czechoslovakia in 1918' in *Czechoslovakia, Crossroads and Crises*, 53.

decided to go to the US the next spring. He intended to achieve three main objectives: to establish closer financial and political cooperation with Czech and Slovak organizations in America; to get support for the transportation of Legionaries from Siberia to Europe; to persuade the Wilson administration, American politicians, and the American public to recognize and support the cause of Czechoslovak independence. During his six month visit (from May to November 1918), Masaryk achieved rapid success in his first goal. On 31 May 1918, in Pittsburgh, Czech and Slovak organizations in America signed, under the presidency of Masaryk, an agreement regarding the creation of a Czecho-Slovak state on an equal basis for both nations.[10] While Masaryk had no recognition for acting in the name of Czechs and Slovaks, this agreement played an important role in legitimating the Czechoslovak movement and himself as its leader. At this time, the State Department decided to change its position on the Czechoslovak question and support the Czech and Slovak movement with two main purposes: to destabilise the Austro-Hungarian Empire from the inside so as to shorten the war; using the Czechoslovak Legion in Russia to weaken the Bolshevik's positions along the Trans-Siberian railroad, and to destabilise Japanese influence on the Russian Far East. Secretary of State Robert Lansing in a declaration on May 1918 stated that the 'nationalistic aspirations of Czechoslovaks and Yugo-Slavs for freedom' had the 'earnest sympathy' of the US government. Five days later, on June 3, the French, British and Italian prime ministers noted the American declaration 'with pleasure' and hastened to 'associate themselves' with it.[11] In June 1918, Czechoslovak Legionaries arrived in Vladivostok. By Masaryk's request for assistance, on 6 July, Wilson approved sending American US troops 'to help the Checho-Slovaks consolidate their forces and get into successful cooperation with their Slavic kinsmen and to steady any efforts at self-government or self-defence in which the Russians themselves may be willing to accept assistance.'[12]

Later, in summer 1918 when the Czechoslovak National Council was recognized by the French and British governments, Lansing put the question of the Czechoslovaks to the president. After searching for the most suitable wording, on 3 September 1918, the State Department declared that the United States recognized 'the Czecho-Slovak National Council as a de facto belligerent government clothed with proper authority to direct the military and political affairs of the Czecho-Slovaks.'[13] This decision primarily allowed for the provision of financial aid to the Council for the Legion's activities. But nothing was mentioned about Czechoslovakia as a state. However, in October 1918, the US refused the Austro-Hungarian proposal to start peace

---

10 Mamatey, *The United States and Czechoslovak Independence*, 72.
11 *A History of the Czechoslovak Republic*, 21.
12 Murphy, *Initiative help*, 44.
13 *FRUS, 1918*. Supplement 1. Volume1, 824.

negotiations on the basis of the 'Fourteen points.' Washington added that the program was not in line with the recognition of the Czechoslovaks's right to self-determination.[14]

Soon after that, on 18 October 1918, Masaryk published in Washington the Declaration of Czechoslovak Independence, and personally handed it to Wilson.[15] On 28 October the Czechoslovak National Committee in Prague proclaimed the independence of Czechoslovakia, and established its power in Bohemia and Moravia. Masaryk was elected in absentia as the first president of the state. In November 1918, he left the US for Europe.[16] The main goals of his visit had been achieved. The third one – the return of the Czechoslovak Legion from Russia was performed partially. The US promised to promote its transportation across the Pacific Ocean. The Czechs's propaganda managed to attract the sympathy of Americans and created a positive image of Czechoslovaks, which could be used at the upcoming peace conference. But although France, Britain and Italy accorded *de jure* recognition to Czechoslovakia in October, the United States did not take such a step.[17]

American diplomacy and the Czechoslovak question at the Paris Peace Conference of 1919

In 1919, the delegations of the victor countries gathered in Paris to discuss and sign peace treaties and create a new territorial and political order. Leaders of the three main allied powers played the principal roles at the meetings: David Lloyd George of Great Britain, George Clemenceau of France and Woodrow Wilson of the United States. It was the first American experience in such a global forum as an equal Great Power. Wilson became the first acting US president to go abroad to personally lead the American delegation.

The Allies had a common goal – to prevent aggressions and a new war, but they saw different ways of achieving it. Entente leaders intended to radically change the balance of power in Europe and to weaken their former enemies' geographic and economic positions. President Wilson aspired to change the

---

14   Unterberger, *The United States*, 314.
15   Viktor Mamatey, *The Unated States and East-Central Europe 1914–1918. A study in Wilsonian Diplomacy and Propaganda*. Princeton: Princeton University Press, 1957, 331. Herbert A. Miller, 'What Woodrow Wilson and America Meant to Czechoslovakia' in *Czechoslovakia: Twenty Years of Independence*, edited by Robert J. Kerner. Berkley: University of California Press, 1940, 71–87.
16   *Chehia i Slovakia v XX veke: Ocherki istorii*, edited by Valentina V. Mar'ina. Kniga 1. Moskva: Nauka, 2005, 88–92.
17   Murphy, *Initiative help*, 50.

whole international relations system. He proposed to use the principle of national self-determination to create new interstate borders based on ethnic boundaries and the people's free opinions in every disputed territory. Wilson supposed that while his plan could present new conflicts between nations, it would also provide conditions for economic recovery and development in Central Europe, and it would allow new states to protect themselves from external and internal threats.

The Czechoslovak delegation in Paris, led by Masaryk's close companion in the fight for independence, Edvard Beneš, presented its territorial demands in February 1919. He proposed to draw the Czechoslovak borders according to historical, economic, military and strategic considerations. Beneš and his colleagues wanted to create a strong state, and demanded the inclusion of vast areas with German populations in Bohemia and Moravia (Sudetenland), Hungarians in Southern Slovakia, Poles in a small but important industrial area of Teschen in Czech Silesia, and Ruthenians in the East. The Czech army occupied Sudeten areas before the Conference began. The same happened with Slovakia in 1919. But in Teschen, they met strong resistance from Poland. Beneš also mentioned Lusatia (Slavic area in Germany) and Burgenland (the corridor along the new border between Austria and Hungary to Yugoslav state). Thus, Czechoslovakia was supposed to become a little multinational empire like the defunct Austria-Hungary, but with the dominance of the Czechs. Beneš explained that all these areas were needed for the existence of the State.[18]

French delegates were the main supporters of Czech demands. They wanted to create a strong counterweight to Germany and its former allies in Central Europe, as well as a *cordon sanitaire* against the spread of Bolshevism from Russia. For the same reasons, the British agreed. A member of the Inquiry and the American delegation, Charles Seymour, wrote in his memoirs that the French and the British wanted to create Czechoslovakia with defendable borders and a solid economic foundation.[19]

Inquiry experts suggested using primarily language lines, but took into account historical, administrative and economic factors. Their preliminary

---

18   *FRUS, Paris Peace Conference..* Volume3, 877–87; *Dokumenty československé zahraniční politiky, Československo na pařížské mírové konferenci*. Svazek 1. Praha: Ústav mezinárodních vztahů, 2001, 131–41; Elena P. Serapionova, 'Chehoslovatzkiy vopros na Parizhskoy mirnoy konferencii' in *Vostochnaya Evropa posle Versalya*, Sankt-Peterburg: Aleteya, 2007, 94.

19   Edward Mandell House and Charles Seymour (eds.), *What really happened at Paris. The story of the Peace Conference, 1918–1919*. New York, C. Scribner's Sons, 1921, 97.

report favoured an independent Czechoslovakia, including historically Czech lands, Slovak territories of Hungary and Ruthenia. The main reason was the desire of their population to live in one state. But the position of Austrian, German and Hungarian borderlands, inhabited by non-Slavic citizens was subject for further research and discussion.[20] Investigating the situation and real wishes of the population, American experts visited different areas of the former Austria-Hungary. Some of them were in opposition with Czech demands for very vast territories.

The main decisions were made by the Czech Committee of the Peace Conference, and the Counsel of Ten, which included representatives of the main powers. American delegates had to move away from the original Wilsonian position. Most of Beneš's demands were granted, excluding Lusatia and Burgenland. The question of Teschen was handed over for special discussion between Prague and Warsaw. Later, the president wrote to his Secretary of State, Robert Lansing that 'ethnic lines cannot be drawn without the greatest injustice and injury' in Bohemia.[21] However, the Czechs's excessive territorial claims were reduced and Prague had to guarantee the rights of national minorities. But contrary to the Pittsburgh agreement, the republic was created as a unitary state (Czechoslovakia, not Czecho-Slovakia). Ruthenians, Germans, Hungarians and Poles did not receive broad autonomy.

The behaviour of European allies as well as the growing nationalism of the small nations caused disappointment in American society. The Congress refused to ratify the Paris Peace Treaties. In the 1920 elections, the Republican Party defeated the Democrats. The new administration declared the return to isolationism as a traditional course of American foreign policy. As a result, in the 1920s, the US withdrew from direct involvement in European international politics.

The United States and Czechoslovakia, 1920–1930s: from politics to economy

The years of the Paris Peace Conference marked the beginning of political and economic relations between the United States and Czechoslovakia. In June 1919, the first American minister, Richard Crane, son of Charles Crane arrived in Prague. His brother-in-law and son of Tomáš Masaryk became the

---

20   Lawrence E. Gelfand, *The Inquiry. American preparations for peace, 1917–1919*. New Hawen and London: Yale University Press, 1963, 204.
21   Arthur S. Link and David W. Hirst (eds.), *The Papers of Woodrow Wilson*. Volume 61. Princeton: Princeton University Press, 1989, 371.

first Czechoslovak chargé d'affaires to the US in December 1919.[22] These appointments stressed close personal ties between the two countries.

Even before establishing official political relations, Washington started giving financial help to the Czechoslovaks. In 1918, the Czecho-Slovak Council received the first US loan for Legion operations in Russia.[23] In February 1919, the American Relief Administration (ARA), under the direction of Herbert Hoover, began its mission in Prague.[24] Its activities in Central Europe were directed at rebuilding commercial links so as to start reconstruction and prevent hunger, poverty and political radicalism. The ARA was engaged in providing food supplies to the war-torn republic; American experts worked on the restoration of Bohemian industry and trade relations in the region. Soon, the Czechoslovak government succeeded in getting a US loan to purchase raw cotton for the textile industry.[25] All of this laid a good foundation for further cooperation. It also gave American experts better understanding of the region's economic and political features and made a base for further cooperation.

The Republicans, who replaced the Democrats in power in 1921, sought to change the Wilsonian course of active intervention in European political affairs to isolationism. But after the war, the United States were strongly connected with European countries in financial and economic areas.[26] The growing American economy was looking for new markets and one of them could be Central Europe. Reducing political relations, the Americans did not want to abandon financial, economic and trade cooperation. But further development and deepening of these ties required the settlement of a number of contradictions.

There were two major problems which dominated Washington's decision-makers regarding its contact with the government in Prague. The first problem, inherited from Wilson's Administration, was connected to the huge war debts of former American allies in Europe, including Czechoslovakia. During the war and the settlement period, the US provided loans for military and food supplies and the restoration of the economy. Their pay was delayed due to difficulties in the economic recovery. In 1922, the US Congress

---

22 Polišenská, *Diplomatické vztahy Československa a USA 1918–1938*, 138, 255.
23 Polišenská, *Diplomatické vztahy Československa a USA 1918–1938*, 46.
24 Murphy, *Initiative help*, 114.
25 US Senate, *Loans to Foreign Governments*. Washington. D.C.: US GPO, 1921, 241–5; Suda L. Bane and Ralph H. Lutz (eds.), *Organization of American Relief in Europe, 1918–1919*. Stanford: Stanford University Press,1943, 686–703.
26 Zsuzsa L. Nagy, *The United States and the Danubian Basin, 1919–1939*. Budapest: Akadémiai kiadó, 1975, 10.

established the World War Foreign Debts Commission to determine the exact amounts of debts which could be used by the State Department to conclude repayment agreements with all debtors. France, Britain and Italy were the main American debtors, Czechoslovakia had the seventh position in the list.[27] The official Czechoslovak debt to the US in the early 1920s was $110 million. It included different loans for the ARA's relief supplies, repatriation of the Legionaries from Russia, purchases of military materials and accrued interest.[28] The government in Prague recognized most of the Czechoslovak war debts, but tried to obtain more favourable conditions for their payment. Negotiations lasted for a few years and finished in 1925 when the State Department blocked negotiations between Czech and American financial representatives over new loans and credits. As a result, Czechoslovakia was forced to sign the debt agreement which provided a 62 year term of payment and the total final amount of $312 million.[29] This opened the way for further American investment in the Czechoslovak economy.

However, the economic crisis of 1929 resulted in a sharp fall in international trade and a reduction in foreign exchange. In 1931, US President Herbert Hoover suggested a one-year moratorium on all inter-state debts and reparations to support the European economy. The following year, the Lausanne Conference suspended World War I reparations. After that, the main US debtors – France and Great Britain – raised the question of suspending payments to the United States. The new administration of Franklin D. Roosevelt, which came to power in 1933, tried to work out new agreements.[30] Nevertheless, all debtors stopped payments in 1934. By that year, Czechoslovakia had paid about $ 20 million.

The White House raised the debt question again in December 1937 when the Czechoslovak government showed interested in new loans from the United States. Also, Prague, which had been in difficult international conditions and facing a potential conflict with Germany, looked for political support in Washington. The Czechs notified the US about their readiness to start new discussions on a debt agreement.[31] However, the occupation of Czech lands by Germany in March 1939 put an end to these intentions. The US Congress

---

27   *Combined Annual Reports of the World War Foreign Debt Commission. Fiscal Years 1922, 1923, 1924, 1925, 1926.* Washington: US Government Printing Office, 1927, 10.
28   Murphy, *Initiative help*, 320.
29   *Minutes of the World War Foreign Debt Commission*, 112–115; *Combined Annual Reports of the World War Foreign Debt Commission*, 193–204; Charles I. Bevans (ed.), *Treaties and Other International Agreements of the United States of America 1776–1949*. Volume 6. Washington, D.C.: US Government Printing Office, 1971, 1253–9.
30   *FRUS, 1934*. Volume 1, 556–7.
31   *FRUS, 1937*. Volume 1, 847.

proposed to shift the Czechoslovak debts to Germany, but the hope of resolving this problem was very small.[32]

The second main concern among American politicians regarding Czechoslovakia in the 1920s and 1930s was related to the regulation of trade and the protection of American business interests. World War I had destroyed the united Austro-Hungarian market. During the Paris Peace Conference, ARA experts were unsuccessfull in trying to rebuild economic ties between successor states, which were necessary for political stability and strength.[33] But in the 1920s, American diplomats and politicians left this idea and highlighted another task – the promotion and defending of American business interests.

In post-war conditions, the highly developed and export-oriented Czech economy looked attractive for foreign investment. On the other hand, Czechoslovak industry needed new sources of raw materials and export markets. But there were some obstacles to the development of trade relations – protectionist trade barriers and import licensing.[34] The State Department's attempts to overcome this system were a part of its common policy pursuing the liberalization of international trade. In 1923, the State Department initiated the most favourable national trade agreement with Prague. But because of Prague's unwillingness to abandon its import licensing system protecting Czech industry, the treaty was concluded with mutual concessions in import quotas and duties as a temporary *modus vivendi* for only two years. In 1924, it was declared termless and continued to operate for the next 10 years.[35]

On the basis of the most favourable nation, US diplomats tried to lobby American business interests, ensuring additional import license provisions from Prague. But Czechoslovak manufacturers often blocked the growing demands of their competitors. Complaining about discrimination, the American Minister in Prague and the State Department attempted to apply pressure on the government in Prague by threatening retaliatory measures against Czechoslovak products.[36] However, these actions were not too active because the trade was not very large.

---

32   US Congress, *Congressional Record*. Volume 84, Part 3. Washington, D.C.: US Government Printing Office, 1939, 2845–51.
33   Murphy, *Initiative help*, 536.
34   Rudolf Olšovsky, *Svetovy obchod a Československo 1918–1938*. Praha: Statni nakladatelství politické literatury, 1961, 136–138.
35   *FRUS, 1923*. Volum 1, 866–80; *FRUS, 1924*. Volume 1, 615–7; *Treaties and Other International Agreements*, 1244–6.
36   *FRUS, 1928*. Volume 2, 692–717.

During the Great Depression, Herbert Hoover's administration tried to return to ARA's policy of support for economic rapprochement with Central European countries and their speedy recovery. In 1931–1932 American diplomats took part in discussions about establishment of the Danubian Confederation and the creation of a customs union in the region, which would also include Czechoslovakia. The State Department agreed to maintain Czechoslovakia as the most favoured nation of the union states, if they would not provide special trade privileges to other countries. But Washington refused direct financial support, and because of this political controversy, negotiations stalled and the project was never realised.[37]

Economic crises caused the rise of protectionist tariffs and duties in all countries. Along with the revival, the US began a new program of international trade liberalization. Since 1934 the Department of State had negotiated bilateral agreements with the main trading partners on the basis of unconditional most favoured nation treatment, intending to spread this regime gradually to the whole international trade.[38] In 1935, the State Department studied conditions of mutual trade with Czechoslovakia in response to the Czech request. But American experts found that the Czechoslovak government discriminated against some American goods, while giving additional trade privileges to neighbouring countries of the Danubian area. As a temporary measure in 1935, Washington and Prague signed a new *modus vivendi*, stipulating the application of all trade benefits given to other countries to mutual American-Czechoslovak commercial relations.[39]

After that, the Department of State suggested to the Czechoslovak government to negotiate trade agreement conditions corresponding more to American interests. The process was complicated by the Czechs's wishes to have a special regime for Danubian trade and for some kinds of American products. Notwithstanding, in the context of rising conflict with Germany and a reduction of external commercial relations, the Czechoslovak economy was extremely interested in the trade agreement with the United States.[40] Negotiations lasted for about a year; then in early 1938, the Americans declared to the Czechs that the US was ready to refuse the new trade agreement if their proposals were not accepted and on 7 March 1938 the agreement was signed.[41] The deal was criticized on both sides. The State

---

37   FRUS, 1932. Volume 1, 846–59.
38   Richard A. Harrison, 'The United States and Great Britain: President Diplomacy and Alternatives to Appeasement in the 1930s in' *Appeasement in Europe: A Reassessment of United States Policy*, edited by Richard D Challener and David F. Schmitz. New York: Greenwood Press, 1990, 114.
39   FRUS, 1935. Volume 2, 137–63.
40   FRUS, 1937. Volume. Volume 2, 238–55.
41   FRUS, 1938. Volume 2, 223–30. Treaties and Other International Agreements,

Department's concessions to Czechoslovakia were attacked in the Congress by representatives and senators who were afraid of rising competition for American shoes manufacturers.[42] The agreement with Czechoslovakia was in place for less than a year. On the next day after the German occupation of Bohemia and Moravia, the Congress requested the abolishment of all trade preferences for Czechoslovakian goods, and to increase duties on the basis of trade conditions with Germany. The State Department approved this decision on 17 March 1939.[43]

The American reaction to the Czechoslovak-German conflict of 1938–1939

In the second half of the 1930s, Czechoslovakia faced not only trade and economic recovery, but also a serious of political changes. In 1935, President Tomáš Masaryk resigned at the age of 85 because of health problems, and was succeeded by his close friend and associate, Minister of Foreign Affairs, Edvard Beneš. But more important for Czechoslovak's future was the change of political regime in neighbouring Germany, which was governed by the National Socialist Party beginning in 1933. Focusing on the injustice of Versailles Peace Treaty, the new Nazi Chancellor Adolf Hitler raised the question of discrimination against Germans in neighbouring states, including Czechoslovakia. The Hungarian and Polish authorities expressed similar claims to Prague.[44]

In such circumstances, Prague tried to reinforce old alliances with new guarantees and allies. In 1934, the Czechoslovak government established diplomatic relations with the USSR (a year after the US). In 1935, Moscow and Prague signed a treaty of mutual assistance providing military support to Czechoslovakia that was regarded by Hitler as a new threat to German security. Afterwards, he directly supported the Sudeten-German nationalist movement in Czechoslovakia. Thus, Berlin aimed to destabilize the republic.[45]

From the American point of view, the Czechoslovak crisis appeared in the background of other international tensions in Europe and Asia. Holding its

---

1285–93.
42 Congressional Record. Volume 83, Part 9, 914.
43 The New York Times, 17 March 1939.
44 Joseph S. Roucek, 'Czechoslovakia and Her Minorities' in Czechoslovakia: Twenty Years of Independence, 174.
45 Vera Olivova, 'The Czechoslovak Government and its 'Disloyal' Opposition, 1918–1938' in The Czech and Slovak Experience. Selected Papers From the 4th World Congress for Soviet and East European Studies, edited by John Morison. New York: St. Martin's Press, 1992, 100.

isolationist policy, the US was mostly interested in the Far East situation. But Roosevelt's administration, as well as the Congress and the public were strongly concerned with the crisis in Central Europe, fearing a new great war that the Americans did not want to be drawn into. Condemning the aggressive actions in Europe, Roosevelt and the State Department were only outside observers, not wanting to be drawn into the Czechoslovak-German conflict. In April 1937, the Czechoslovak chargé d'affaires in Washington, Otakar Kabeláč reported to Prague that the US desired 'to beware of any military conflict.' He noted a lack of awareness and interest of the American public in the development of the Czechoslovak situation.[46]

The Undersecretary of State Sumner Welles was the first to allow the possibility of a US intervention. Welles, who visited Europe in the fall of 1937, proposed an international conference in Washington to review the conditions of the Versailles Treaty. But both the President and Secretary of State (Cordell Hull) were opposed to direct involvement in Europe.[47] An important debate over the different perspectives on the Czechoslovak crisis was launched between the American representatives in Europe. The Ambassador to the UK, Joseph Kennedy, taking a pro-British position, supported Neville Chamberlain's appeasement policy. Thus, Kennedy stated the need for Czechoslovak concessions to Germany and the federalization of Czechoslovakia.[48] The Ambassador to France, William Bullitt, insisted on concessions too, seeing them as the only way to avoid war. He laid some part of responsibility on Beneš, and even made accusations against him in an effort to provoke a Franco-British clash with Germany. In May 1938, Bullitt proposed to Franklin D. Roosevelt to initiate an international conference which could force Prague to make concessions or, in case of failure to do so – to free France from its allied obligations to Czechoslovakia. Later, he repeated this sentence several times. Actually, that was an offer to sacrifice Czechoslovakia for the sake of peace. The main supporter of Prague was American Minister to Prague Wilbour Carr, who believed that the United States, as one of the co-creators of Czechoslovakia and all European post-war settlements, was responsible for the fate of the republic and had to support it.[49]

---

46   Documenty československé zahraniční politiky. Československá zahranicní politika v roce 1937. Svazek I. Praha: Ústav mezinárodních vztahů, 2007, 309–16.
47   Frederick W. Marks, 'Six Between Roosevelt and Hitler: America's role: the Appeasement of Nazi Germany' in American Foreign Policy in the 1930s, edited by Melvyn Dubofsky and Stephen Burwood. New York: Garland, 1990, 69–71.
48   E. L. Woodward and Rohan Butler (eds.), Documents on British Foreign Policy, 1919–1939.Third Series. Volume 3, 1938. London: H.M.S.O., British Information Services, 1949, 238.
49   Orville H.H. Bullitt (ed.), For the President, Personal and Secret: Correspondence Between Franklin D. Roosevelt and William C. Bullitt. Boston: Houghton Mifflin

In May 1938, the Czechoslovak Minister in Washington, Vladimir Hurban, reported to Prague that the threat from Germany significantly increased American attention towards and sympathy for Czechoslovakia.[50] By the fall of 1938, correspondents of leading American newspapers and radio stations were sent to Prague and Berlin to report directly on the development of the crisis.[51] At its peak, after the German ultimatum to Prague on 23 September 1938 to transfer the Sudeten German regions before 1 October 1938 under threat of war, Czechoslovakia was on the front pages of American newspapers and major radio stations released updates regularly.[52] The Secretary of the Interior, Harold Ickes, pointed out in his diary that, in those days, the government's attention was completely focused on the situation in Europe, which was in danger of a general war.[53]

This pushed President Roosevelt to make his first appeal. On 26 September 1938, he asked Germany, Czechoslovakia, Great Britain and France not to interrupt the negotiations. On 27 September, in the second appeal, Roosevelt called on all concerned states to resolve the conflict in a conference. American participation in this meeting was not mentioned. Moreover, President Roosevelt asked Italian Prime Minister Benito Mussolini to persuade Hitler to continue negotiations. By Washington's request, the appeal was supported by Latin American states.[54] It had to demonstrate Roosevelt's concern and desire for preventing war while holding with isolationism policy.

On 28 September, Mussolini appealed to the German chancellor with a proposal to hold a conference on the Sudeten problem but with a narrow list of participants – France, Britain, Germany and Italy, excluding Czechoslovak representatives. That was a serious distortion of the American plan. The Munich agreement, signed on 30 September 1938, approved Hitler's demands for the Sudetenland. As Prague found itself one-on-one against

---

Company, 1972, 232–8, 261–5; *FRUS, 1938*. Volume 1, 508–12.
50   *Československá zahraniční politika v roce 1938*. Svazek II (1. červenec – 5. říjen 1938). Praha: Ústav mezinárodních vztahů, 2007, 42–5.
51   Richard M. Ketchum, *The Borrowed Years 1938–1941. America on the Way to War*. New York: Random House, 1989, 51–2.
52   Donald A. Ritchie, *Reporting From Washington: the History of the Washington Press Corps*. Oxford: Oxford University Press, 2005, 56–7; Ketchum, *The Borrowed Years*, 51–2.
53   Harold L. Ickes, *The secret diary of Harold Ickes*. New York: Simon and Schuster, 472–3.
54   *FRUS, 1938*. Volume 1, 658, 684–5; S. Shepard Jones and Denys P. Myers (eds.), *Documents of American Foreign Relations. January 1938 – June 1939*. Boston: World Peace Foundation, 1939, 286–94; *For the President*, 282–3; Donald B. Schewe (ed.), *Franklin D. Roosevelt and Foreign Affairs. Second Series: January 1937–August 1939*. Volume 11. New York: Clearwate, 1969, 214–5, 226–8.

Berlin, it was forced to accept the Munich agreement. Soon Hungary and Poland, using the weakening of Czechoslovakia, had also obtained some territories of Czechoslovakia.

The first reaction on the peaceful end of the Czechoslovak crisis in the United States was a relief. The State Department concluded that the crisis was overcome and Secretary of State Hull said that the achieved results caused a 'general sense of relief.' But the US refused to give their official approval.[55] A large part of the US population sympathized with the Czechs. According to one poll, 70% felt that the Munich agreement and the German attachment of the Sudetenland were unfair. At the same time, the majority supported British and French actions for preventing a new war.[56] According to the Czechoslovak delegation in Washington, the American press felt mistrust towards the agreement, believing that peace rested on very insecure and shaky grounds.[57]

President Beneš, under pressure of Berlin, was forced to resign and left to the UK. In February 1939, he went to the United States for lectures. In America, Beneš received a very warm welcome. He was grateful to Roosevelt for his appeal before Munich, but was quite unhappy with the attitudes of the US ambassadors to Britain, France and Germany, as well as the support for appeasement among some US politicians.[58]

The next German step – the invasion of Czecho-Slovakia (after Munich, the republic was reorganized into a federation) on 15 March 1939 – met a strong US opposition. After the republic was divided into three pieces – the Protectorate of Bohemia and Moravia (attached to Germany), Slovakia (nominally independent) and Ruthenia (annexed by Hungary). On 17 March, Welles officially condemned the German acts of 'wanton lawlessness and of arbitrary force' against Czechoslovakia, 'which have resulted in the temporary

---

55   FRUS, 1938. Volume 1, 703; Documents of American Foreign Relations, 297; Cordell Hull, The Memoirs of Cordell Hull. Volume 1. New York: Macmillan, 1948, 595–6; Julius W. Pratt, Cordell Hull, 1933–1944. Volume 1. New York: Cooper Square, 1964, 300; Documents on British Foreign Policy, 625; Grigory N. Sevostyanov, Evropeisky krizis i poziciya SShA. 1938–1939. Moskva: Nauka, 1972, 156; US Department of State, Peace and War. United States Foreign Policy, 1931–1941. Washington, D.C.: United States Government Printing Office, 1943, 429.
56   Marcia L. Toepfer, Preconceptions: American governmental attitudes towards the Soviet Union during the 1938 Czechoslovakian crisis. PhD dissertation. University of Virginia, 1976. Ann Arbor, Mich.: University Microfilms International, 1978, 238.
57   Československá zahraniční politika v roce 1938. Sv. 2, 526–7.
58   Edward Taborsky, President Edward Beneš: between East and West, 1938–1948. Stanford Calif.: Hoover Institution Press, 1981, 44; Memoirs of Eduard Benes. From Munich to New War and New Victory. Cambridge: The Riverside Press, 1954, 167.

extinguishment of the liberties of a free and independent people with whom, from the day when the Republic of Czechoslovakia attained its independence, the people of the United States have maintained specially close and friendly relations.' At a press conference on 24 March, Secretary Hull called German actions an international lawlessness. The State Department announced that the US had not recognized the new status of Bohemia and Moravia.[59] It also rejected the recognition of the independent Slovakia and Hungary's annexation of Ruthenia. However, the German occupation of Czechia was recognized as de facto. American Legation in Prague was closed (while maintaining the consulate) and the Minister was recalled to the United States. At the same time, the Czechoslovak diplomatic mission in Washington, headed by Vladimir Hurban (who was assigned by Beneš and refused to resign at Berlin's request), continued its existence as an official representation of the temporarily occupied republic.

The United States and the restoration of Czechoslovakia during World War Two

The Munich agreement and occupation initiated a new wave of emigration and exile from Czechoslovakia to the West. The US, as 25 years before, became one of the main centers of the Czech national movement. But the majority of American Slovaks supported the creation of the First Slovak Republic. In 1939, American Czechs established a new Czechoslovak National Council, and elected Beneš as the head of the national liberation movement. Since March 1939, he returned to politics and actively promoted the idea of liberation and restoration of pre-Munich Czechoslovakia.[60] While in the US, he tried to meet Roosevelt for support, but the president instructed the State Department to tell Beneš 'not come to Washington at this time nor ask for an appointment with him.'[61]

However, for his 55th birthday, on 28 May 1939, Beneš was invited to Roosevelt's residence at Hyde Park for a private unofficial and confidential meeting. Beneš put forward to the president the idea of organizing a provisional government and military forces. But Roosevelt's answer was just sympathy for Czechs and disapproval of German actions against Czechoslovakia.[62] He did not want to give direct and public support for anti-German struggle in the US, believing that Washington's decision of non-

---

59 FRUS, 1939. Volume 1, 50, 59.
60 George V. Rimek, *Presidency Of Edvard Beneš*. PhD Thesis. University Of Ottawa, Canada, 1975, 437–40.
61 Taborsky, *President Edward Beneš*, 46.
62 Valentina V. Mar'ina, *Vtoroy president Chehoslovakii Edward Benesh: politik i chelovek. 1884–1948*. Moskva: Indrik, 2013, 264.

recognition of Munich and saving Czechoslovak Legation were enough. Beneš was satisfied by this policy and the president's comment to recognize the Czechoslovak government in exile when the time came.[63] Roosevelt acted accordingly with public mood – Americans had no desire to intervene in European conflicts, keeping a distance and speaking only about the moral deprecation of military aggression.

The beginning of World War 2, on 1 September, had not brought any important changes in the American position on Czechoslovakia. For three years, Beneš and the Czechoslovak National Committee, established in Paris from political refugees (later moved to London and transformed into the government-in-exile of the Czechoslovak Republic), was trying to achieve official recognition from the US. The State Department had consistently rejected Czech requests explaining that there was a lack of continuity between the Czechoslovak and Beneš governments.[64] But the real reason was probably its reluctance to get involved in a conflict with Germans, Hungarians and Poles because of Czechs.

The first changes in the American position came in the middle of 1941. In July 1941, after the German invasion of the USSR, London and Moscow gave full de jure recognition to Beneš as a president-in-exile.[65] On 30 July, Roosevelt in a personal message to Beneš, informed him of the US decision to establish a permanent relationship with Beneš as a 'president of the provisional Czechoslovak government' through ambassador Anthony J. D. Biddle, who performed a similar function for other governments in exile in London.[66] But the official *de jure* recognition of Beneš as a president of Czechoslovakia followed only in October 1942 after the US entry into the war.[67]

Despite the establishment of official ties with the Beneš government, Americans demonstrated little interest in the Protectorate and Slovakia. There were only occasional mentions related to Beneš or Nazi crimes and terror in diplomatic correspondences or in the press. Often the question of Czechoslovakia was closely intertwined with Poland and other countries of Central Europe. In discussions and interviews Beneš was perceived by American diplomats and journalists mostly not as a president, but as an expert in European and international relations and Soviet foreign policy.

In 1943, when the first signs of German weakness and the possibility of

---

63 Taborsky, *President Edward Beneš*, 48.
64 *FRUS, 1941*. Volume 2, 21–31.
65 *FRUS, 1941*. Volume 1, 239.
66 *FRUS, 1941*. Volume 2, 32.
67 *Memoirs of Eduard Benes*, 180.

victory came, Beneš decided to improve his position by direct negotiations with two new main allied powers – the US and the USSR. In the US, he wanted to strengthen his position in the American Czech community and to establish cooperation with Slovak organizations. They supported the United States in the war not only against Germany, but also against the Slovak Republic, which as a German ally declared war on the US in December 1941. Beneš also sought American support before his visit to the USSR in December 1943. In Moscow, the Czechoslovak president intended to sign a treaty of friendship with the Soviet government. In this regard, Beneš wanted to use the United States as a counterweight to Soviet influence in accordance with his post-war foreign policy program – reliance on new allies against Germany (instead of France and the UK, responsible for the Munich borders) and equal orientation to the West and the East.[68]

The visit to the United States lasted from 8 May to 9 June 1943. Americans met the Czechoslovak President with official honours, Beneš made a speech at the Congress, and he held meetings with the Secretary of State, politicians, public figures, and Czech and Slovak community leaders. Touching upon the problems of post-war Europe, Beneš argued the need to develop close cooperation with the Soviet Union, owing to its growing power in Europe.[69] American diplomats and experts accepted this argument, as long as Czechoslovakia turned to the USSR not as a forced but as a natural step. According to Beneš, Roosevelt had supported demands for pre-Munich boundaries, agreed with the transfer of a number of Germans from Czechoslovakia, and expressed satisfaction with Czechoslovak-Soviet relations, but he did not express a desire to sign a similar agreement.[70] The participation of American troops in the liberation of Czechoslovakia was not discussed.

By 1945, Americans did not show much interest in the Czechoslovak issue. The State Department was not active in establishing closer cooperation with Beneš' government.[71] The situation in the Protectorate and Slovakia was observed mostly as relevant for the war operations planning and anti-German propaganda activities. It was obvious that liberation of Czechoslovakia would

---

68   Elena P. Serapionova, 'Eduard Benes: Plany poslevoennogo razvitiya Czechoslovakii i realnosť in *Totalitarizm: istoricheskiy opyt Vostochnoy Evropy. 1944–1948.* Moskva: Nauka, 2002, 119.
69   *President Benes On War And Peace. Statements by Dr. Edvard Beneš, President of the Czechoslovak Republic, during his visit to the United States and Canada in May and June 1943.* New York: Czechoslovak Information Service, 1943; *The New York Times*, 13 May 13 1943, 23–4.
70   *Memoirs of Eduard Benes*, 193.
71   Lynn E. Davis, *The Cold War Begins. Soviet-American Conflict over Eastern Europe*. Princeton, N.J.: Princeton University Press, 1974, 161–2.

come from the Red Army, and the Soviet Union would have the main impact in the region. Beneš, as he stated in 1943 in Washington, thought it was inevitable and was trying to build close relations with Moscow.

The State Department's Division of Central European Affairs in its memorandum of 11 January 1945 stated that 'the Czechoslovak government's relations with the British and Soviet governments are excellent, and present no problems. Czechoslovak-American relations remain excellent, as they have been in the past.' The Division recommended to restore Czechoslovak republic in pre-Munich borders and to maintain relations with it, contributing in democratic changes and elections.[72]

By the beginning of 1945, the Red Army had begun liberating the eastern part of Slovakia and continued to go west. US troops, moving from France and Italy, were approaching Bohemia. Soviet influence was growing but there were no strong desires from Roosevelt to dispute Moscow's intention to forge closer relations with Prague, supported by Czechs. In Yalta and other meetings, the American and Soviet sides agreed that Czechoslovakia would be liberated by both armies and two occupation zones would be created. Both approved restoration of pre-Munich borders, the creation of a democratic multiparty government and deportations of German and Hungarian minorities. The future of post-war Czechoslovakia had to be decided in upcoming democratic elections.

In March 1945, Beneš visited Moscow again and reached new agreements about the government structure and post-war political orientation of Czechoslovakia. Some important positions in the coalition People's front government were given to communists, and others belonged to the democratic parties. Gathered in the Slovak city, Košice, the Czechoslovak government announced its program of post-war development on 5 April 1945, which presupposed socialist reforms and closer relations with the USSR.[73] Without disputing the results of the Moscow talks, the State Department protested only twice: when Moscow refused to allow American diplomats to Košice, and after Soviet annexation of Ruthenia, agreed upon by Beneš. In April 1945, American troops entered Bohemia and came close to Prague. Having real opportunities to liberate the Czechoslovak capital in May before the Red Army (that was the desire of the British, supported by some State Department officials), they stopped on Dwight D. Eisenhower's order at the agreed borderline of the Soviet and American zones. The general did not want to dispute Moscow's positions in the region and sacrifice American

---

72   *FRUS, 1945*. Volume 4, 420–2.
73   Valentina V. Mar'ina, *Sovetskiy Soyuz i cheho-slovatzkiy vopros vo vremia Vtoroy mirivoy vojny, 1939–1945. Kniga 2, 1941–1945*. Moskva: Indrik, 2009, 322–3.

soldiers in vain.⁷⁴ After the end of war, US troops were located in Western Bohemia through the end of 1945, when they were withdrawn simultaneously with the Red Army by agreement between Truman and Stalin.⁷⁵

American diplomatic representation in Prague was re-established in late May 1945. The following months, the Red Army and US troops were trying to implement allied agreements in their zones. But unlike the Soviet Union, America was not interested in strengthening its military presence or deepening relations with the Czechoslovak government, and refused to enter into any additional civil agreement. Despite their dissatisfaction with Soviet and Communists actions, and calls for support from Czechoslovak democratic forces, the United States showed no intentions of increasing its influence or playing an active role in the life of the republic. Apparently, American diplomats had hoped for the performance of Soviet promises not to interfere in Czechoslovak internal affairs, and waited for the impending democratic elections, which were to strengthen democratic pro-Western forces. However, over the next three years, the Communists were able to gradually increase their influence, and in 1948, Czechoslovakia entered the Soviet zone of influence for the next 40 years.

In conclusion, it can be noted that the US manifested a little interest towards Czechoslovakia, except during the crisis years. The most active American involvement in Czechoslovakia was observed in 1918–1919, during the founding of the state. During World War I, the US was concerned with the possible destabilization of Central Europe in the case of the collapse of the Austro-Hungarian Empire and thus it delayed recognition of the national movement of the Czechs and Slovaks. After the war, American experts and diplomats tried to work out a new territorial arrangement to create stable borders and restore economic ties in Central Europe in order to avoid new conflicts and wars. But Wilson's desire to use new principles in international relations encountered difficulties. After his demission in 1921, the US turned back to isolationism and relations with Czechoslovakia shifted to economic and financial areas. Although the US policy towards Czechoslovakia was positive and friendly in nature, the State Department never demonstrated great interest in deepening political or economic relations. The impulse came primarily from the Czechoslovak side, who considered the United States an important potential force for Central Europe, capable of becoming an additional guarantor of Czechoslovak freedom and independence, as well as

---

74   Walter Ullmann, T*he United State in Prague, 1945–1948*. Boulder, New York: East European quarterly, 1978, 320; *FRUS, 1945*. Volume 4, 449–50; Davis, *The Cold War Begins*, 361.
75   Perpiska Predsedatela Soveta Ministrov SSSR s prezidentami SShA I premier-ministrami Velikobritanii vo vremia Velikoj Otechestvennoy vojny 1941–1945. Moskva: Gospolitizdat, 1958, 273–5.

a profitable trading partner. But both the Americans and the Czechs were able to defend their own interests, especially in economic relations.

In the 1930s, a new international crisis caused new public interest in Czechoslovakia in the US. The main aspiration of American leaders was the prevention of war, even at the expense of concessions to Germany. Roosevelt did not want to intervene directly in the conflict, and only at its peak took the initiative to resolve it. But direct aggression by Germany in March 1939, which led to the destruction of Czechoslovakia and the redrawing of borders in Central Europe, was strongly condemned as a violation of international law.

During World War II, the US refused to recognize the disappearance of Czechoslovakia, and it was neither in a hurry to support President Beneš' activities for liberation, nor wanting to get involved in international disputes between Central European nations. By the end of the war, Washington adopted Beneš' plan of stabilization, based on the restoration of former borders and transfers of national minorities. In fact, it was a return to the idea of ethnic lines. Roosevelt also agreed with growing Soviet influence and its priority interests in Czechoslovakia, but hoped for the maintenance of democratic traditions and cooperation between different political forces. But, unlike the Soviet Union, the US did not have a program for the development of relations with Czechoslovakia. Finally, Moscow offered Prague more favourable conditions for cooperation, which led to a gradual strengthening of Moscow's influence and Czechoslovakia's change to communism.

Part Three

Propaganda and Perceptions

6

The Great War and the Polish Question in Imperial Russia: A Case Study of Its Reflections in Kiev's Press, 1914–1917

IVAN BASENKO

German-Russian antagonism was a common feature for the information space of the Russian Empire before the Great War. It was manifested in press with an abundance of ostentatious warmongering rhetoric.[1] In general, that reflected an all European trend: the notion of war was utilised by the contemporary literature and mass media as a source of constant public interest and, therefore, of commercial profit. Otherwise, war eloquence was interpreted as an ordinary, often non-hazardous instrument of international political bargaining.[2] The Russian Empire's regional press of Kiev basically followed this pattern. The Polish question – a central point of this survey, remained in a shade of the profound anti German sentiment of the Kiev press. Yet, in the pre war months of 1914, the first signs of Polish involvement in the potential German Russian war had already appeared. Referring to the statement of Roman Dmowski, a leader of the Polish National Democratic movement in Russia, the local newspaper *Kievljanin* expressed its contempt for Polish political speculations. Prophetically, Dmowski forewarned the tsardom that imperial Poles would support the probable German invasion

---

1 Boris Kotov, 'Obraz Germanii v russkoj presse v period 'gazetnoj vojny' vesny 1914 goda,' *Vestnik Moskovskogo gosudarstvennogo oblastnogo universiteta*, 3 (2011): 87–97.; Nikolaj Judin, 'Problema podgotovlennosti obshhestvennogo mnenija stran Ant- anty k vojne na primere 'Gazetnoj vojny' 1914 goda,' (paper presented at the International scientific youth forum 'Lomonosov-2011', Moskva, MGU imeni M.V. Lomonosova, Rossi- ja, 2011).
2 Niall Ferguson, *The Pity of War*. Bath: The Penguin Press, 1998, 11–20.

unless they were granted a separate Kingdom of Poland.³

This study uncovers the evolution of the Kiev press's attitude towards the Poles within the context of the German-Russian clash in the First World War. It examines the various techniques, by which the Polish theme was incorporated into the Russian war effort against *Kaiserreich*. The focus of the study derives from the fundamental wartime discourse of the German Russian confrontation. It should be noted that the other rival holding a significant part of the Polish territories, the Austro Hungarian monarchy, was only viewed as a secondary power, subordinated to Berlin's will. Chronologically, the study covers a period of Russia's active military commitment: from the outbreak of the war in 1914 to the Bolshevik Uprising in November of 1917, which led to the end of hostilities with the Central Powers. The article is divided into three subchapters, revealing the enthusiastic war agitation of 1914, the disillusionment of the subsequent years and the disintegration of Romanov's Empire in 1917. Geographically, it is focused on the Southwestern Krai – a large borderland region of the Russian Empire, formed on the Southeastern territories of the former Polish-Lithuanian Commonwealth and thus contested between Polish and Russian cultural influences. Despite the region's predominantly Ukrainian ethnic composition,⁴ tsarist authorities and Russian public opinion considered it to be naturally Russian.⁵

Kiev city was an administrative, economic and cultural centre of the Russian Southwestern Krai.⁶ The Kiev press was a major media actor, traditionally speaking on behalf of the whole region.⁷ At the same time, it resembled a typical provincial media, dependent upon mainstream discussions in the newspapers of Petrograd and Moscow. In 1914, the daily press of Kiev was issued in four different Slavic languages, yet more than 70% of the market

---

3   'Nelepoe zapugivanie,' *Kievljanin*, 16 January 1914, 2.
4   In 1917 the Ukrainians amounted for the 75.5% of the region's total population while the Russians – only 3.4 % and the Poles – 9 % respectively. See: Tamara Lazans'ka, 'Narodonaselennya Ukrayiny' in: *'Ukrayins'ke pytannya' v Rosiys'kiy imperiyi (kinets' XIX – pochatok XX st.)*, Part 1, Kyiv: Instytut istoriyi Ukrayiny, 1999, 78–81.
5   Ukrainians were considered to be a part of the all Russian nation by both the state ideology and the Russian public opinion of the late imperial era. See: Alexei Miller, *The Romanov Empire and Nationalism. Essays in the Methodology of Historical Research*, Budapest–New York: Central European University Press, 2008, 161–81.
6   According to Isaac Bisk, in 1917 Kiev's population amounted approximately 470,000. The largest share of 49.9% was ethnic Russian while the Ukrainians held only 12 % of the city dwellers, another 4.4 % identified themselves as the Little Russians (Malorossy); the Poles consisted 9.1%, other nationalities – 24.95 % of the population. See: Lazans'ka, 'Narodonaselennya Ukrayiny', 78–111.
7   Volodymyr Molchanov, *Zhyttyevyy riven' mis'koho naselennya Pravoberezhnoyi Ukrayiny (1900–1914 rr.)*, Kyiv: In-t Istoriyi Ukrayiny NAN Ukrayiny, 2005, 181–2.

belonged to Russian media.[8] At the beginning of the war, the sole Ukrainian newspaper *Rada* was labelled disloyal and compulsorily closed;[9] later, in 1915 the Czech newspaper ceased to exist.[10] The Polish *Dziennik Kijowski* remained the only non Russian daily until 1917. Being situated on the frontlines of WWI, the Kiev press functioned under the supervision of civil and military censors. Both were designed to suppress the anti government moods of the media.[11] However, after the February Revolution of 1917, civil censorship was abolished by the Russian provisional government and military censorship became de facto afunctional.[12] Also, the old regime wartime prohibition on Ukrainian and Jewish printed products became obsolete. The officially octroyed freedom of speech facilitated the emergence of diverse non Russian and leftist newspapers.[13]

This study is based on analysis of Kiev's Russian language prominent daily newspapers: the rightist *Kiev*, conservative *Kievljanin*, 'progressive' (liberal/ socialist) *Kievskaja Mysl*, *Poslednie Novosti* and *Juzhnaja Kopeika*. These newspapers reflect the entire spectrum of the city's Russian political thought as well as the dynamics of its development. Pro regime, partially state subsidised *Kiev* and *Kievljanin* enjoyed relatively small circulation in 1914 (six and 16,000 respectively). *Kiev* embodied the local Russian nationalist group while *Kievljanin* was adherent to conservative ideas.[14] On the contrary, the independent 'progressive' newspapers were more popular (each with circulations between 55,000 and 80,000) and local censors deemed them influential.[15] The term 'progressiveness' designated these newspapers' affiliations as reformist and critical to the reactionary tsarist regime. Censors

---

8   Mihail Shhegolev, 'Prilozhenie k otchetu po periodicheskoj pechatiza 1914 god.' Kiev, 1 July 1915, 4 // Tsentral'nyy derzhavnyy arkhiv Ukrayiny u m. Kyyevi (The Central State Historical Archive of Ukraine in Kyiv (hereafter, TsDIAK Ukrainy)), Collection 295, Box 1, Folder 579, page 53 rev., Kyiv, Ukraine.
9   Shhegolev, 'Prilozhenie k otchetu po periodicheskoj pechatiza 1914 god,' 22.
10 Mihail Shhegolev, 'Otchet po periodicheskoj pechati Kievskogo vremennogo komiteta po delam pechati za 1915 god.' Kiev, 7 aprelja 1916, 4 // TsDIAK Ukrainy, Collection 295, Box 1, Folder 579, page 75 rev., Kyiv, Ukraine.
11 Oleksandr Kyriyenko, 'Viys'kova tsenzura tylovykh huberniy Kyyivs'koho viys'kovoho okruhu (1914–1917 rr.),' *Ukrayins'kyy istorychnyy zbirnyk*, 13/1 (2010): 182–92.
12 Oleksandr Kyriyenko, 'Rosiys'ka viys'kova tsenzura v ukrayins'kykh huberniyakh za chasiv Tymchasovoho uryadu,' *Problemy istoriyi Ukrayiny XIX – pochatku XX st.*, 19 (2011), 27–36.
13 Oleksandr Mukomela, *Na zlami vikiv: Ukrayins'ka zhurnalistyka na pochatku XX st.*, Kyiv: Hramota, 2010, 48.
14 Shhegolev, 'Prilozhenie k otchetu po periodicheskoj pechati za 1914 god,' 6, 12.
15 Mihail Shhegolev, 'Otchet po periodicheskoj pechati Kievskogo vremennogo komiteta po delam pechati za 1914 god.' Kiev, 15 April 1915, 2–3 // TsDIAK Ukrainy,

maintained that these newspapers were under the Jewish auspice and promoted harmful 'pseudoliberal' and 'leftist' ideas.¹⁶ Additionally, this study incorporates the two leading Ukrainian daily newspapers of the 1917 revolutionary era: the social liberal *Nova Rada* (15,000 circulation) and the organ of the Ukrainian Social Democratic Labour Party *Robitnycha Hazeta* (9,000 circulation).¹⁷ The paper concludes that Russian Ukrainian tensions diverted the press' attention from the Polish question in late 1917.

Methodologically, the paper is built upon the concept of imagology, which explores national stereotypes and images of 'otherness' in conjunction with the actor's own identity.¹⁸ Also, Walter Lippmann's theory of mass media is a valuable asset for this study. Lippmann suggested that the readership of newspapers participates in an everyday poll by buying a particular kind of newspaper and thereby complying with its style, information and political affiliation. Based on the experience of WWI, Lippmann's survey asserts that the press not only influences but also reflects public opinion.¹⁹ In Imperial Russia, the press was considered to be a primary source of public opinion since the Great Reforms of the 1860s – 1870s.²⁰

However, only during the pre-1914 decade did the printed media cover the needs of all the urban classes and partially infiltrate the rural areas. Great War demand for information finally boosted the imperial press to the level of mass media.²¹ The Empire's public education programme facilitated such a development: already in 1913, 54% of men and 26% of women above nine-years-old were literate.²² No less important was the affordability of press: in 1913, even Kiev's lowest ranking labourer spent about 5–9 roubles annually (or 1–2 % of his total income) on cultural and information needs. By

---

Collection 295, Box 1, Folder 579, pages 11 rev.–12, Kyiv, Ukraine.
16 Shhegolev, 'Prilozhenie k otchetu po periodicheskoj pechati za 1914 god,' 5–6.
17 Komissar g. Kieva Dorotov, 'Spisok proizvedenij pechati na ukrainskom jazyke, vypushhennyh v svet v gor. Kieve v 1917 g. po 4 dekabrja i zaregistrirovannyh v kancel-jarii komissara po gorodu Kievu.' Kiev, 5 December 1917, 1 // Derzhavnyy arkhiv m. Kyyeva, Collection 292, Box 1, Folder 62, page 34, Kyiv, Ukraine.
18 Manfred Beller, 'Perception, image, imagology,' in: *Imagology: the cultural construction and literary representation of national characters: a critical survey*, edited by Manfred Beller and JoepLeerssen, Amsterdam and New York: Rodopi, 2007, 3–16.
19 Walther Lippmann, *Public Opinion*, New Brunswick: Free Press, 1997, 317–337.
20 Boris Mironov, *Social'naja istorija Rossii perioda imperii (XVIII-nachalo XX v.)*. Volume 2, Saint-Petersburg: Dmitrij Bulanin, 2000, 252.
21 Svetlana Mahonina, *Istorija russkoj zhurnalistiki nachala XX veka*, (Moskva: Flinta, 2004) – Vremja i pressa (1890-e—1918 gg.), accessed June 09, 2015, http://evartist.narod.ru/text1/84.htm.
22 Boris Mironov, *Social'naja istorija Rossii*, 294–5.

comparison, the annual subscription to a penny newspaper (such as *Juzhnaja Kopeika*), amounted to only three and a half roubles.[23] Kiev's censorial reports shed light on the distribution of press. For example, the readership of *Kievskaja Mysl* included the bureaucracy, clergy, military and even 'the commonalty' of Kiev. Moreover, thanks to the railroad network it was distributed amongst the teachers, priests, paramedics and authorities in the rural areas of the Krai.[24]

The Polish question during World War I has already been examined by a large number of prominent researchers. Among English language scholarship, Andreas Kappeler thoroughly presented the Polish question within the context of the Russian Empire's national movements.[25] More specifically, the First World War's impact on the Polish movement is assessed by Aviel Roshwald,[26] Eric Lohr[27] and Joshua Sanborn.[28] Roshwald uncovers the binary nature of Polish nationalism, which was developed separately by its two leaders – Jozef Pilsudski and Roman Dmowski. Eric Lohr and Joshua Sanborn depict the Great War as a catalyst for the national movement and decolonization process in the Romanov Empire. There are also some important studies in Russian that analyse Petrograd policy towards the Poles.[29] Also, considerable work on the topic is performed by Polish

---

23   Volodymyr Molchanov, *Zhyttyevyy riven'*, 182.
24   Mihail Shhegolev, 'Prilozhenija k Otchetu po periodicheskoj pechati Kievskogo vremennogo komiteta po delam pechati za 1913 g.' Kiev, 17 July 1914, 9 // TsDIAK Ukrainy, Collection 295, Box 1, Folder 438, page 302, Kyiv, Ukraine.
25   Andreas Kappeler, *The Russian Empire: A Multiethnic History*, Harlow: Longman, 2001.
26   Aviel Roshwald, *Ethnic Nationalism and the Fall of Empires: Central Europe, Russia and the Middle East, 1914-1923*. London: Routledge, 2001.
27   Eric Lohr, 'War nationalism,' in: *The Empire and Nationalism at War*, eds. Eric Lohr, Vera Tolz, and Alexander Semyonov, 91–108, Bloomington: Slavica, 2014.
28   Joshua Sanborn, *Imperial Apocalypse: The Great War and the Destruction of the Russian Empire*, Oxford: Oxford University Press, 2014.
29   Nikolaj Dobronravin, 'Rossija i nepriznannye gosudarstva v period Pervoj mirovoj vojny 1914–1916 gg.,' *Novejshaja istorija Rossii: mezhdisciplinarnyj nauchno-teoreticheskij zhurnal*, 3/10, (2014): 60–73; Svetlana Fal'kovich, 'Pol'skij vopros v treh rossijskih revoljucijah,' in: *Revoljucionnaja Rossija 1917 goda i pol'skij vopros: Novye istochniki, novye vzgljady*, 20–7, Moskva: Institut slavjanovedenija RAN, 2009; Gennadij Matveev, 'Fevral'skaja revoljucija v Rossii i pol'skij vopros,' in: *Revoljucionnaja Rossija 1917 goda i pol'skij vopros: Novye istochniki, novye vzgljady*, 85–92, Moskva: Institut slavjanovedenija RAN, 2009.'; Aleksandra Bahturina, 'Pol'sha, Ukraina, Galicija v politicheskih planah Rossijskoj Imperii, Avstro-Vengrii i Germanii v 1916 g.,' in: *Politika Rossijskoj Imperii v Vostochnoj Galicii v gody Pervoj mirovoj vojny*, 203–13, Moskva: AJRO-XX, 2000.

historians,[30] and their Ukrainian colleagues.[31] The two studies, most relevant for this research are those of Laura Engelstein and Aleksandr Astashov.[32] Both scholars reconstruct the Russian attitude towards the Germans in the context of Berlin-Petrograd's rivalry over Poland. Engelstein's article is centered onto the Kalisz incident of August 1914 – an example of the German military outrage that developed into a symbolic propaganda construct. Astashov's work reveals the logic of the Russian Slavic war propaganda and, particularly, Russian policy in the Polish case.

The Polish question and the 1914 war enthusiasm

The 'Polish question', being a constant cultural challenge and a dangerous example of separatism, was the most difficult of the national policy of the Romanov Empire since the end of 18th century. Long standing Polish state tradition preserved by the native gentry resulted in two unavailing anti-tsarist uprisings in 1830–31 and 1863. By the end of the 19th century, the Polish movement had developed into a modern national form and was highly influential for the nation building processes of the neighbouring Lithuanian, Belarusian and Ukrainian ethnic groups. The Congress Poland played an essential role in the 1905 Russian Revolution, compelling tsarist authorities to consider the Polish autonomy project.[33]

---

30 Andrzej Nowak, 'Imperialna polityka Rosji wobec Polski 1795–1914,' in: *Polacy, Rosjanie i Biesy. Studia i szkice historyczne z XIX i XX wieku*, 11–24, Kraków: Arcana, 1998; Andrzej Chwalba, *Polacy w służbie Moskali*, Warszawa—Kraków: Wydawn. Nauk. PWN, 1999; Leszek Jaśkiewicz, 'Carat i sprawy polskie na przełomie XIX i XX wieku,' Pułtusk: Wyższa Szkoła Humanistyczna, 2001; Aleksander Achmatowicz, *Polityka Rosji w kwestii polskiej w pierwszym roku Wielkiej Wojny, 1914–1915*, Warszawa : Instytut Historii PAN, 2003; Marian Zgórniak, 'Terytorium Polski w planach wojennych państw centralnych i Rosji w chwili wybuchu pierwszej wojny światowej – 1914 rok,' *Kwartalnik poświęcony historii* XX w., 36/3 (2004): 16–32.

31 Vladyslav Boyechko, 'Aktyvizatsiya pol's'kykh natsional'nykh syl u period Pershoyi svitovoyi viyny (1914–1918) ta vidrodzhennya Nezalezhnoyi Pol'shchi,' *Naukovi pratsi. Istoriya*, 195 (2012): 40–48; Morushko Oleksandr, 'Pol's'ke pytannya na pochatku Pershoyi svitovoyi viyny,' *Visnyk NU Derzhava ta armiya*, 408 (2000): 183–7; Mariya Pan'kiv, 'Polyaky v rosiys'kiy imperiyi. Ohlyad suchasnoyi pol's'koyi istoriohrafiyi,' *Skhid-Zakhid: Istoryko-kul'turolohichnyy zbirnyk*, 9–10 (2008): 319–34.

32 Laura Engelstein, 'A Belgium of our own" the sack of Russian Kalisz, August 1914,' in: *Fascination and Enmity: Russia and Germany as Entangled Histories, 1914–1945*, ed. Michael David-Fox, Peter Holquist, Alexander M. Martin, 13–38, Pittsburgh:University of Pittsburgh Press, 2012; Aleksandr Astashov, 'Slavjanskaja' propaganda Rossii protiv 'germanizma',' in: *Propaganda na Russkom fronte v gody Pervoj mirovoj vojny*, (Moskva: Speckniga, 2012) http://propagandahistory.ru/books/Aleksandr-Astashov_Propaganda-na-Russkom-fronte-v-gody-Pervoy-mirovoy-voyny/, accessed 23 July 2018.

33 Kappeler, *The Russian Empire*, 213–46, 328–69.

As a former territory of the Polish-Lithuanian Commonwealth, the Southwestern Krai was a bone of contention between the old Polish and the new Russian elite throughout the 19th century.[34] At the end of the 19th century, Russian authorities had succeeded in marginalizing local Poles. However, this dispute accelerated the emergence of the indigenous Ukrainian national movement.[35] Thus, in the early 20th century, the imperial administration became concerned with the rise of a separate Ukrainian identity.[36] Consequently, on the eve of WWI the Polish question lost its initial importance in the Krai, yet it was still frequently covered by the Kiev press.

With the outbreak of the Great War, the Russian press became fully focused on the grand clash of the European empires, leaving the Polish factor as an inessential component of the geopolitical balance of power. Several articles published in Kiev presented the attitude towards the war of the Poles in *Deutsches Reich*. It was stated that these Poles preserved their loyalty to the Slavic heritage[37] and were unwilling to take the 'strangers' (German) side in the war.[38] The Polish theme reached a new level of importance shortly after the *Deutsches Heer* invasion of Congress Poland in early August 1914.[39] The enemy's army excesses in the border city of Kalisz on August 4[40] triggered a press campaign of 'the German atrocities.'[41] The Kalisz incident allowed media to question a popular pre war stereotype of the 'highly cultured' German nation.[42]. This notion was challenged by the vivid, realistic accounts of the enemy's 'unimaginable barbarism' against the civilians of the peaceful city.[43] The responsible commander, Major Preusker became a well known symbol of the 'Prussian lieutenant's brutality.'[44] By the end of August, the Kalisz episode was also interpreted as an example of German cowardice. It was believed that a massacre occurred due to the invader's panic – fright of

---

34 Leonid Gorizontov, 'The Geopolitical Dimension of Russian-Polish Confrontation in the Nineteenth and Early Twentieth Centuries,' in: *Polish Encounters, Russian Identity*, ed. David Ransel and Bozena Shallcross, 122–43, Bloomington: Indiana University Press, 2005.
35 Roshwald, *Ethnic Nationalism*, 24.
36 Kappeler, *The Russian Empire*, 328–69.
37 'Demonstracija v Poznanskomcirke,' *Poslednie Novosti*, 23 July 1914, 2.M. (morning issue).
38 'Nastroenie poljakov v Germanii,' *Poslednie Novosti*, 23 July 1914, 2.M.
39 Sanborn, *Imperial Apocalypse*, 55.
40 The study employs a Gregorian calendar. However, footnotes to the newspapers's articles are presented according to the original Julian calendar.
41 Hereafter the quotation marks are used to indicate the original labels of the press.
42 D. Skrynchenko,'Vot tak kul'tura!..,' *Kiev*, 1 August 1914, 2.
43 'Prusskaja gnusnost',' *Poslednie Novosti*, 1 August 1914, 1.E. (evening issue).
44 A. Kacheurov, 'Vozmezdie,' *Juzhnaja Kopejka*, 6 August 1914, 2.

the possible Russian counterattack.[45] Above all, the Kalisz incident has demonstrated that the Kiev press associated the city's indigenous Polish population with the (politically) common Russian people. In fact, the Kiev press's reactions mirrored the broader all-Russian response: the sack of Kalisz acquired a state-wide symbolic value, thus presenting the fierce advancement of Germandom onto the Russian civilization.[46]

At the 1914 stage of the war, Kiev's press intensively promoted an all-Russian identity concept. The German invasion of the Congress Poland provided a necessary background to strengthen imperial patriotism.[47] Its pathos was directed onto the diverse empire's population and aimed to fuse a politically homogeneous nation. For instance, the Kalisz incident was utilised as an insult to 'the Russian soul and Russian conscience'[48] with the press demanding revenge on the enemy and the capture of Berlin.[49] The war had enforced a supra-ethnic connotation of the term 'Russian.' Occasionally, both liberal and rightist newspapers wrote about the 'bodies of Russian martyrs'[50] and murdered Russian citizens of the small Polish town of Kalisz without referring to their ethnic origin.[51]

Since Kalisz, the press had been striving to create a rigid image of the enemy by providing numerous examples of the German crimes in Congress Poland.[52] The most notorious was the occupation of Czestochowa on 16 August 1914. Newspapers reported the desecration of Czestochowa's famous shrine of Jasnogorski monastery. Scenes of the German brutal pillaging and sexual abuses there were intended to form the image of the German 'antichristianity.'[53] Grotesque 'avarice' and 'ignorance' were also commonly attributed to the German invaders. For instance, the press mocked one German lieutenant who had allegedly demanded a loot in the form of red caviar after the capture of the small Congress Poland town of Konin. According to the journal, the German fallacious perception depicted the whole

---

45   G. Dorofeev, 'Germanskaja psihika,' *Kiev*, 29 August 1914, 1.
46   Engelstein, 'A Belgium of our own', 19–25.
47   'Nemcy v Kalishe. Zapiska revizora kalishsko petrovskogo akciznogo upravlenija inzhener tehnologa Jedmunda Ivanovicha Oppmana,' *Kiev*, 24 August 1914, 2.; Vl. Sokolov (uchenik V klassa Kievskoj 6 jgimnazii), 'Slavjanam,' *Kiev*, 27 August 1914, 2.
48   Aleksandr Jablonovskij, 'Nemeckie neistovstva,' *Kievskaja Mysl'*, 4 August 1914, 1–2.
49   Omikron, 'Malen'kij fel'eton. Pred nachalom,' *Kiev*, 9 August 1914, 2.; Figaro, 'Nenavist' k nemcam,' *Kiev*, August 10, 1914, 3; JakovNivich, 'Til'zit,' *Kiev*, 15 August 1914, 3.
50   Jablonovskij, 'Nemeckie neistovstva,' 1–2.
51   Figaro, 'Nenavist' k nemcam,' 3.
52   Vladimir S***,'Mysli vsluh,' *Juzhnaja Kopejka*, 13 August 1914, 2.
53   'Germanskie zverstva v Chenstohove,' *Juzhnaja Kopejka*, 5 August 1914, 1–2.

Russia as a 'country of red caviar.'[54]

The official manifesto to the Poles, which was issued on 14 August 1914 by the Russian Supreme Commander Grand Duke Nicholas, marked the increasing political significance of the Polish question for the tsarist regime.[55] It proclaimed the goal of reunion of the separated Polish nation within the frame of an autonomous Poland that was 'free in its faith, language and self government.' However, Russian state elites were hesitant to implement the manifesto, which they perceived to be the sole instrument capable of retaining control over the region. Imperial policy of the forthcoming years proved Petrograd's unwillingness to grant Poles any of the promised facilities.[56] Despite this, back in 1914, the manifesto was extensively popularised by the press. It promised 'to unify all the parts of Poland under the sceptre of the all-Russian Tsar, and King of Poland.'[57] The press interpreted the manifesto's vague notion of the future Poland's boundaries as limited solely to the ethnic Polish territories.[58] Noteworthy, this vision was also relevant for the subsequent period.[59] The press rejected the idea of a greater historical Poland because of contested lands, such as the Austro-Hungarian Galicia province – for which the Russian Empire had its own ambitions.[60]

In the agitation campaign, the press appealed to Polish historical feelings. The successive forms of German statehood – from the Teutonic Order and the Kingdom of Prussia to the Wilhemine Empire – were depicted as an ultimate cause of all of the Polish misfortunes. At the same time, press unanimously evaded the Russian Polish negative historical context. Thus, St Petersburg's role in the partitions of the Polish-Lithuanian Commonwealth was either disguised or totally omitted. Kiev's progressive and rightist media eloquence slightly differed. The progressives were much more concerned with Berlin's violations of Polish civil liberties, such as anti Polish state legislation,

---

54 Aleksandr Jablonovskij, 'Na voennye temy,' *Kievskaja Mysl'*, 17 August 1914, 2.
55 Mihail Dolbilov, Aleksej Miller (eds.), *Zapadnye okrainy Rossijskoj imperii*. Moskva: Novoe literaturnoe obozrenie, 2007, 413.
56 Sergey Poznyak, 'Pol'skij vopros' vo vlastnyh strukturah imperatorskoj Rossii nakanune i v gody Pervoj mirovoj vojny'. *Rossijskie i slavjanskie issledovanija*: 1 (2004); 159–73.
57 Volynec, 'Nemcy i poljaki,' 2; A. Volynec, 'Nemcy i poljaki,' *Kiev*, 6 September 1914, 1.
58 Ani, 'Galickaja Rus'. III.,' *Kiev*, 8 September 1914, 2.
59 A. Lunacharskij, 'Dva referata,' *Kievskaja Mysl'*, 26 April 1915, 2.
60 Russian propaganda considered the Austro-Hungarian territories of Galicia, Bukovina and Carpathian Ruthenia as historical parts of Russia and referred to their population as to the 'Russian people'. Therefore, it proclaimed the goal of liberation and subsequent reunification with the Russian 'Motherland' (See: Astashov, ''Slavjanskaja' propaganda Rossii protiv 'germanizma',').

land property issues and cultural oppression.[61] In contrast, rightists emphasised the Teutono Slavic confrontation and agitated for the revival of 'Polish Russian fraternization' against the common enemy. The 1410 Battle of Grunwald, where Polish, Lithuanian and Russian troops defeated the Teutonic knights was chosen as a symbol.[62] The rightist press envisioned Russia's historical mission in its resistance to the German '*Drang nach Osten*'[63] expansion.[64] In fact, it favoured the expulsion of all German colonists out of the Polish region, blaming them to be 'ethnic strangers,'[65] 'spies and traitors.'[66] In late 1914, deportation campaigns and the pass of the law on enemy real estate expropriation were equally supported by the rightist press.[67]

Russian rightists portrayed the Polish nation's lifespan under the rule of Romanov's dynasty as a 'century of prosperity' if compared to the horrible 1795–1807 period of 'Prussian domination' in Poland.[68] They argued that the Poles should have been contented with being part of 'the great and independent Slavic state' of Russia, where Polish life had flourished 'better than in a former Poland.'[69] Examples of famous and successful Polish writers and scientists from Congress Poland, such as Adam Mickiewicz, Joachim Lelewel, Teodor Narbutt, Henryk Sienkiewicz and others, were provided to reinforce the statement.[70]

As a method of agitation, the press illustrated the anti German and pro Russian attitudes of Polish public opinion. It quoted average Russian Poles, for instance an old Polish man from Warsaw who cursed the Germans as '*Psia krow, podly szwb*' (sic!) ('Dog's blood, mean Swabian') at the same time praising the Russian soldiers – 'our brothers by blood.'[71] Media also referred

---

61   L. L–skij, 'Poljaki v Prussii,' *Juzhnaja Kopejka*, 4 August 1914, 1; L. L–skij, 'Bor'ba protiv poljakov v Prussii,' *Juzhnaja Kopejka*, 7 August 1914, 1; 'Pol'sha,' *Kievskaja Mysl'*, 8 November 1914, 2.
62   'Grjunval'denskaja bitva,' *Kievljanin*, 6 August 1914, 2.
63   German '*Drang nach Osten*' denotes the 'Drive to the East'. It was broadly used by the Entente propaganda (Vejas Liulevicius, *The German Myth of the East*, Oxford: OUP, 2009, 13).
64   Knigochij, 'Iz proshlogo Vostochnoj Prussii,' *Kiev*, 27 August 1914, 2.
65   A. Volynec,'Nasha vnutrennjaja nemetchina. I.,' *Kiev*, 18 September, 1914, 1; A. Volynec,'Nasha vnutrennjaja nemetchina II.,' *Kiev*, 20 September 1914, 1.
66   D. Skrynchenko,'O nemcah v Rossii,' *Kiev*, 24 August 1914, 1.
67   'Nemeckoe zemlevladenie v Rossii,' *Juzhnaja Kopejka*, 23 February 1915, 4; A. Kajskij, 'Germanskaja kolonizacija,' *Kiev*, 18 March 1915, 3.
68   A. Volynec, 'Nemeckie appetity na Pol'shu,' *Kiev*, 8 August 1914, 2.
69   A. Volynec, 'Nemcy i poljaki,' *Kiev*, 14 August 1914, 2.
70   Volynec, 'Nemcy i poljaki,' 2.
71   Man, 'Iz razgovorov na vokzale,' *Kiev*, 31 July 1914, 4.

to the front experience: a group of Russian Siberian Riflemen were thrilled to receive a warm welcome 'even here in [Russian] Poland,' where the locals willingly presented them with 'the brimful baskets of food and clothes.'[72] The Kiev press glorified those Poles who preserved their loyalty to the state,[73] sheltered Russian escapees[74] or were fighting the enemy.[75] It agitated the public for donations to the Polish war refugees,[76] several waves of which fled from the Congress Poland to the other regions of the empire and constituted a challenge to both the authorities and social organizations.[77] Another part of the image concerned those foreign Poles who were levied to the *Deutsches Heer* and Austro Hungarian army. They were presented as victims of state coercion, keen to surrender or even to join the Russian side.[78]

In general, in 1914, the Polish question in the press of Kiev developed as an integral part of the broad anti German, war supporting campaign. It should be examined within the context of an all-European 'civilization confrontation' – 'holy war' between 'European culture' and 'German barbarism,'[79] 'Christian Europe' and 'German nihilism,'[80] the peaceful nations of the world and the 'warlike descendants of the Teutons.'[81] These and similar clichés reflected the common approach of the Entente's early war propaganda.[82]

The Polish question and the war routine (1915–1916)

The disastrous Russian military campaign of 1915 significantly affected press rhetoric. In the absence of victorious reports from the front, newspapers were

---

72 'Okolovojny. Sibirskie strelki,' *Juzhnaja Kopejka*, 1 November 1914, 4.
73 'Rasstrel portreta knjazja Radzivilla,' *Poslednie Novosti*, 28 October 1914, 2.M.
74 Nik.Ivanov, 'Jepizody. (Iz Carstva Pol'skogo). I. Iz plena.,' *Kievskaja Mysl'*, 13 December 1914, 3.
75 'Uzh ne nachalo li konca?' *Kiev*, 5 October 1914, 2.
76 Jenzis, 'Iz nabljudenij v nemeckom plenu. IV. Djoberic.,' *Kievskaja Mysl'*, 6 October 1914, 1–2; Garol'd, 'Rifmy dnja. Segodnjashnij plakat 'Kiev – Pol'she',' *Kievskaja Mysl'*, 4 November 1914, 5; A. Ezhov, 'Poslednie da budut pervymi!' *Kievljanin*, 20 January 1915, 2.
77 Tetyana Lykhachova, 'Pol's'ki bizhentsi chasiv pershoyi svitovoyi viyny u suchasniy istoriohrafiyi,' *Zbirnyk naukovykh prats' Kharkivs'koho natsional'noho pedahohichnoho universytetu imeni H. S. Skovorody*, 46 (2012): 215–9.
78 Nemo, 'Sredi plennyh,' *Kiev*, September 13, 1914, 3; 'Nashvrag,' *Juzhnaja Kopejka*, 27 October 1914, 2.
79 'Vsepobezhdajushhaja sila,' *Kievljanin*, 2 August 1914, 1.
80 F. L'vov, 'Kulachnoe pravo,' *Kiev*, 21 August 1914, 1.
81 Bajan, 'Voinstvujushhij germanizm,' *Kiev*, 1 August 1914, 2.
82 Nikolaj Judin, 'Sozdanie obraza vraga v propagande stran Antanty v nachale Pervoj mirovoj vojny (avgust-dekabr' 1914),' *Izvestija Saratovskogo universiteta. Novaja serija. Serija 'Istorija. Mezhdunarodnye otnoshenija'* series, 12/3 (2012): 50–9.

unable to maintain a triumphant tone.[83] As a result, the media lost their positive argument for the restoration of unified Poland and substituted it for a no less mobilising, but essentially different, concept of the evil German occupation. The occupation theme first appeared at the end of 1914, and culminated in 1915. It consisted of several storylines, namely: German atrocities and the *Reich*'s economic and political rule in Congress Poland. Additionally, the press dealt with the problem of Polish resistance and collaboration with the enemy.

German atrocities in Poland were portrayed either as spontaneous or as purposeful acts against the innocent civilian population. A typical list of outrages included robbery and looting, vandalism, desecration of churches, drunkenness, rape and murders.[84] Media tended to dramatise these misdeeds by adding numerous horrifying details. For instance, it was reported that the Germans had slaughtered all the inhabitants of the Polish Pomjany village. After the victims were driven together and locked in a building, the village was set on fire and shelled by enemy artillery. Most surprisingly, the alleged explanation for that 'barbarity' was the simple German desire 'to preserve secrecy' – so that the villagers could not have pointed out the direction of retreat to the advancing Russians.[85] The press often spoke with a gloomy irony about the acts of the 'cultured Germans,' who shot an old man upon his remark about soldiers looting, or who mercilessly strapped to a cannon's side a son for his complaints about his old mother being killed by the *Deutsches Heer* shelling.[86] Additionally, press uncovered images of German sexual exploitation of Polish women. Most of the stories were of a tragic and moralising nature, and presented on average a group of German soldiers led by an officer, who had raped and killed young girls or women of aristocratic origin, or committed other crimes until they were killed or captured by the Russian vanguard.[87] Stories also aimed to entertain the public with a happy ending. For example, an account of Ms. Brzezowski illustrated an adventure of a pretty Polish lady who found herself captive at the German organised

---

83   Aleksandra Bahturina, 'Vozzvanie k poljakam 1 avgusta 1914 g. i ego avtory,' *Voprosy istorii*, 8 (1998), 134.
84   'Hronika vojny. Pod igom prussakov,' *Kiev*, 9 March 1915, 2; 'Nemeckie zverstva,' *Poslednie Novosti*, 9 March 1915, 2; 'Sredi nemcev,' *Kievljanin*, 14 June 1915, 3; 'Nemeckoe nashestvie (Rasskaz postradavshego),' *Juzhnaja Kopejka*, 8 December 1914, 2; 'Shpionomanija,' *Poslednie Novosti*, 15 May 1915, 1; 'Nemcy nasil'niki,' *Poslednie Novosti*, 28 September 1915, 2; 'Ugroza komendanta g. Chenstohova,' *Kievljanin*, 2 June 1915, 2; E. Jan–ok, 'Pust' krasnejut!' *Juzhnaja Kopejka*, 19 July 1915 , 3.
85   'Varvarstvo prussakov,' *Kiev*, 14 February 1915, 3.
86   'Nemcy v Privisljan'e,' *Kiev*, 6 March 1915, 3.
87   'Varvarstvo nemcev,' *Poslednie Novosti*, 1 April 1915, 2; 'Chernye dni krasavicy Varshavy,' *Juzhnaja Kopejka*, 10 August 1915, 1; 'Okolo vojny. V Loviche,' *Juzhnaja Kopejka*, 1 November 1914, 4.

'maid market.' She had been sold to the German Baron von Hessling and successfully endured his numerous molestations before the baron's unfaithfulness was discovered by 'his pious German wife.' Consequently, the baron's wife made a scene, liberated Ms. Brzezowski and helped her with a train ticket to Russia.[88] Apart from the sexual abuses, the Germans were stereotyped for their cynical black humour. Newspapers covered plenty of cases where the German military issued fake requisition receipts to unaware Polish owners. In one of these it was stated that: 'The presenter of this receipt is liable to be hanged after the end of the war;' in the other: 'Being grateful for the riding horse.'[89] Prussian officers allegedly boasted about the capital punishment of civilians[90] and seized jewellery out of the Warsaw stores with a promise of payment 'when Russia will pay a billion reparations to Germany.'[91]

Berlin's economic rule in Poland was depicted as a malicious exploitation. The press reported of the looted Polish factories, the enemy pillage of valuable industrial resources,[92] and of the army food requisitions that brought the local population to the verge of starvation.[93] It was claimed that occupational authorities intentionally created unbearable conditions in order to secure Polish labour migration to the *Reich*[94] and facilitate German colonization in return.[95] In general, the Russian press continued to perceive the Polish case within the 1914 paradigm of Teutono Slavic confrontation.[96] It asserted the German historical guilt for the 1772–1795 Partition of Poland[97] while presenting the tsarist empire as 'the last Slavic state' – a new victim of Prussian expansion.[98] The media uncovered the *Kaiser* grand plan for Russia's partition through the creation of loyal 'buffer states' – the 'Duchy of

---

88   'Rynok nevol'nic,' *Poslednie Novosti*, 14 May 1915, 1.
89   'Okolovojny. Prusskoe ostroumie,' *Juzhnaja Kopejka*, 22 September 1914, 2.
90   'Prusskaja shutka,' *Juzhnaja Kopejka*, 16 November 1914, 5.
91   'Germancy v Varshave,' *Kievljanin*, 24 August, 1915, 2.
92   'Vyvoz nemcami medi iz Lodzi,' *Kiev*, 13 February 1915, 3.
93   A. A–ch, 'Iz Chenstohova,' *Juzhnaja Kopejka*, 7 January 1915, 1–2; A. A–ch, 'Hozjajnichanie nemcev,' *Juzhnaja Kopejka*, January 12, 1915, 1; 'Vesti iz Chenstohova,' *Kievljanin*, 14 April 1915, 2; 'Hronika vojny. Iz okkupirovannoj germancami Pol'shi,' *Kievskaja Mysl'*, 16 September 1915, 3; 'Germanskij rezhim v Lodzi,' *Kievljanin*, 10 December 1915, 2.
94   A. A–ch, Nemcy v pol'skoj provincii,' *Juzhnaja Kopejka*, 18 January 1915, 2; A. A–ch, 'Nemcy v Bendine,' *Juzhnaja Kopejka*, 3 February 1915, 1; 'Vesti iz zanjatyh germancami mest,' *Poslednie Novosti*, 1 December 1915, 2.
95   'Nemeckie plany,' *Kievljanin*, 12 July 1915, 3.
96   V. Elatomskij, 'Rossija, slavjanstvo i 'zheleznyj kancler',' *Kiev*, 19 March 1915, 1; Ch–r, ' 'Sobcy' v slavjanstve,' *Kiev*, 9 December 1915, 1–2.
97   A. L. I., 'Vekovaja bor'ba slavjanstva s nemcami. Slavjane i Gogencollerny,' *Kievljanin*, 2 August 1915, 4.
98   Chestmir, 'Germanskie uzhasy i slavjanskie mechty,' *Kiev*, 13 October 1915, 1.

Poland' and 'Ukraine.'[99] They were concerned with the enemy policy of Germanisation,[100] such as incorporation of the Polish lands into the Hohenzollern Empire[101] and the imposition of *Reich* citizenship on the Poles.[102]

The press counteracted a hypocritical enemy propaganda image of Berlin as a 'saviour of the rightless nations.'[103] It uncovered the alleged *Deutsches Heer* loathing for the Poles who were portrayed as 'these scoundrels' and 'Polish slobs' in intercepted enemy correspondences.[104] In return, media emphasised anti Prussian Polish sentiments by referring to the opinion of famous Polish writers, such as Boleslaw Prus,[105] Wladyslaw Reymont,[106] Henryk Sienkiewicz[107] and Szymon Askenazy.[108] For instance, an excerpt from the pen of W. Reymont depicted a scene of Germanisation in school, where a fat red haired German tutor harassed a little Polish girl for her refusal to repeat the prayer in German; likewise, the press referred to Askenazy's work, *Rosja - Polska: 1815–1830*, presenting an idea of a 'Teutonic threat' to the Slavic nations.

In the first half of 1915, when Petrograd was still controlling the main body of Congress lands, the press continued to commend Polish loyalty. It was implied that a 'Polish patriot' should defend his motherland against the 'gluttonous imperialism of Iron Prussia.' As a reward, Poland's restoration was promised – but only 'under the sceptre of the Russian Tsar' and only after the war.[109] On the contrary, pro Kaiser Polish forces were considered politically marginal.[110] The press stigmatised Polish legionnaires – volunteers in the Austro Hungarian army[111] – as petty looters and drunkards – the 'pets of

---

99   N. P., 'Nemeckij mir,' *Poslednie Novosti*, 29 October 1914, 1. E.; Jenzis, 'Chego hotjat nemeckie imperialisty,' *Kievskaja Mysl'*, 14 August 1915, 1.
100   A. Kajskij, ' 'Blagodejanija' nemeckoj kul'tury,' *Kiev*, 3 December 1915, 2.
101   'Nemcy v Sosnovicah (Ot nashego Varshavskogo korrespondenta),' *Juzhnaja Kopejka*, 13 November 1914, 4.
102   'Nemcy v Pol'she,' *Kievljanin*, 1 July 1915, 3.
103   'V Lodzi,' *Poslednie Novosti*, 3 July 1915, 2; 'V Chenstohove,' *Kievljanin*, 16 January 1915, 2.
104   'Nashestvie gunnov,' *Poslednie Novosti*, 27 January 1915, 2.
105   L. Kozlovskij, 'Nemeckie zavoevateli v proizvedenijah Boleslava Prusa,' *Kievskaja Mysl'*, 7 August 1915, 2.
106   St. Vl. Rejmont, 'V prusskoj shkole (perevod s pol'skogo),' *Poslednie Novosti*, 21 August 1914, 3. M.
107   Osipov, 'Iz dnevnika istorii.Vechnye vragi,' *Juzhnaja Kopejka*, 1 March 1915, 2.
108   N. P.,'Galicija i Poznan',' *Kievljanin*, 9 July 1915, 3.
109   'Pol'skij vopros,' *Kievljanin*, 18 January 1915, 1.
110   'Vosstanovlenie Pol'shi,' *Kiev*, 9 February 1915, 3.
111   Volunteer Legions were an example of wartime nationalist activism which intended to win support for the final goal of self determination of the nation via military

Germany.'[112] Unlike the volunteers, the enemy conscripts of Polish origin were treated in a conciliatory manner. The press noted the tragedy of the Polish nation, whose sons were forced to battle each other because of the whim of the 'God damned German Lucifer [Kaiser Wilhelm II].'[113] It promoted the idea that the Poles from *Deutsches Heer* would peacefully surrender to their 'Polish brothers,' who were fighting on the 'right' Entente's side both in the West[114] and on the Eastern front.[115]

By the end of summer 1915, Russian newspapers were greatly depressed with the 'heaviest German stroke' which resulted in the loss of a 'Beautiful Poland.'[116] In the new circumstances, the question of Polish resistance and collaboration became the primary interest of the press. Media endeavoured to secure Polish loyalty, or at least to counteract the growing enemy influence by appealing to the Polish national sentiment.

Russian rightist press was the most active in presenting the Polish resistance image. This was because the progressive media's general reorientation shifted from the war theme towards the internal problems of the state, such as living standard deterioration. Instead, rightists tended to overshadow the Grand Retreat topic with examples of Polish gallantry.[117] Most prominent was the story of Warsaw school teacher Stanislav Poleszczanski, who barricaded himself in the apartment and fired back at the invading German troops until he was wounded heavily, captured and hanged.[118] The press created an atmosphere of the all-nation resistance, reporting about the numerous executions and imprisonments of Polish sympathisers of Russia[119] and, in general, of 'everyday clashes' between the people and the 'German punitive raid forces.'[120] For instance, newspapers informed about public unrest in Czestohowa and Lodz, where occupants attempted to steal the church icons, and in Warsaw, where Poles participated in bread riots[121] and lynched

---

participation in the host country's war effort. Volunteer legions were extensively used by both the Entente and the Central Powers.

112 'Pol'skie sokoly v Lodzi,' *Kievljanin*, 10 January 1915, 3; A. A–ch, 'Nemcy v Bendine,' *Juzhnaja Kopejka*, 3 February 1915, 1.
113 Ju. Revjakin, 'Nerazluchnye (ocherk),' *Kievljanin*, 15 January 1915, 2.
114 'Pol'skie dobrovol'cy,' *Kievljanin*, 16 January 1915, 4.
115 A. Filatov, 'Pered Varshavoj,' *Kievljanin*, 1 July 1915, 3.
116 Ju. Larin, 'My i sojuzniki,' *Kievljanin*, 24 August 1915, 1–2.
117 'Zverskaja rasprava s pol'skimi druzhinnikami,' *Kievljanin*, 26 July 1915, 3.
118 'Rasprava nemcev nad poljakami,' *Kievljanin*, 25 August 1915, 2.
119 'Germancy v Varshave,' *Kievljanin*, 24 August 1915, 2.
120 'Vesti iz Germanii,' *Poslednie Novosti*, 16 October 1915, 1.
121 M. Cvjatkovs'kij,'Sredi vragov,' *Kievljanin*, 25 October 1915, 3.

drunken 'German looters.'[122] Passive resistance was equally commended.[123] For example, newspapers greeted the sabotage, performed by the Central Residents' Committee of Warsaw (Polish self governance authority) towards a red carpet welcome of the arriving German Prince Leopold of Bavaria.[124]

In spite of being negative to 'Polish national egotism,' rightist press utilised it to create an image of German Polish enmity.[125] By doing this, it aimed to undermine the existing and also potentially pro Berlin Polish sentiments. For instance, it was reported that a *Deutsches Heer* Lieutenant of Polish origin, Count Poninski was executed for his anti German conversation with local Poles.[126] Another episode described the occupants's prohibition of the arrival of the popular Polish legion's leader Jozef Pilsudski[127] to Warsaw for an arranged patriotic meeting.[128] Politically, the press attempted to prove that pro Berlin Poles – those 'Prussian servants' – failed to achieve their goal of Poland's independence by means of collaboration with the *Reich*.[129] Its government, stated the press, had been pursuing solely its own adverse policy.[130] In late autumn 1915, shortly after the Austro-German conquest of Congress lands, the Polish question had almost entirely disappeared from the public space. Occasional news concerned the notorious problem of 'German atrocities'[131] and, more specifically, of starvation in Poland. Russian rightists presented starvation as an intentional 'horrible German policy,' aimed at the Polish nation's annihilation and ensuing Polish land grab.[132] In the first half of 1916, rightist *Kiev* was the only newspaper contributing to the Polish theme. Yet, it had articulated the question ambiguously and in the context of Pan Slavic doctrine.[133] In essence, *Kiev* supported the idea of an 'ancient Polish state' restoration on the basis of Polish ethnic lands[134] – of Prussia, Russian

---

122   'Poslednie vesti iz Varshavy,' *Kievljanin*, 8 September, 1915, 2.
123   'V Varshave,' *Kievljanin*, 30 August 1915, 2.
124   M. Cvjatkovs'kij, 'Sredi vragov,' *Kievljanin*, 23 October 1915, 2.
125   Cvjatkovs'kij, 'Sredi vragov,' 2.
126   'Rasstrel grafa Poninskogo,' *Kievljanin*, 17 June 1915, 2.
127   Remarkably, the conflict was presented in a clear ethnic category as a clash between the commanding German power and its Polish subjects – despite the fact that Jozef Pilsudski's Polish legion's units were subordinated to the Austro-Hungarian army.
128   'V Varshave,' *Kievljanin*, 5 September 1915, 2.
129   'Poljaki i nemcy,' *Poslednie Novosti*, 28 September 1915, 2.
130   Jenzis, 'Pol'sha pod voprositel'nym znakom,' *Kievskaja Mysl'*, 11 September 1915, 2.; N.P.,'Germanija i Rossija,' *Poslednie Novosti*, 20 September, 1915, 1; 'V Varshave,' *Kievljanin*, 21 October 1915, 2.
131   'Dva goda zverstv,' *Poslednie Novosti*, 23 July 1916, 1.
132   L. Sosnin, 'Osnovnye principy nemeckoj politiki i nemeckoj taktiki,' *Kiev*, 14 June 1916,2.; N. M.,' 'Proekt' germans'kogo doktora (Genca Potgofa),' *Kievljanin*, April 2, 1916, 1.
133   Chestmir, "Kroty' v slavjanstve,' *Kiev*, 9 January 1916, 2.
134   The Polish part of the Austro Hungarian Galicia province was omitted in the

Congress Poland and even some of the ethnographically disputable parts of the Russian Suwalki and Grodno provinces.[135] Furthermore, it was stated that Petrograd had recognised the right of self determination for the Slavic nations and sought no political control over Poland.[136] On the contrary, the same newspaper proclaimed the goal of Russia's supervision over the supposed Slavic alliance: 'Not a single Slavic state but a family of Slavic states in which the Russ – the big brother' was destined to protect the 'younger brothers' from the German intrigues – 'the betrayal of the Slavs.'[137]

The Polish question was instigated once again in reaction to the Central Powers's proclamation of the Kingdom of Poland on 5 November 1916. The press unanimously stigmatised the Act as obvious 'German hypocrisy.'[138] The Act was interpreted as 'irretrievable' to the German Russian relations, yet hardly effective to spoil Russian Polish relations. The press's optimism derived from the following considerations: first, 'German made' Poland was incomplete without the Polish ethnic lands in Prussia; second, it was Petrograd's only authority to legitimise part of its own territory as an independent Poland; third, 'the vital interests' of Poland were in its association with Russia.[139]

Impelled by Austro-German activity, newspapers sought the justification of the postponement of the Russian promised restoration of Poland. They argued that the Polish question was 'international' and, therefore, could only be solved by the post-war peace conference.[140] Furthermore, the press insisted on a thorough legal procedure: while Congress Poland *de jure* remained an inherent part of the empire,[141] the decision on its autonomy required the consent of both the tsar and the State Duma.[142]

Media diminished the value of the enemy granted Polish autonomy in order to

---

article. Instead it was claimed that '…the lands, populated by the Russian nation in Galicia, Bukovina and Ugria [Carpathian Ruthenia] should be incorporated into the Russian Empire, embraced with the Russian state boundaries and joined to the common Russian life…' ('Celi vojny,' *Kiev*, 3 March 1916, 1).

135   'Celi vojny,' *Kiev*, 3 March 1916, 1.
136   'Celi vojny,' 1.
137   Chestmir, "Celi vojny',' *Kiev*, 21 March 1916, 2.
138   'Akt o Pol'she i nejtral'naja pechat',' *Juzhnaja Kopejka*, 1 November, 1916, 1.
139   L. Kozlovskij, 'Germanija i pol'skij vopros,' *Kievskaja Mysl'*, 30 October 1916, 2; 'Kiev, 26 October 1916,' *Kievljanin*, 26 October 1916, 1; N. S–kij, 'V okkupirovannoj Pol'she,' *Kievskaja Mysl'*, 19 November 1916, 3.
140   V. Shul'gin, 'Kiev, 25 janvarja 1917 g.,' *Kievljanin*, 26 January 1917, 1–2.
141   V. Shul'gin, ' 'Pod znakom Marsa',' *Kievljanin*, 29 January 1917, 1–2.
142   Chlen Gosudarstvennoj Dumy D. Chihachev 'O porjadke razreshenija voprosa o gosudarstvennom ustrojstve Carstva Pol'skogo,' *Kievljanin*, 14 February 1917, 1–2.

counteract the growth of pro German sentiment. The autonomy was presented as a 'Prussian trap,' designed solely to replace the *Deutsches Heer* losses with Polish manpower.[143] Poles were reminded of a century long 'German treachery' – from the initial settlement of Teutons in the 12th century to the latest agreement with the Prussian king Friedrich Wilhelm II (1786– 97).[144] Press also ridiculed the pro Berlin 'Polish petty patriots,' who had sacrificed their ambition for the united Poland restoration. While leaving Poznan and West Prussia to Germany, these Poles vainly expected to enlarge their country in the East at the expense of Russia.[145] 'The great political scandal' occurred when the Reich's government rejected the claims of the Polish Provisional Council of State for the Courland and Lithuania – i.e. for the lands, which in Polish opinion 'were liberated from the Russian yoke and historically gravitated to Poland.'[146]

In early 1917, common Polish loyalty was publicly questioned for the first time. The rightist press became critical towards the ambivalent Polish identity –'Slavic,' yet committed to the 'Western culture.' *Kievljanin* argued that this Western orientation was intentionally anti Russian. It also acknowledged that Poles were hostile to both Germans and Russians, thus presenting a potential territorial menace for the two empires. However, geopolitically the prospective Poland was deemed to be non self sufficient and evaluated as an object of perpetual Berlin-Petrograd rivalry.[147] Anxious about the retaining of Poland within the Russian sphere of influence, media confronted any idea other than that of Polish autonomy.[148] In a new fashion, autonomy was presented as a 'fraternal' political union with Russia, guided by the principle of 'association of the equal with the equal, of the free with the free' between Poles and Russians.[149] Still, it lacked consistency, stating ad locum that Russia as 'the most powerful and the largest among the Slavic states' was to assume the leading role in the union.[150] Thus, Poland was envisioned as an 'outpost' of the Russian-controlled 'Slavic civilization,' within the context of struggle with the 'German World.'[151]

---

143 'Prusskaja lovushka,' *Poslednie Novosti*, 6 September, 1916, 2; 'V Pol'she pod germanskim igom,' *Poslednie Novosti*, 10 October 1916, 2.
144 Brusilov (general-ad'jutant) 'Prikaz armijam Jugo-zapadnogo fronta,' *Kievskaja Mysl'*, 11 December 1916, 2.
145 V. G.,'Pol'skij gosudarstvennyj sovet,' *Juzhnaja Kopejka*, 28 January 1917, 1.
146 V. G.,'Pol'skij gosudarstvennyj sovet,' 1.
147 Shul'gin, "Pod znakom Marsa',' 1–2.
148 '*Kiev*, 6 February 1917,' *Kievljanin*, 7 February 1917, 1.
149 V. Vojcehovskij, 'Vozmozhno li ozdat' blagoprijatnye otnoshenija mezhdu russ- kimi i poljakami bez idei slavjanskogo ob'edinenija,' *Kievljanin*, 1 February 1917, 2.
150 Vojcehovskij, 'Vozmozhnoli...,' 2.
151 K. B., 'Rol' slavjanstva v proshlom i budushhem mezhdunarodnogo obshhenija (Prof. A. M. Luk'janenko),' *Kievljanin*, 28 February 1917, 2.

The Polish question during the 1917 February Revolution

The February Revolution in Petrograd resulted in the abdication of Tsar Nicholas II (1894–17) and the overthrow of the Romanov dynasty in March 1917. However, besides the radical political transformation of the imperial regime into a parliamentarian form of government, the Revolution had initially no significant impact on either territorial integrity or public identification with the common Russian state. The former empire's Southwestern Krai was just the same. Despite the emergence of the Ukrainian national movement, the region remained an inherent part of the united Russian state until its collapse in early November 1917. For this period, the original Ukrainian aspirations were limited to national cultural autonomy, thus leaving the movement within the legal frames of the state.[152]

The Kiev press continued to exist in a unified all Russian information space. Yet, the revolution changed the discussed theme priorities, with much attention diverted from the war with the Central Powers to the urgent domestic issues of the state.[153] Consequently, the Kiev press's interest in the Polish question also declined.

To start with the most popular, the Russian progressive press of Kiev mentioned the Polish case extremely rarely and mostly in the context of the Revolution. Poland served as an example for the region's most prominent Russian Ukrainian argument over the autonomy of Ukraine. According to the Ukrainian position, the Russian provisional government's reluctance towards Ukrainian aspirations was an act of 'hypocrisy' on the part of the Russian democratic movement – since both Finland's and Poland's political autonomies had already been recognised.[154] Apart from this, the Polish case was also mentioned within the contemporary 'fraternization' discussion.[155]

---

152   Shortly after the February Revolution in Petrograd, an All-Ukrainian council of Central Rada was established in Kiev on 4 (17) March, 1917. Functioning as an assembly of various political, public and cultural organizations, it became a revolutionary parliament of Ukraine on the decision of the All-Ukrainian National Congress (19–21 April 1917). By the Second Universal on 3 (16) July, Central Rada adopted its political subordination to the Russian Provisional Government at the same time acquiring the status of Ukraine's highest provincial authority within Russian Republic (Further reading: Valeriy Smoliy, Hennadiy Boryak, and Vladyslav Verstyuk (eds.), *Narysy istoriyi ukrayins'koyi revolyutsiyi 1917–1921 rokiv*. Volume 1. Kyiv: Naukova dumka, 2011).

153   Boris Kolonizkij, 'Metamorphosen der Germanophobie: Deutschland in den politischen Konflikten der Februarrevolution von 1917,' in: *Verführungen der Gewalt. Russen und Deutsche im Ersten und Zweiten Weltkrieg*, 121–44, eds..von Karl Eimermacher, and Astrid Volpert, München: Wilhelm Fink Verlag, 2005.

154   A. Brynskij, 'Na ulichnyhmitingah,' *Kievskaja Mysl'*, 9 June 1917, 2.

155   With the outbreak of the 1917 February Revolution 'fraternization with the

Namely, the author agitated for 'revolutionary fraternization' with German soldiers of Polish origin who were considered to be peace willing unlike their ethnic German counterparts.[156] Lastly, the press reminded the public of the continuous German intention to create a loyal Polish puppet state.[157]

Revived after the fall of the tsarist regime, the Ukrainian press formed its attitude towards Poland on the grounds of its own national interests. The Ukrainian press utilised the Polish precedent as a supportive example for the Ukrainian 'national cultural autonomy' argument.[158] The leading daily *Nova Rada* was aware of Poland's dependent status in relations to the Central Powers, yet it considered German 'narrow but effective' steps in the creation of 'independent Poland' to be more significant than empty Russian 'broad promises.'[159] Disappointed by the hostility of the Russian democracy, the Ukrainian movement, thus, implicitly considered the Polish pro Berlin example as an alternative solution for its national aspirations.[160] Eventually, *Nova Rada* regarded German and Russian imperial influences as temporary obstacles for Polish national state development.[161]

Nova Rada demonstrated its amicability towards the Polish nation and, in particular, towards the Polish minority in Ukraine. It commended local Poles for their recognition of the Ukrainian right to national self determination and regularly cited encouraging articles of Kiev's Polish daily *Dziennik Kijowski*.[162] The latter affirmed that the Poles were 'the closest and natural allies of the Ukrainian national liberation' from the Russian imperial yoke.[163] While the majority of Poles were regarded as sincere supporters of Ukrainians, *Nova Rada* also mentioned the inimical group of Polish national democrats who were an 'exception from the friendship of the two nations.'[164] On the contrary,

---

enemy' became a widely spread form of antiwar frontline protest of the of Russian army soldiers. It was instigated not only by the revolutionary soldiers' committees but also by the Bolshevik agitators and special Austro-German units. Being a vicious violation of military discipline, fraternization significantly influenced the decay of the Russian army (See: Sergej Bazanov, 'Nemeckie soldaty stali... perepolzat' k russkim 'tovarishham' i bratat'sja s nimi,' *Voenno-istoricheskij zhurnal*, 6 (2002): 43–50).

156 V. Stechkin, 'Komu blizhe krasnoe znamja?' *Juzhnaja Kopejka*, 21 March 1917, 2.
157 'Chto delaetsja v Pol'she,' *Poslednie Novosti*, 8 April 1917, 3.
158 M. Chernyavs'kyy, 'Natsional'ne pytannya v Rosiyi,' *Nova Rada*, 21 June 1917, 1–2.
159 'Nimechchyna i Pol'shcha,' *Nova Rada*, 7 September 1917, 1.
160 'Nimechchyna i Pol'shcha,' 1.
161 Yak. Mk., 'Derzhavnyy borh. II.,' *Nova Rada*, 18 May 1917, 1.
162 'Vystup pol's'koyi hazety,' *Nova Rada*, 9 June 1917, 1; 'Z pol's'koyi presy,' *Nova Rada*, 11 June 1917, 1; 'Z pol's'koyi presy,' *Nova Rada*, 18 June 1917, 1.
163 'Z pol's'koyi presy,' *Nova Rada*, 28 June 1917, 1.
164 'Z pol's'koyi presy,' 1.

the Ukrainian social democratic *Robitnycha Hazeta* focused on the Polish–Ukrainian disagreement. It confronted the above mentioned Polish 'chauvinistic' group's claim for Greater Poland 'from the sea to the sea' – i.e., with the inclusion of Kiev and the large portion of the Ukrainian ethnic lands.[165] Consequently, the newspaper was concerned with the probable Polish military occupation of Ukraine.[166]

Although Russian rightists had initially welcomed the Revolution, shortly after they became both disappointed and profoundly marginalized by its outcome.[167] Russian rightist ideology was founded on the key principle of state territorial integrity and loyalty to the Entente. Therefore, *Kievljanin* acknowledged its amicability towards the Poles, who participated in the Polish national units of the Russian army,[168] struggled against the common German enemy,[169] and supported the 'Russian democratic state' in general.[170] The newspaper continued to evaluate Poland from the context of the idea of the 'One and indivisible Great Russia.' A contemporary Russian imagination embraced Warsaw as '…the heart of a free Poland…beautiful eye of the single all Slavic entity, whose head and body are Russian…'[171] Particularly, *Kievljanin* insisted that Poland simply could not exist 'beyond Russia' because otherwise it would be doomed by the *Deutsches Reich*.[172]

Kievljanin's agitation of 1917 combined traditional appeals towards Polish loyalty[173] and warnings of the Prussian evil[174] with a revolutionary rhetoric,

---

165   Ol. Hrudnyts'kyy, 'Vchorashni kholopy – s'ohodnishni imperialisty,' *Robitnycha Hazeta*, 22 April 1917, 2.
166   D. A., 'Pol's'ke viys'ko,' *Robitnycha Hazeta*, 27 May 1917, 1–2.
167   By 1917 the Russian autocracy lost its support not only in the 'lower classes' of the society but also among its elites. As a result, pro monarchial Russian rigtist parties remained passive and uncoordinted in the outbreak of the Revolution and, consequently, were removed from power. Remarkably, many of the key Russian rightist activists originally supported the Revoultion for the sake of the Russian state or from fear of political opression. However, later on they were dissapointed with the Russian Republic's ineffecive state policy (Jurij Kir'janov, *Pravye partii v Rossii. 1911—1917 gg.*, Moskva: ROSSPEN, 2001, 388–424).
168   'Proshhanie pol's'kogo polka s Kievom,' *Kievljanin*, 24 April 1917, 2.
169   'Parad vojsk Kievskogo garnizona,' *Kievljanin*, 8 March 1917, 1.
170   V. Vojcehovskij, 'Iz pol'skoj zhizni i pechati. Pol'skie politicheskie soveshhanija,' *Kievljanin*, 18 March 1917, 1.
171   Lev M–skij, 'Mne grustno… V svjatuju noch',' *Kievljanin*, 27 April 1917, 1.
172   Lev M–skij, 'Pod belym orlom na krasnom pole. Pol'skij mezhdunarodnyj tribunal. II.,' *Kievljanin*, 22 June 1917, 2.
173   V. Vojcehovskij, 'Iz pol'skoj zhizni i pechati. Novyj kursvAvstro Germanii,' *Kievljanin*, 10 March 1917, 2.; 'Praporshhik Sikorskij,' *Kievljanin*, 23 July 1917, 1–2.
174   Prof. Andrej Stojanovich, 'Vozstanie 'rabov'. IV Senkevich i Gus,' *Kievljanin*, 2 April 1917, 1.

addressed to the 'Eagle of a New Poland' urging to join the free nations's 'fight against the tyranny of imperialist Germany.'[175] However, the Polish Provisional Council of State's reply to Petrograd's provisional government proclamation 'to the Poles' of March 1917[176] worsened *Kievljanin*'s attitude. The newspaper interpreted the 'cold and restrained hostility' of official Warsaw as a sign of its anti Russian policy.[177] Furthermore, the recognition of Germany as Poland's independence guarantor[178] was stigmatised as a Polish statesmen's treachery – implying 'that the enemies of Russia, England, France and America – are the friends of Poland.'[179] Yet, to soften the confrontation, *Kievljanin* soon underlined the unrepresentativeness of the pro-Berlin Polish authority.[180] As a result, the press summoned the Poles in Revolutionary Russia to form their own political centre and disregard the treacherous 'Old Warsaw' (though, with a prospect of its further liberation).[181]

Observing the disintegration of the state from 1917, Russian rightists perceived the German-granted Polish independence as a negative and virulent symbol to follow. Their primary concern in the Southwestern Krai was the Ukrainian national movement, which threatened to replicate the Polish experience. It should be noted that the 'German instigated Ukrainian peril' was another popular topic of the Russian press throughout the war. In 1917, *Kievljanin* confronted the Ukrainian aspiration for autonomy, stating that the Central Council of Ukraine resembled the Polish Provisional Council of State. With a grim irony the newspaper proposed that Ukrainians 'go ahead and ask the German emperor Wilhelm' for 'Polish style' independence.[182]

By autumn of 1917, the Russian Republic was on the brink of collapse due to army decay, unsolved socio economic problems and, ultimately, society's war

---

175   Lev M–skij, 'Pod belym orlom na krasnom pole. Pol'skoe nacional'noe stroi-tel'stvo. III.,' *Kievljanin*, 24 June 1917, 2.
176   On 29 March 1917 the Russian Provisional Government issued a proclamation recognising the right of the Polish nation to form its own state on the basis of Congress Poland, German and Austro Hungarian ethnic Polish territories. However, the final decision on the Polish question was delegated to the prospective all Russian Constituent Assembly. Also, the proclamation assumed the creation of the 'Free military alliance' between Poland and Russia, thus preserving the first within the Russian sphere of influence (Matveev, 'Fevral'skaja revoljucija,' 88–90).
177   G. D., 'Dva Vozzvanija,' *Kievljanin*, 8 April 1917, 1–2.
178   G. D., 'Dva Vozzvanija,' 1–2.
179   V. Shul'gin, 'Kiev, 8 go aprelja 1917 g. (po telegrafu iz Petrograda),' *Kievljanin*, 9 April 1917, 1.
180   'Doklad po pol'skomu voprosu,' *Kievljanin*, 18 April 1917, 2.
181   Lev M–skij, 'Pod belym orlom na krasnom pole. K pol'skomu s'ezdu,' *Kievljanin*, 21 June 1917, 2.
182   V. Shul'gin, '*Kiev*, 8 June 1917 g. (po telegrafu iz Petrograda),' *Kievljanin*, 2 June 1917, 1.

weariness.[183] Kiev press reflected this decadent mood, presenting examples of public acceptance of Russia's war defeat.[184] *Kievljanin* complained about the indifference of the mass of citizens who perceived a possible German 'wealthy country' occupation of Russia as a better option than the misery of their own state. The newspaper reported of the Moscow street mob exclaiming '...we used to live under Nicholas so we could not care less about the life under Wilhelm [Hohenzollern].'[185] These observations led *Kievljanin* to the conclusion of the German victory over the Slavdom and Russia.[186] The emergence of a pro Berlin Polish state was considered an inherent part of this enemy triumph.[187]

The Bolshevik Uprising in November of 1917 marked the end of the Russian democratic regime. It also triggered Russian state disintegration, for the non Russian national periphery had refused to recognise the Bolshevik order. As a result, a *de facto* separate Ukrainian People's Republic was proclaimed in Kiev on 20 November 1917. These events reshaped both the focus and the mood of Kiev's printed media. As with others, the press discussion of the Polish question became completely obsolete. At the same time, the very notion of a common all Russian information space ceded to exist with the start of Soviet Russia's aggression against Ukraine in December 1917.

Conclusion

Throughout the period of 1914–1917, the Polish question in the Russian press was incorporated within the German-Russian Great War confrontation theme. At the outbreak of the war, it was a mere rhetorical construction, applied as a pretext for the anti German campaign and aimed at boosting the empire's war effort. However, the original enthusiastic mood had vanished in 1915 due to war routinisation and the Russian army's Great Retreat from the Congress Poland. The subsequent enemy occupation raised the issue of Polish loyalty. It became a burning question by the time of the Austro German proclamation of the Kingdom of Poland in late 1916. Since then the Polish question was closely connected to the problem of national state building and resembled a Berlin Petrograd contest over Polish sympathy. The 1917 February Revolution marked the decline of interest to the Polish question,

---

183   Peter Gatrell, *Russia's First World War: A Social and Economic History*, Harlow: Pearson Education, 2005, 197–215.
184   Pod'jachev, 'Vchajnoj (iz derevenskih nabljudenij),' *Kievskaja Mysl'*, 2 September 1917, 1; Jarilo, 'Malen'kij fel'eton.Vo vneshnej politike,' *Juzhnaja Gazeta*, 16 September 1917, 6; Vl. Rozanov, 'Mir za schet Rossii,' *Kievskaja Mysl'*, 24 September 1917, 1.
185   A. Lohov (Moskva), 'Dym otechestva,' *Kievljanin*, 31 October 1917, 1.
186   A. Ezhov, 'Vpechatlenija. Slavjanskij jekzamen,' *Kievljanin*, 26 August 1917,1; Petrogradec, 'Petrogradskie otkliki. Oboshli molchaniem,' *Kievljanin*, 15 October 1917, 2.
187   V. Shul'gin, '*Kiev*, 9 go sentjabrja 1917 g.,' *Kievljanin*, 10 September 1917, 1–2.

while the press shifted to domestic political issues. The Revolution also enabled the freedom of speech, thus presenting different opinions on the Polish question.

This research's findings correspond to the Russian imperial borderland region of the Southwestern Krai and not general Russian perception. However, they thoroughly reflect the peculiarities of the Russian information space of the contested western margins of the Romanov's Empire. Furthermore, this study's methodological framework and the supplementary data on the composition of Kiev's population, press distribution and political affiliation, bring a broader conclusion. Namely, that the image of the Poles constructed by the Kiev press both reflected and influenced the attitudes of its mass readership. In general, this article illustrates the painful process of the collapse of the Russian imperial worldview: from a once stable observation of Polish inclusion into Russia's body, to the bitter apprehension of Poland's loss. Apparently, the Russian press's recognition of the existence of a separate pro Berlin Poland was conditioned by the 1917 Russian Empire's disintegration process. For the Russian press in Southwestern Krai, this took the form of a Ukrainian national movement challenge. Eventually, the Polish question became obsolete when the region's ruling Russian minority faced the question of Ukrainian autonomy – an issue of 'another Poland' for the all Russian nationalism in the impending Russian Ukrainian struggle of the Revolutionary era.

7

The Baltic Dream of a 'Handicapped' Great Power: The Weimar Republic's Policies towards the Baltic-Germans

AGNE CEPINSKYTE

Perceiving a state as a living creature could well be seen as insane. However, this was precisely the idea of Friedrich Ratzel, a German geographer and ethnographer, also known for coining the now infamous term '*Lebensraum*,' which was later misused by Nazis. Ratzel's concept of the state's borders as a naturally evolving chief 'organ' of the state was his suggested rationale for Germany's potential territorial expansion. He wrote: 'A nation does not remain immobile for generations on the same piece of territory: it must expand, for it is growing.'[1] In the 1920s, for Germany, such an approach was acceptable, as it gave hope to the German people that their state's decline was only temporary and there was still a prospect of territorial expansion.

Following similar thinking, Manfred Langhans-Ratzeburg insisted that regardless of its miserable post-war state, Weimar Germany still belonged to the Great Powers and was only temporarily 'disabled' by the Allies.[2] Its status as a recovering Great Power was implicitly recognised by the League of Nations in 1926, when Germany was given a permanent member's seat on the League's Council. In April of that year, several months before Germany was admitted to the League, Foreign Minister Gustav Stresemann (1923–29)

---

1   Mark Bassin, 'Imperialism and the nation state in Friedrich Ratzel's political geography', *Progress in Human Geography*, 11/3 (1987): 473-95, 473.
2   Manfred Langhans-Ratzeburg, *Die Großen Mächte Geojuristisch Betrachtet*. München und Berlin: R. Oldenbourg, 1931.

explained in his speech at the national assembly of the German People's Party (*Deutsche Volkspartei* – DVP) that one of the conditions that Germany raised for its entrance to the League was 'the obvious recognition of the German Great Power status (*Großmachtstellung*).'[3]

There is thus something volatile about a 'handicapped' Great Power. Even during the times when such a state complies with unfavourable international demands and humiliating constraints out of necessity, its self-perception as a Great Power (even if a temporarily restrained one) is likely to be as solid as ever and its domestic nationalists may be feeding on revanchist theories. Indeed, ideas invigorating the myth of the Third Rome and the mission of 'special civilisations' spread in Germany in particular during the 1920s.[4] Such theories, at first aimed at merely remedying the dissatisfaction of the masses, may acquire a whole new intensity when political, economic and historical circumstances change and enable those in power to turn ideas into reality.

The ambivalent nature of the interwar German Great Power status is evident in the Weimar Republic's approach and policies towards the Baltic States. On the one hand, pressed by economic demands and troubled international and domestic circumstances, post-WWI Germany had to quickly shift its wartime annexationist plans. This was necessary for pursuing pragmatic cooperation with the newly independent Baltic States that would potentially open the doors to Eastern (primarily Russian) economic markets. On the other hand, revanchist and imperialistic discourse was quietly but steadily streaming below the surface of the carefully considered diplomatic efforts.

For most of the 1920s, Gustav Stresemann led German foreign policy. At first, as the Reich's Chancellor for a hundred days in 1923, then as foreign minister from 1923 to his death in 1929, Stresemann guided the devastated state throughout its most difficult years. Historians have disagreed as to whether he was a pioneer of European diplomacy or an adamant advocate of pan-German expansion. For his diplomatic achievements Stresemann has been named Weimar's greatest statesman and the founding father of the German politics of international law (*Völkerrechtpolitik*).[5] Nevertheless, historian Fritz Fischer for one suggested the so-called continuity thesis (*Kontinuitätsthese*). He argued that Stresemann's policies, particularly those towards national minorities abroad, formed a bridge between the pan-German imperialism of

---

3   Gustav Stresemann, speech in the assembly of DVP. Stuttgart, 18. April 1926.
4   See, for example, Arthur Moeller Van den Bruck, *Das Dritte Reich*. Berlin: Ring Verlag, 1923.
5   Jonathan Wright, *Gustav Stresemann: Weimar's Greatest Statesman*. Oxford: OUP, 2002; Hans Morgenthau, 'Stresemann als Schöpfer der Deutschen Völkerrechtspolitik', *Die Justiz* 5/3 (1929), 169–76.

the Wilhelmine era and the *Lebensraum* doctrine of the *Third Reich*.[6]

This paper takes a discursive approach to foreign policy and proposes that with regards to Weimar *Ostpolitik*, both positions are correct. That is, the political discourse of the Weimar Republic towards the Baltic States had several 'layers' operating simultaneously.

The study builds on the analytical model developed by Ole Waever, who introduced the idea of layered discursive formations. According to him, the deeper discursive structures are more abstract and more solidly sedimented. For that reason they are more difficult to politicise and change.[7] Therefore, the change usually happens on the surface level of political discourse, while on the deeper level continuity may persist. Thus, analysing political discourse as a layered structure allows discovering a complex picture: instead of simply tracing the change or establishing continuity, one can specify 'change within continuity.'[8]

This study focuses on the first half of the 1920s. While German *Ostpolitik* was dynamic throughout the whole Weimar period, the most radical shift in its policies towards the Baltic States occurred precisely in the early years of the Weimar Republic. The study analyses political discourse as it appears in Gustav Stresemann's speeches and policy documents. However, the remainder of the study that outlines the context that this political discourse operated in relies on various other sources, both secondary (studies by other scholars) and primary (memoirs, diaries, archival material etc.).

The first part of the study addresses the issue of revisionism and revanchist ideas in post-WWI Germany – something that was reflected at the 'deepest' level of political discourse. The second part discusses the shift in German policies towards the Baltic States that were constructed at the surface level of political discourse. The final part analyses political discourse as it appeared in Stresemann's speeches and policy documents. The aim is to unearth the aforementioned discursive layers that enabled the co-existence of revisionist ideas and pragmatic policies. The most attention will be paid to Stresemann's minority discourse that played a significant role in reconciling the two extremes.

---

6   Fritz Fischer, *Bündnis der Eliten: Zur Kontinuität der Machtstrukturen in Deutschland 1871–1945*. Düsseldorf: Droste Verlag, 1979.
7   Ole Waever, 'Identity, communities and foreign policy: Discourse analysis as foreign policy theory' in: *European Integration and National Identity: The challenge of the Nordic states*, edited by Lene Hansen and Ole Wæver, 20–50. London: Routledge, 2002, 32.
8   Waever, 'Identity, communities and foreign policy', 31.

Imperialistic revisionism in the mutilated Weimar Republic

> You must carve in your heart
> These words as in stone:
> What we have lost
> We will restore![9]
>
> Paul Warncke, '*Was wir verloren haben*,' 1920.

Post-WWI Germany, the successor of a defeated empire, faced the challenge of coming to terms with a significant decrease in population and territory, the loss of military might and the consequent sense of injustice and humiliation. This provoked a desperate search for an explanation as to why it had failed. Such an explanation was offered by geopolitical theory that pointed to other Great Powers, the Allies, as responsible for the German fall. Perhaps even more importantly, ideas of classical geopolitics suggested that the 'wrongful' outcome of the war could be reversed.

Geopolitical thought in Weimar Germany was developed and popularised around the claim of the injustice of Germany's newly redrawn territorial borders. The theory took advantage of widespread resentment towards the Treaty of Versailles. The Treaty deprived Germany of around one-eighth of its pre-war territory, one-tenth of its population and, in the German view, imposed 'dictated peace.'[10] At the time, when Germans might have been divided on many issues, their hatred of the Treaty of Versailles was the common ground. In March 1921, Stresemann cast doubt on the Treaty's legal implications: 'The Treaty of Versailles is devoid, morally speaking, of any legal basis (...) The fact that we signed the Treaty under compulsion after being disarmed does not alter in any way the legal position.'[11]

Similarly, despite their differences, all German political parties agreed that the Peace Treaty had to be revised. Historian Bastiaan Schot wrote in his study that all German political parties were of the position that 'at all costs the impression should be avoided that the Reich recognised the 1919 territorial provisions as binding.'[12] Grievances against the Treaty were also widespread

---

9   Original German: 'Ins Herz sollst du dir graben/Dies Wort als wie in Stein:/Was wir verloren haben/Darf nicht verloren sein' (translation by A.C.).
10   Robert John O'Neill and Robin Havers (eds.), *World War II: Europe 1939–1943*. New York: the Rosen Publishing Group, 2010, 17.
11   *Essays and Speeches on Various Subjects by Gustav Stresemann*, translated by Christopher R. Turner. Freeport, NY: Books for Libraries Press, 1930, 114–5.
12   Bastiaan Schot, *Nation oder Staat? Deutschland und der Minderheitenschutz : zur Völkerbundspolitik der Stresemann-Ära*. Marburg/Lahn: J.G. Herder Institut, 1988, 27.

among the German people. Harry Kessler, an Anglo-German count, diplomat and writer, described in his diary the mood in Berlin in the summer of 1919, a few days before the Treaty of Versailles was signed:

> This morning, students and soldiers removed the French flags we are supposed to surrender from the Arsenal and burned them in front of the statue of Frederick the Great. This afternoon, since the Entente has declined to accept our signature under reservation, the military leaders have announced their resistance to the government, the Centre Party has withdrawn its Agreement to signature, and the government has decided to resign. This evening the ultimatum expires. The tension is terrific. Very oppressive weather. Counter-revolution, war, insurrection threaten us like the nearing thunderstorm.[13]

New geopolitical ideas provided the German people with hope that results of the war need not to be permanent. Historian David Thomas Murphy accurately noted that the geopolitical criticism of the Treaty (i.e. that it violated the 'natural' political geography of Central Europe, that it unjustly excluded millions of Germans from their homeland etc.) – was not particularly unique or significantly different from the criticism made by non-geopoliticians. However, geopoliticians at the time argued that their critique was scientific and therefore it was accepted as more objective and credible than other critiques.[14] As American geopolitician Nicholas Spykman would later say: 'Geography does not argue. It just is.'[15]

In 1920s Germany, geopolitical ideas were not limited to narrow academic and political circles. They were introduced in German schools in order to persuade the new generation that the emergence of new states in the East was unnatural and unjust and therefore their existence was only temporary. Likewise, geographical institutes at German universities offered lectures and seminars on geopolitics. Geopolitical rhetoric in educational institutions not only suggested that the borders in East-Central Europe were illegitimate, but also included teachings that the German people outside Germany's borders were still a part of the homeland.[16]

---

13   Charles Kessler (ed.), *Berlin in Lights: The diaries of Count Harry Kessler (1918–1937)*. New York: Grove Press, 1999, 102.
14   David Thomas Murphy, *The Heroic Earth: Geopolitical Thought in Weimar Germany, 1918–1933*. Kent: Kent State University Press, 1997, 46.
15   Nicholas J. Spykman, 'Geography and Foreign Policy II', *American Political Science Review* 32/2 (1938), 236.
16   Murphy, *The Heroic Earth*, x.

The overall idea about territorial borders in the geopolitical theory was that natural and stable state borders were those determined by ethnic and geographic factors as opposed to the 'inherently unstable' borders resulting from political agreements. German geopolitician Adolf Grabowsky contended that 'a border can rest on the conditions of space and on conditions of ethnicity. In both cases, it is not artificial, not a mere treaty border, but a natural one.'[17] Grabowsky revived the ideas that had already been proclaimed by German philosophers such as Johann Gottlieb Fichte and Johann Gottfried Herder, who insisted that borders must be in harmony with 'peoples' spirit' (*Volksgeist*). In other words, in determining legitimate state borders 'natural' forces, such as geography, race, ethnicity, should prevail over law and politics.[18] Such an argumentation constituted a potential basis for justification of revisionist policies and territorial expansion.

Karl Haushofer, one of the leading geopoliticians of the Weimar era and arguably of all times, explicitly favoured German territorial expansionism. He, among a number of other geopoliticians, suggested that Germany's growing population needed new space – *Lebensraum*.[19] Haushofer defined *Lebensraum* as the right and duty of a nation to provide ample space and resources for its people. It was the duty of the stronger state with a growing population to expand at the cost of the weaker one.[20] Interestingly, there was also another body of geopoliticians, led by Friedrich Burgdörfer, who argued to the contrary, i.e. that the German population was actually critically declining.[21] However, they too advocated for more space.

Their argument was that the decrease in population was allegedly a result of people gathering in the cities, which prompted urbanisation, the decline of moral standards, and changes in the social role of women.[22] Germans, now being forced to crowd into the cities, were supposedly intentionally restricting family size, as they knew they would not be able to provide for their families under the miserable conditions of post-WWI Germany.[23] It was for this reason that Germany needed new space with agricultural lands. Such were the lands

---

17   Adolf Grabowsky, *Staat und Raum: Grundlagen Räumlichen Denkens in der Weltpolitk*, Berlin: Zentralverlag, 1928.
18   Murphy, *The Heroic Earth*, 32.
19   The term was first introduced in Friedrich Ratzel, *Der Lebensraum. Eine biogeographische Studie*. München, 1901.
20   Holger H. Herwig, 'Geopolitik: Haushofer, Hitler and Lebensraum,' *Journal of Strategic Studies*, 22/2–3 (1999), 218–41, 226.
21   Friedrich Burgdörfer, *Volk ohne Jugend. Geburtenschwund und Überalterung des Deutschen Volkskörpers*, Berlin: Kurt Vowinkel, 1934.
22   Murphy, *The Heroic Earth*, 37.
23   Friedrich Burgdörfer, *Der Geburtenrückgang und Seine Bekämpfung. Die Lebensfrage des Deutschen Volkes*. Berlin: R. Schoetz, 1929, 46, 63, 102–3.

located in the East, primarily in the Baltics, where people of German descent had been cultivating them for centuries. These and similar assertions were intended to give legitimacy to the eventual expansion of German territory.

Furthermore, geopoliticians invoked the threat of de-Germanization of the already shrinking body of the German population. Burgdörfer referred to the example of the oppressed German minority in the East-Central European states and explained how their national identity was jeopardised as they were exposed to assimilation in a 'mixed people zone' (Völkermischzone).[24] He then concluded that '[o]nly an indigenous, procreative peasant population, tied to the soil, would be in the position to resist the pressures of excess Slavic population and successfully secure the German ethnic soil in the East.'[25]

Geopolitical theory is claimed to have become an intellectual underpinning for Nazi policies in the 1930s and during WWII. Historian Bruno Hipler described Karl Haushofer as Hitler's teacher, who during the 1920s through the mediation of his friend Rudolf Hess had largely formed Hitler's ideology.[26] In fact, Haushofer killed himself right after WWII, ending the suicide note with the words: 'I want to be forgotten and forgotten.'[27] He allegedly did this out of grief and remorse prompted by reflection on Nazi crimes.[28] Such a conclusion seems to be supported by a sonnet written by Haushofer's son, Albrecht Haushofer, who was executed by Nazis shortly before the end of WWII: 'My father broke the seal open/He did not see a touch of evil/Yet let the demon escape into the world.'[29]

As these lines suggest, Hitler found ideological background for his heinous crimes in Karl Haushofer's ideas without the latter ever intending to become an *éminence grise* of the Nazi atrocities. Murphy made a similar observation, stating that while geopolitics and originally geopolitical terms (notably: *Lebensraum*, *Raumforschung*, *Blut-und-Boden*, *Rasse-und-Mum* etc.) played an important role in the domestic propaganda of the 1930s, Nazis saw in geopolitics 'convenient ex post facto rationalizations for a course of policy developed independently of strict geopolitical considerations.'[30] Thus, as demonstrated in Murphy's study, it was particularly the Weimar period when

---

24 Burgdörfer, *Volk ohne Jugend*, 419, 423.
25 Burgdörfer, *Der Geburtenrückgang*, 160.
26 Bruno Hipler, *Hitlers Lehrmeister: Karl Haushofer als Vater der NS-Ideologie*. St. Ottilien: EOS Verlag, 1996, 7.
27 Colin S. Gray, Geoffrey Sloan (eds.), *Geopolitics, Geography and Strategy*. New York: Routledge, 2013, 237.
28 Murphy, *The Heroic Earth*, 241.
29 Cited in Hipler, *Hitlers Lehrmeister*, 18.
30 Murphy, *The Heroic Earth*, viii, xi.

revisionist geopolitical ideas had the most ideological significance.

Imperialism interrupted: *ex oriente lux* and pragmatic turn

After Germany's defeat in WWI and its consequent decline, many Germans were disappointed with their homeland and resentful towards the West. To make sense of their time, in search for a way out of their problems and to a better future they turned to the East.[31] Hermann Hesse, one of Germany's foremost authors of the 20th century (whose father happened to be a Baltic-German from Estonia) reflected on this phenomenon in his novel 'Journey to the East' (*'Die Morgenlandfahrt'*):

> [I]mmediately after the end of the World War – our country was full of saviours, prophets, and disciples, of presentiments about the end of the world, or hopes for the dawn of a Third Empire. Shattered by the war, in despair as a result of deprivation and hunger, greatly disillusioned by the seeming futility of all the sacrifices in blood and goods, our people at that time were lured by many phantoms (...).[32]

His narrator then embarked on the pilgrimage to the East in the quest for the ultimate truth. This Eastern mysticism (whether referring to the Far East, Russia or East-Central Europe) was a common motive in Weimar Germany's literature. However, it was not only the writers and disenchanted ordinary Germans who were mesmerised by the East. The Weimar Republic's Ostpolitik was one of the principal concerns of German foreign policy makers. They realised that if managed properly, relations with the newly independent states in the East might build a foundation for a brighter tomorrow. Thus, as another German writer summed it up, "*Ex oriente lux*' [Light from the East] was Germany's hope for the future.'[33]

Throughout history, German territorial borders were constantly changing from the pre-unification period to the boundaries of 1871, the suddenly expanded post-Brest-Litovsk Empire of spring and summer of 1918, and the humiliatingly reduced territory of the Weimar Republic. Not one of these states represented ethnic, linguistic, and cultural homogeneity.[34] Thus, the

---

31	John A. Williams (ed.), *Weimar Culture Revisited*. New York, N.Y.: Palgrave Macmillan, 2011, 133.
32	Hermann Hesse, *Die Morgenlandfahrt*. Berlin: Suhrkamp, 1933, 10.
33	Kurt Wolff, *Kurt Wolff: A Portrait in Essays and Letters*. Chicago, IL: the University of Chicago Press, 1991, 127.
34	Annemarie H. Sammartino, T*he Impossible Border: Germany and the East (1914–1922)*. Ithaca, NY: Cornell University Press, 2010, 5.

question as to 'what was German' posed a constant dilemma for German authorities as well as for the German people within and outside the perpetually changing borders.

Having lost the war and much of its territory, Germany faced national identity confusion and the need to redefine what was German. This dilemma – or rather how it was seen by the soldiers continuing to fight in the Baltics when the war was already over – is described in the excerpt from Ernst von Salomon's novel based on his own experience fighting in the German paramilitary units *Freikorps*:

> Where was Germany? Was it where the nation was? But the nation was screaming for food (...) Was it the State? But the State was busy searching for its constitutional form. (...) Germany was at its borders. The provisions of Versailles Peace Treaty told us where Germany was.

This excerpt illustrates the understanding of a *Freikorps* soldier as to what Germany was in 1919. The soldiers felt that the lands in the East where they were fighting were also German, but admitted with bitterness that it was ultimately the Peace Treaty that dictated where Germany was. Von Salomon wrote that they were German soldiers who were nominally not German soldiers and protecting German lands that were nominally not German lands.[35]

That being said, before the outbreak of WWI, the prevailing ideology in Germany was that of a nation-state, where state, nation, and territory coincide. The pan-Germans (a movement founded in 1891) were concerned that millions of Germans continued to live outside of the borders of the unified German Empire. They were especially interested in Germans residing in East-Central Europe, who were allegedly subject to growing assimilationist pressures in the expansive and dangerous Slavic territory.[36] On the eve of WWI, the increasingly popular nationalist (*völkisch*) right in the *Reich* was challenging the legitimacy of the German Empire because of its failure to include all of those who belonged to the German nation.

During the course of the war, discussions about Baltic annexation intensified in the German media and among the stakeholders from business, industry

---

35   Ernst von Salomon, *Freikorps: die Geächteten*. Salenstein, Schweiz: Unitall Verlag, 2011, 55.
36   Rogers Brubaker, *Citizenship and Nationhood in France and Germany*. Cambridge, MA: Harvard University Press, 1992, 116.

and academia. The Baltic Trust Council (*Die Baltische Vertrauensrat*), an organisation established in 1915 by Baltic-German émigrés, attempted to convince the German government about the benefits of incorporation of the Baltic lands into the *Reich*, and addressed the Reich's Chancellor with a memorandum, which read: 'We have only two alternatives – to be annexed by Germany or to be massacred by Russia.'[37]

Their prayers seemed to have been answered in March 1918 with the Treaty of Brest-Litovsk, by which Russia ceded the Baltics to Germany. Shortly after the Treaty had been signed, Gustav Stresemann declared in the *Reichstag* that only the union of the Baltic territories with the German Empire would secure Germany's Eastern border.[38] However, the Treaty was effectively terminated later that year as a result of Germany's capitulation to the Allied powers. The November Revolution and the collapse of the German *Kaiserreich* thwarted any further attempts to create German rule in the Baltics.[39] This urged the German government 'finally to throw overboard the policy of the conservative German-Baltic barons and to conduct a purely German policy in Latvia and Estonia, built on an honourable basis.'[40]

The most sensitive issue with regards to Lithuania was the situation with Memel (Klaipėda) territory. This territory, previously a part of the Kingdom of Prussia, pursuant to the Treaty of Versailles was to remain under the control of the League of Nations until a later date when the people of this region would vote on whether to return the land to Germany or not. Germany never ceased to consider the people in Memel as part of the German nation. In 1922, Stresemann urged Foreign Minister Hans von Rosenberg (1922–23) to not forget the Memel question and to persist claiming 'the right of self-determination for the Germans there who are at the mercy of international arrangements (…) for they were once politically united with us.'[41]

In 1923, disregarding the provisions of the Peace Treaty, Lithuania seized the Memel territory. Despite profound indignation over Lithuanian actions, the

---

37   Brubaker, *Citizenship and Nationhood*, 116.
38   Hans Erich Volkmann, *Die Deutsche Baltikumpolitik Zwischen Brest-Litovsk und Compiegne*. Cologne, Vienna: Bohlau Verlag, 1970, 122–3.
39   John Hiden, *The Baltic States and Weimar Ostpolitik*. Cambridge: Cambridge University Press, 1987.
40   Letter from 'Ostexport', an organ for goods exchange between Germany and East-Central Europe (22 April 1920), quoted in Karl Heinz Grundmann, *Deutschtumspolitik zur Zeit der Weimarer Republik: Eine Studie am Beispiel der deutsch-baltischen Minderheit in Estland und Lettland (Beiträge zur baltischen Geschichte)*. Hannover-Döhren: Verlag Harro v. Herschheydt, 1977, 245.
41   Stresemann, speech in the Reichstag, 25 November 1922, translated in Turner, *Essays and Speeches*, 148.

Weimar Republic was forced to maintain relatively soft policies concerning this issue. It had to eventually endorse Lithuanian actions, as it was motivated to have Lithuania on its side and thus prevent the isolation of East Prussia.[42] It should be mentioned, however, that in March 1939, Hitler rushed to recapture Klaipėda as the *Reich*'s last territorial acquisition before the outbreak of WWII. This was even before signing the infamous secret protocol of the Molotov-Ribbentrop Pact, as if the suppressed revisionist bitterness had been impatiently waiting for the right time to erupt.

As discussed above, Germans nearly unanimously opposed the new borders imposed at Versailles and many thought of the German minority abroad (*Auslandsdeutsche*) as a symbol of the German historical claim to territory in East-Central Europe. However, in the tense post-war environment, when Germany was under strict surveillance by the Allied powers, any indications of irredentist ambitions in German foreign policy would have been politically destructive. Needless to say, the demilitarised, impoverished and vanquished German state would have had little chance to actually enact such aspirations.

Instead, foreign policy makers started viewing the Baltic-German community as irreplaceable for the vital task of preserving and promoting German culture in the East, and strengthening the ties between the Baltics and the *Reich*. As historian John Hiden noted, 'The Baltic-Germans as a whole exemplified the model of a German minority which had enjoyed a long-standing and prominent economic role abroad and which might be expected to pick up the threads again after 1919.'[43] In other words, the German government was interested in pursuing its own pragmatic interests in the Baltic provinces while the interests of the Baltic-Germans, as such, were of secondary importance.[44]

In addition, Baltic-German refugees in the Weimar Republic formed a bridge to the 'German element' in the Baltic countries. Therefore, the German government was eager to support and protect the Baltic-German community on both sides of the border, primarily by funding the relevant minority organisations.[45] While the preference was given to economic rather than to cultural survival, the cultural support for the Baltic-Germans in the Baltics (e.g. schooling, subsidies to the German theatre, the school visits, visiting professors and student exchanges) was necessary to cement together the

---

42   Miroslav Klusek, *Gustav Stresemanns Osteuropa Politik in den Jahren 1923– 1929: unter besonder Berücksichtigung seines Verhältnisses zur USSR*. Berlin: Weidler, 2011, 103.
43   Hiden, *The Baltic States and Weimar Ostpolitik*, 44.
44   'Im Namen und Auftrage des Baltischen Nationalausschusses, 21 Juli 1919' // Bundesarchiv Lichterfelde (hereafter, BArch). R 8054–27 fol. 1, p. 15.
45   Grundmann, *Deutschtumspolitik*, 240, 297.

disparate elements of the Baltic-German community.[46]

Another factor that pressed Germany to pursue politics of understanding and cooperation with the Baltic States was the British interest in the region. Already in 1919, when the Bolsheviks retreated from the Baltics and the *Freikorps* turned against the Baltic people, British advisors arrived to train the Baltic forces to fight against the *Freikorps*, and the Entente increased its pressure on the German government to withdraw all support from the *Freikorps*.[47]

The German-Baltic National Committee (*Deutsch-Baltische Nationalausschuss*), an organisation founded in 1918 to represent the Baltic-German population in Latvia and to maintain ties with Germany, then declared that, even though there was a rumour in Germany that after the revolution the Baltic countries sought for British protection, no Baltic-German would ever think of such a thing.[48] The Committee insisted that this 'would be a betrayal of the future of the German nation to which the Balts would always belong physically and spiritually. It [was] the duty of every Balt to oppose such talks and such projects by all means with the greatest vigour and with ruthless candour.'[49]

However, despite such reassurances, Great Britain clearly had an interest in the newly independent Baltic States. In 1920, Dr. Rosenstock, a Baltic-German attorney residing in Latvia, wrote to the German Ministry of Foreign Affairs:

> It is well known that at the moment England is making its efforts to alienate the Baltic-Germans against the Reich in order to use them for the purposes of English politics. Efforts are being made to encourage the Baltic-Germans to return and they are being promised that pressure on the Baltic governments will be exerted, if the Baltic-Germans are willing to turn their backs to the Reich and to place themselves at the service of the English policy. (...) Thus, if Germany does not help the Baltic-Germans, it will inevitably drive them into the arms of England and the Baltic States.[50]

---

46   Hiden, *The Baltic States and Weimar Ostpolitik*, 47, 53.
47   Sammartino, *The Impossible Border*, 59.
48   At the time, the Baltic-Germans referred to themselves as 'Balts', as they considered themselves the true Baltic people.
49   'An unsere baltischen Landsleute in der Heimat' // BArch. R 8054–27, fol. 1, p. 11.
50   Letter from Dr. Rosenstock, Kodlin to the Reich's foreign ministry // BArch.

Dr. Rosenstock further reminded that the Baltic-Germans, who had been the pioneers of the German culture in the Baltics for 700 years, 'can only count on Germany to help them preserve the acquired rights (*Besitzstand*) in the Baltic provinces.' He then advised that helping them was in the interest of Germany, as the newly independent Baltic States would form an economic bridge to Russia. Germany thus 'must pursue a farsighted policy aimed at preserving the German element in the Baltic provinces, which is an absolute economic necessity.'[51] Heinrich von Baer, a Baltic-German from Estonia, provided similar observations: 'England sought, above all, to destroy any German influence in the Baltic provinces, without at the same time allowing the advance of the Russians.'[52]

The German government's pursuit of policies of understanding and cooperation was, however, at odds with the interests of increasingly active conservatives in the *Reich*. Historian Henry L. Bretton accurately described this clash of interests:

> By force of necessity, German foreign policy had to be peaceful, bare of all reference to the use of arms. On the other hand, the peace settlement had created enough dissatisfaction among the German masses to render a rational and moderate foreign policy highly impractical from the point of view of domestic politics.[53]

Domestic nationalists were not prepared to accept rapprochement with the Western powers. This resulted in growing alienation between Gustav Stresemann and his adherents on the one hand and the bourgeois nationalist circles on the other.[54] Thus, the policy makers in Weimar Germany found themselves in a difficult position between a rock and a hard place. They had to measure up to the demands of the Allied Powers, while at the same time avoiding the alienation of nationalists in Germany. Stresemann's leadership was remarkable, not least because he managed to skilfully balance between the two extremes.

R901/80982, fol.1, 62, 64.
51 Letter from Dr. Rosenstock, Kodlin to the Reich's foreign ministry // BArch. R901/80982, fol.1, 62.
52 Heinrich von Baer, *Mein Erlebnis der Brüderlichkeit: Aufzeichnungen aus dem Jahre 1979*. Norderstedt: Books on Demand, 2012, 23.
53 Henry L. Bretton, *Stresemann and the Revision of Versailles: a Fight for Reason*. Stanford: Stanford University Press, 1953.
54 Bastiaan Schot, *Stresemann, Der Deutsche Osten und der Völkerverbund*. Stuttgart: Franz Steiner Verlag Wiesbaden, 1984, 5.

Continuity, change and national minorities in Stresemann's political discourse

Henry L. Bretton summarised Stresemann's political struggle and success as follows: 'His unusual political acumen was combined with a mental agility and flexibility that enabled him to represent one political extreme and the other without any detriment to his career. His international attitude developed from one of revengefulness and chauvinism to one of enthusiastic, intense internationalism.'[55]

Bretton further commended Stresemann for proving over the course of his political career that 'a militarily weak and defeated nation could arise from under a severe peace settlement without resorting to armed force.' He noted, that '[i]f Stresemann appeared to be belligerent at times, it was primarily because it was necessary to appease the extremists at home.'[56] Indeed, while constantly emphasising the lack of irredentist or revisionist motives behind his foreign policies in order to reassure suspicious Allied powers, Stresemann would also make sure that he did not appear feeble in the eyes of the nationalists at home.

Thus, the foreign policy leader constantly manoeuvred between satisfying the Western powers and the German nationalists. Even though one might say that actions speak louder than words, it was to a large extent through language that Stresemann achieved his success. In 1923, when speaking in the *Reichstag* he himself addressed the criticism about allegedly too much talk and too little action:

> A distinction is often drawn nowadays between speech and action by certain people (...) But what do they mean by action in the present state of international affairs? (...) Action as regards foreign nations can assume various forms. It can take the form of parliamentary and diplomatic 'feelers,' of speeches in parliament, of notes and proposals. The choice of methods must depend upon circumstances.[57]

Under the circumstances of the time, when Germany was severely restricted in its capabilities and had to 'give proof of its goodwill' to the international community, language became Stresemann's main means of pursuing foreign

---

55   Bretton, *Stresemann and the Revision of Versailles*, the inside cover.
56   Bretton, *Stresemann and the Revision of Versailles*, the inside cover, 54.
57   Stresemann, speech in the Reichstag, 17 April 1923, in: *Essays and Speeches*, 150.

policy goals.[58] More specifically, it was a multi-layered political discourse that underlay Stresemann's speeches and policy documents. Professor of International Relations Ole Waever suggested the idea that 'discourse forms a system which is made up of a layered constellation of key concepts.' When the change happens in political discourse (and accordingly in policies), it is likely that this change only occurs on the superficial level, whilst the deepest discursive level remains unaltered. Thus, Waever's main point is that a change in discourse is not the same as the change of discourse: 'Change is not an either/or question, because we are not operating at one level only.'[59]

Following Waever's model, three layers (or levels) can be indicated in political discourse that appears in Stresemann's speeches and texts. The first and deepest level is the imperialistic Great Power discourse. At this level, Germany is positioned vis-à-vis the world – as the 'handicapped' Great Power state, entitled to revise the 'unjust' consequences of WWI. The second level of discourse reveals the basic conceptual relation between the nation and the state. The crucial question here is who are defined as national minorities abroad and what is their relation to the kin-state. The third level addresses specifically the role of national minorities abroad in Germany's foreign policy. Such a role was largely dependent on what national interests were prioritised at the time.

This study suggests that the 'pragmatic turn' in Weimar Germany's political discourse towards the Baltic States and the Baltic-Germans in the early 1920s took place particularly at the third level. Meanwhile, the imperialistic Great Power discourse with its revisionist claims persisted at the deepest level. The dynamics at the second level were arguably the most interesting ones. The relation between the nationals abroad and the German state had to be redefined in such a way that allowed for change at the surface level to occur and for the revisionist discourse at the deepest level to continue. At the middle level, the discourse was largely related to minorities, both abroad and within the German *Reich*, and to their conceptual relation to the kin-state.

Stresemann realised early on that Germany had to re-establish itself in the international arena as a peaceful Great Power and erase the image of a menacing belligerent state. He declared in the *Reichstag* in 1921: 'Let us make no mistake – we have got to change the hearts of those who were responsible for the Treaty of Versailles. Unless we succeed in doing so we shall never be able to recover our political and economic independence.'[60] A

---

58 Stresemann speech in the Reichstag, 6 October 1923, in: *Essays and Speeches*, 171.
59 Waever, 'Identity, communities and foreign policy', 29, 31.
60 *Essays and Speeches*, 127.

few years later, he was still explaining that it was 'essential that [one] should act with the utmost caution in the present situation,' when a voice from the public reproached: 'too much caution.' The foreign minister then replied persistently: 'we shall not make any progress unless we show caution.'[61]

Similarly, Stresemann noted in the DVP convention: 'Our liberty in foreign politics has hitherto been severely circumscribed and is likely for some time to remain so. We are finding out how hard it is for a defenceless nation to carry on a foreign policy.'[62] He tried to show sympathy and understanding in order to appease the dissatisfaction of nationalist party members who were impatient to remedy Germany's position (in which Germany, as they saw it, had been put in unfairly by the Allies), and perceived Stresemann's strategy as not assertive enough.

Moreover, Stresemann encouraged to find unity not only among members of his own party, but also among different parties, regardless of any political disagreements. In fact, he considered that only in unity can a defeated state re-establish itself as a Great Power: 'There is another weapon at the disposal of a Foreign Minister of a defenceless State. I am referring to that national unanimity which transcends party differences and enables him when the time comes to reject impossible terms.'[63] On a different occasion, Stresemann declared: 'Party strife was never less undesirable than at a time like the present, when the enemy is at our gates. Never before has such a call come to us to rise superior to party strife and devote all our efforts to the preservation of our nation and our fatherland.'[64]

In the early years of Germany's first parliamentary democracy, which conservatives perceived as a humiliating concession made on the ruins of the empire, friction and disagreements between different political parties were inevitable. However, the unity that Stresemann was talking about existed at the deeper level of Great Power discourse. Bastiaan Schot concluded in his study that all German political parties – from the communist left to the extreme nationalist right – were at least in agreement that the Treaty of Versailles had to be revised with all available means.[65] This illustrates exactly the thought of Ole Waever, who stated in his layered discourse theory that even if a certain position is perceived as in 'opposition' or 'marginalised' 'it means only that it is "outside" and "different" at the level of manifest politics,

---

61 *Essays and Speeches*, 176.
62 *Essays and Speeches*, 210.
63 *Essays and Speeches*, 191.
64 *Essays and Speeches*, 148.
65 Schot, Stresemann, *Der Deutsche Osten*, 27.

most likely it shares codes at the next (deeper) level of abstraction.'[66]

Thus, even Stresemann, who took a 'more circuitous but more peaceful approach through an understanding with the West,' had never relinquished revisionist claims concerning the territories in the East.[67] In his speeches, he was emphasising different points depending on whether he was speaking in Berlin or in an international forum. When addessing the German community, Stresemann would never discard the future prospect of the extension of German territory. For instance, in his speech in the *Reichstag* in the spring of 1925 he stated:

> Germany does not have the power to force through an alteration of her frontiers nor does she have the desire to do so. Since Article 19 of the Covenant of the League of Nations, however, states expressly that treaties which have become inapplicable can be altered, no one can expect Germany to renounce, for all time, her right to take peaceful advantage of this principle and to reopen the question at some future date.[68]

Stresemann used a slightly different rhetoric when campaigning in the League of Nations for the right of national minorities to national and cultural self-determination. There he would always point out that this principle was not meant to become a tool for territorial revisionism, but rather it was aimed primarily at the liberation of minority nations from the domination of their states. Furthermore, he would usually speak in an abstract, neutral and almost academic manner. He carefully omitted references to the situation of minorities in the individual states. Even if the implications were meant for particular states, such as the Baltics, Stresemann limited his statements to the general theoretical principles that, in his opinion, should be respected by the member-states of the League of Nations.[69]

The question of national minorities and the League's Covenant were closely related to one another. Germany joined the League of Nations precisely to secure a position enabling it to pursue minority policy. In fact, this was the only way for a disarmed and weak Weimar Republic to lead effective minority policy and to potentially extend its influence beyond the borders. As Bretton put it, '[i]f Germany's role was to be that of a guardian over the minorities (...), the League and its machinery could achieve what only strong armies could

---

66 Waever, 'Identity, communities and foreign policy', 31.
67 Bretton, *Stresemann and the Revision of Versailles*, 125.
68 *Kolnische Zeitung*, 13 March 1925, no. 190.
69 Schot, *Stresemann, Der Deutsche Osten*, 48–9, 60.

otherwise have accomplished.'⁷⁰ Stresemann even managed to convince the sceptical nationalists at home about the benefits of Germany's membership in the League by assuring them that the League would provide Germany with a platform to control German minorities abroad from Berlin.

Admittedly, there was also external pressure for Germany to join the League. The international pressure increased particularly after signing the Dawes Agreement in August 1924. American creditors hinted in loan negotiations with the German banks that they saw Germany's early entry into the League of Nations as the best guarantee for Germany's stable development.[71] However, when entering the League, in order to appease domestic conservatives and to demonstrate that the Reich would not give up important national interests, Stresemann made the entry of Germany contingent on certain conditions, including the permanent seat on the League's Council and obtaining the same privileges within the League as other Great Power states.

Furthermore, the foreign minister made it seem in his speeches that membership in the League of Nations would not constrain Germany any further. Quite the opposite: it would allow for influencing the nationals beyond its borders without raising a suspicion of the Allies. This is evident in Stresemann's speech delivered on 9 February 1926, about a half-year before Germany officially entered the League:

> The frontiers of Europe were altered by the peace treaties of 1919. Millions of German citizens have been brought under foreign supremacy, a proceeding that was utterly inconsistent with the idea of the right of self-determination of the nations, the principle, which was so proudly proclaimed during the war. We have recognised the situation created by these treaties and have surpassed every other nation on earth in fulfilling the conditions imposed upon us by an inhuman peace. But the right of the German people to feel for and sympathise with their own kith and kin who inhabit another State is an indisputable right of which no one can deprive us.[72]

One of the principal goals was to keep the German element in the Eastern territories intact by ensuring there would be no absorption or assimilation of the minorities by the titular nations. While open irredentism was out of the question for Germany at the time, it seemed to have been merely delayed until a more convenient time in future, when Germany re-established itself as

---

70   Schot, *Stresemann, Der Deutsche Osten*, 127.
71   Schot, *Nation oder Staat?*, 140.
72   *Essays and Speeches*, 256.

a Great Power. Stresemann claimed that eventual territorial revision was a perfectly legitimate consideration: '[f]rankly, I do not think that we have in the present century established a state of affairs which is eternal and that idea is very clearly expressed in the Covenant of the League of Nations.'[73]

It was precisely the plan to use the League of Nations as a framework for demonstrating Germany's interest in the destiny of the kin-minorities, without giving an impression that this could endanger territorial sovereignty of East Central European states. Still, some scholars alleged that Stresemann's minority policy was a concealed revisionism. The memorandum of 12 January 1925 raised much debate on this issue. It stated that '[t]he creation of a state, whose political boundaries include all of the German people, who live within the borders of the areas of Central Europe settled by Germans and wish the union with the *Reich*, is the distant goal of German hopes.'[74] Historian Fritz Fischer referred to this memorandum as the evidence for his thesis that the minority policy of Stresemann provided a link between pan-German and Nazi expansionism. To an extent this is true – the Great Power imperialism as reflected at the deepest level of Stresemann's political discourse was indeed characteristic of all three German *Reichs*. However, Weimar imperialism was much more obscure and virtually non-existent at the most visible surface level of political discourse.

That being said, Stresemann's imperialism revealed itself at the second level of discourse, when he advocated for a unique relation between the nation and the state. This relationship would take the form of *Personenverbandsstaat* – a concept, revived from medieval and early-modern times, which can be roughly translated as an 'association of people.' It essentially defines a polity centred on individuals and the relations between them. In the original sense, it meant relationships between the rulers and the nobility. Stresemann redefined the concept as one that could be juxtaposed with the concept of the modern territorial state. *Personenverbandsstaat* thus lacked the coincidence between sovereignty and territory that was the foundation of the modern state.[75]

One of the crucial aspects of *Personenverbandsstaat* was the recognition that every national minority had a right to cultural freedom, which could only be protected, if this minority constituted a self-governing body. As a result, the principal feature of German minority politics in the League was advocating for the principle that national minorities should have cultural autonomy in their

---

73 League of Nations, *Official Journal*, Council, X (April 1929), 520–2.
74 Stresemann, Memorandum from 13 January 1925, cited in Schot, *Stresemann, Der Deutsche Osten*, 6.
75 Schot, *Stresemann, Der Deutsche Osten*, 9.

host-states. This *inter alia* implied the right to establish intensive connections with the government of their kin-state, without being accused of disloyalty to the host-state. Stresemann argued that such relationships, transcending the borders of one state, 'cannot be regarded as an inadmissible political interference with the domestic affairs of a foreign power.'[76]

The promotion of *Personenverbandsstaat* had repercussions in Germany's domestic policies. Cultural autonomy had to be introduced for national minorities within the Reich as well. Stresemann's memorandum of 12 January 1925 is sometimes called the birth certificate of the minority policy of the Weimar Republic. In the memorandum, he stated that the German Reich had to show to the whole world that every nation had the inherent right to cultural self-preservation, and that such an argument would lose its credibility if the *Reich* itself denied such rights to national minorities within its own jurisdiction.[77] This was problematic given the autonomy of German local governments.

Nevertheless, *Personenverbandsstaat* was arguably the only way to ensure that German minorities in East-Central European countries would receive almost complete equality with the Germans of the *Reich* and gain legitimate access to Germany's financial resources. Stresemann's commitment to minorities in the League of Nations was accompanied by financial support for the Germans abroad. This included loans, legal aid and subsidies for the organisations of Germans in East Central Europe.[78] As John Hiden noted, such financial aid to German minorities living abroad was considered an aid to, not a substitute for, self-help. That is, German minorities were expected to eventually support themselves through their participation in the economic lives of their host-countries, which would in turn help the German government build economic bridges to the new states.[79]

Hiden further explained that the German government accepted the drastic change in the position of the Baltic-Germans and developed a policy which was 'cautious, tactical and yet consciously directed towards long-term aims which were clarified largely in the general context of the problem of all *Auslandsdeutschen*.'[80] Since Stresemann avoided talking about minorities in specific countries to prevent suspicions of revisionist motives, there is barely

---

76   Bretton, *Stresemann and the Revision of Versailles*, 133.
77   *Essays and Speeches*, 146.
78   Georg Arnold, *Gustav Stresemann und die Problematik der Deutschen Ostgrenzen*. Frankfurt/M: Peter Lang, 2000, 118.
79   John Hiden, *German Policy Towards the Baltic States of Estonia and Latvia 1920–1926*. London SSEES, 1970, 75.
80   Hiden, *German Policy*, 48.

any mention in his speeches of the Baltic-Germans specifically. However, the Baltic case presents a unique example that evidences the dynamics of policies, which were justified and constructed through Stresemann's political discourse on national minorities.

The Baltic-Germans, exiled from what used to be their homelands since the Middle Ages, were outcasts in the post-war Germany. Von Salomon wrote in his novel: 'Germany was defeated, [they] could not return home either (....), [they] were homeland-less and ill.'[81] To remedy the feeling of 'homeland-lessness' (*Heimatslosigkeit*), the Baltic-Germans gathered into various organisations in Germany and continued to be interested in the future of the Baltic States, their fellow Baltic-Germans who remained there and generally – in the fate of the Baltic-Germandom. It is estimated that in the time period from 1919 to 1939 there were thousands of the Baltic Germans within Germany that belonged to multiple Baltic-German minority organisations.[82]

One example was the Baltic Trust Council (*Die Baltische Vertrauensrat*), which was established already in 1915 in Berlin. It was a successor organisation to the Association of the Balts (*Die Vereinigung der Balten*) that had existed since 1908. The Council was significantly funded by grants from the German Ministry of the Interior. To ensure the smooth functioning of aid, the competent *Reich* authorities – especially the Foreign Office and the Ministry of the Interior – transferred various tasks related to nationals abroad to the Council as well as to other similar organisations. Because of their private character, they were able to work in the 'border-states' without major obstacles.[83] Since these organisations were financed from the *Reich*'s budget, it meant that their activities had been recognised by the *Reich* and had to remain in compliance with the *Reich*'s policies.[84]

All in all, the concern with national minorities abroad was one of Stresemann's foreign policy priorities. The other two objectives, the reunion of Austria and Germany and the revision of Germany's eastern boundaries, depended upon the successful campaign for control of the minorities.[85] In March 1929, shortly before he died, Stresemann wrote to his friend, emphasising the importance of minority policies in his political career: 'I feel that I am obliged to remain in office until the last issue of the minority question

---

81   Salomon, *Freikorps*, 340.
82   Carla Siegert, 'Deutschbalten in Deutschland in der Zwischenkriegszeit. Versuch einer politischen Einordnung,' *Nordost-Archiv*, Band V: 1996, H. 2, 325.
83   Grundmann, *Deutschtumspolitik*, 336.
84   Reich's office for emigration (Berlin 30 August 1928), BArch, R 8054/30 fol. 1, p.4.
85   Bretton, *Stresemann and the Revision of Versailles*, 126.

has been addressed. I would consider myself a deserter, if I abandoned the issue, which I have started fighting for before the world.'[86]

The promotion of minority rights served both long-term and short-term Germany's interests. The minority discourse and policies were congruent with Germany's urgent need to resume economic relations in the East, and they facilitated the diplomatic manoeuvring between German nationalists and the Allied powers. In the long-run, German minorities abroad had the potential to facilitate the path to eventual territorial revision. As this study suggests, minority discourse was intertwined with the discourse of the relation between the state and the nation. This discourse operated between two other discursive layers: the surface discourse of specific minority policies and the deep-level discourse on Germany's Great Power role in the world that implied revisionist ambitions. It allowed for the imperialistic discourse to continue while pragmatic change was taking place at the level of specific policies.

Conclusion

Post-WWI Germany had to accept the implications of its defeat and war-guilt and was 'handicapped' by the victors. As a consequence, it was impelled to swiftly rearrange its national priorities: imperialistic ambitions had to give way to economic necessities. Having declared independence, the Baltic States not only slipped away from the German sphere of influence, but they also deprived the Baltic-Germans of their previous ruling status and effectively forced most of them to flee. However, the German government was not in the position to challenge that and compromise its relations with the Baltics. Instead, it had to seize the opportunity to build economic bridges to the Baltic States. To that end, it developed prudent political discourse and constructed policies of understanding and cooperation.

Nevertheless, regardless of this cardinal change and adjustment, some authors have alleged that imperialism never ceased to exist in the Weimar Republic. Indeed, revisionist ideas flourished among the German people, academics and politicians. There were also occasional revisionist references – sometimes obscure and sometimes manifest – in Gustav Stresemann's speeches and policy documents. This shows that perceiving German political discourse towards the Baltic States in the early 1920s as either reflecting a change or a concealed continuity of imperialism is an oversimplified approach. This political discourse was multi-layered: at the most visible surface level it presented a pragmatic change, while at the deepest level imperialistic Great Power discourse continued from the Wilhelmine *Reich* into the Third Reich.

---

86   Letter from Stresemann to Kahl (13 March 1929), *Vermächtnis*, III, 438.

There was also a discursive middle layer operating between the two. At this level, foreign policy makers reconsidered the relationship between the state and the nation, giving the utmost importance to the question of belonging of the national minorities abroad. The League of Nations offered Stresemann a forum for minority discourse. The League also enabled the transformation a specific German interest into a matter of international concern. The German foreign policy leader was able to campaign for general minority rights within the capacity entrusted by the League, this way ensuring that no one was able to accuse him of a secret revisionist agenda. At the same time, Germany was empowered to spread its influence beyond the borders and overcome its 'handicap.' In such a way, German foreign policy makers managed to both develop pragmatic and internationally accepted policies towards the Baltics, and appease nationalists at home by giving them hope for the future.

8

Herbert C. Hoover and Poland, 1929–1933: Between Myth and Reality

HALINA PARAFIANOWICZ

In Europe, and particularly in East-Central Europe, Herbert C. Hoover was one of the best-known American politicians after World War I. The son of an Quaker blacksmith, Hoover was educated at the newly established Stanford University and became a successful engineer and expert in mining and a wealthy businessman. He was a man of immense success, an incarnation of the American Dream – an incredible life and career 'from rags to riches.'

As the Director of the American Relief Administration (ARA) and assistant to President Woodrow Wilson, he played an important role during and after the Paris Peace Conference. His successes and great popularity as a public servant pushed him directly towards a rapid and enduring political career. He became the Secretary of Commerce in the Republican administrations of Warren G. Harding (1921–23) and Calvin Coolidge (1923–29). The years of American prosperity in the 1920s, when he had been a successful Cabinet member elevated him to the White House after the victory in the presidential election in 1928.

After such a remarkable career and electoral victory, he entered the presidency as an eminent personality of American life and one of the best-educated American presidents, familiar with economic, financial and political problems and knowledgeable of world affairs. It is paradox and irony indeed that such a great and amazingly swift career was challenged during his presidency and that Hoover's image rapidly reversed. After the Great Depression, his positive, legendary image immediately crumbled and soon disappeared. Instead, a new one emerged – a leader unsuccessful in dealing with economic disaster, heavily criticized, unpopular and then defeated by a rival, Franklin D. Roosevelt.

In practice, Hoover functioned as two different and opposite myths – the earlier one: the legendary hero, cherished and acclaimed (the so-called 'white myth') and, later on, as an unsuccessful, do-nothing 'Depression president' (the 'black myth'). The latter image was fostered in the years to come by his successor and opponents – mostly Democrats, and millions of disappointed countrymen.

Over decades, Herbert Hoover was also generally criticized by most historians for his domestic policy in particular. His foreign policy was not of a special interest to scholars.[1] Certainly, in his biographies and books on the presidency, there are parts dealing with his foreign policy.[2] Some of his diplomatic achievements, such as the good neighbour policy, non-recognition doctrine during the Manchurian crisis and pacifism received more attention and some recognition as well.[3] Moreover, there are a few interesting and useful historical books that illustrate and explain – to a certain extent – Hoover's approach towards Poland.[4] Nonetheless, in the whole writing on Hoover's presidency in English, it is difficult to find more substantial and deeper insight into his policy towards Poland.

The purpose of this chapter is to provide an outlook on Herbert C. Hoover's

---

[1] There are just a few books devoted to the subject which had been published a several decades ago: William Starr Myers, *The Foreign Policies of Herbert Hoover, 1929-1933.* New York: C. Scribner's Sons, 1940; Robert H. Ferrell, *American Diplomacy in the Great Depression. Hoover – Stimson Foreign Policy, 1929–1933.* New Haven: Yale University Press, 1957.

[2] The most useful are: Edgar Eugene Robinson, and Vaughn David Bornet, *Herbert Hoover, President of the United States.* Stanford: Hoover Institution Press, 1975; Joan Hoff Wilson, *Herbert Hoover, Forgotten Progressive.* Boston: Little, Brown, 1975; David Burner, *Herbert Hoover, a Public Life*, New York: Knopf, 1979; George H. Nash, *Life of Herbert Hoover.* New York, 1983; Richard Norton Smith, *An Uncommon Man: The Triumph of Herbert Hoover.* New York: Simon & Schuster, 1984; Glen Jeansonne, *The Life of Herbert Hoover: Fighting Quaker, 1928–1933.* New York: Palgrave Macmillan, 2012.

[3] Alexander DeConde, *Herbert Hoover's Latin-American Policy.* Stanford: Stanford University Press, 1951; Earl R. Curry, *Hoover's Dominican Policy and the Origins of the Good Neighbor Policy.* New York: Garland Publ. 1979.

[4] Let me mention the most useful, such as: Neal Pease, *Poland, The United States, and the Stabilization of Europe, 1919-1933.* New York – Oxford: Oxford University Press 1986; Piotr S. Wandycz, *The United States and Poland.* Cambridge: Harvard University Press, 1980; *Herbert Hoover and Poland. A Documentary History of a Friendship*, compiled and with an introduction by George J. Lerski, Stanford: Hoover Institution Press 1977.

policy towards Poland during his presidency. This study is based on my own, extensive research on President Hoover and his activities.[5] My intention is to demonstrate the US approach towards Poland and Polish matters during Hoover's presidency in the context of East-Central European policy. The chapter hopefully casts some new light on the matter – especially as the chapter is based on important, yet rarely used Polish and American archival sources, newspapers and the most useful literature on the subject.

A humanitarian and his legend

It is impossible to present Hoover's policy towards Poland during his presidency without a brief comment on his previous years of public activities as the director of the American Relief Administration (ARA) and Secretary of Commerce in the 1920s. His name was better known in Europe and associated with his humanitarian activities during and after the World War I.

The ARA, directed by Hoover, was an important element of US policy in relation to post-war Europe. As an agency of help and reconstruction of the 'Old World', it distributed food, clothing and medical aid to the countries which had suffered the most during and after WWI. Formally, the ARA started its operation on 24 February 1919, after its approval and assignation by the US Congress of $100 million for its activities. Its first, still informal then, agencies appeared in Europe as early as the fall of 1918. The agency functioned until 30 June 1919 and covered more than 20 countries, mainly European, with its activities. Then, as a private organisation, it helped numerous states, including Soviet Russia. It is worth remembering that among the humanitarian personnel there were many women, Quakers and dedicated pacifists with a great passion to 'improve the world.'[6]

The ARA has always been a source of controversy and interpretation arguments. Apart from its charitable motives, which have never been questioned, its ideological and economic causes have been discerned from

---

5   For more see, my two books in Polish on the subject – *Polska w europejskiej polityce Stanów Zjednoczonych w okresie prezydentury Herberta C. Hoovera (1929–1933)*. Białystok: Dział Wydawnictw Filii Uniwersytetu Warszawskiego w Białymstoku, 1991 and *Zapomniany prezydent. Biografia polityczna Herberta Clarka Hoovera*. Białystok: Versus, 1993.
6   There is abundant literature on the ARA and Hoover's role in it. For more on its activities in Poland see, Alvin B. Barber, *European Technical Advisers Mission to Poland, 1919–1922*. New York (unknown publisher) 1923; Harold H. Fisher, *America and the New Poland*. New York: Macmillan, 1928; Hugh S. Gibson and Samuel Vauclain, *Poland, Her Problems and Her Future*. New York: American Polish Chamber of Commerce and Industry, 1920.

its expanded activities. The ARA was described as an attempt to find new outlets for American overproduction or as a tool to stop spreading communism. The organization had its devoted supporters as well as fierce adversaries, depreciating its role and the effectiveness of its activities on both sides of the Atlantic. Back then, Hoover was an extremely powerful persona, a 'dictator of food' and a sort of legendary 'superman,' especially in heavily devastated Central Europe which was desperately in need of food and various products for rehabilitation and economic reconstruction. As one of Hoover's collaborators and friends remarked later:

> Mr. Hoover at once went abroad with two points of view in mind. One was to find a market for the American producer and the other was to see that Bolshevism did not spread through Europe because of starvation (...). The activities of ARA and the American uniform became the symbol of reconstruction in Europe (...). In broad lines as we can say that our country under Mr. Hoover's guidance came to the rescue of the disorganized and tarnished peoples who had been crushed by Germany in the war and brought to them not only food, but hope.[7]

Sending aid and technical advisers, Hoover played quite an active role in shaping up certain American decisions on several Polish issues. His friendly activities in the newly reborn Poland, his close contact to Ignacy Jan Paderewski, then Prime Minister of Poland, and the involvement of Americans in the reconstruction of the economic and political life of the country are worth noticing.[8]

In mid-August 1919, during his summer journey in Central Europe, Hoover visited Poland. It was a semi-official visit to recognize the condition of the country and identify its needs ('instead' of President Woodrow Wilson, as it was portrayed in media). In Poland, Hoover stayed between 12 and 19 August 1919, visiting Warsaw, Lvov and Cracow and talking to Polish officials.[9] Hugh S. Gibson, the first US minister in Poland and close, lifelong

---

7   'Herbert Hoover – A Personal Sketch' by Ray Lyman Wilbur, 1938 // Herbert Hoover Presidential Library (hereafter, HPL), Herbert Hoover Papers (HHP), Box 261. West Branch, USA.
8   Paderewski was one of the most effective proponents and champions of the closer association and assistance with America what played a visible and vital role especially during his prime-ministership. For more, see Bogusław Winid, *W cieniu Kapitolu. Dyplomacja polska wobec Stanów Zjednoczonych Ameryki, 1919–1939*. Warszawa: Wydawnictwo PoMOST, 1991.
9   Herbert Hoover, *The Memoirs, v. I, Years of Adventure 1874–1920*. New York: The Macmillan Company, 1951, 355–62.

friend of Hoover, attended many of the meetings focusing mostly on Polish economic needs and getting more American aid, mostly distributed by the ARA. Hoover talked to the Poles about programs for the economic and financial reconstruction of the country and the prospects of future assistance from the United States.[10]

In the years to come, Hoover – as the 'benefactor' who saved millions of Europeans from starvation – was admired and almost worshiped by millions of Poles and other East-Central Europeans as well as by Belgians and Finns. He symbolised and personified the best of America – its idealism, humanity and charity – and he seized the opportunity of a prosperous, abundant and wealthy country which shared ideals and wealth with needy Europeans. Hoover's life itself was an excellent instance of a 'rags to riches' career, a powerful and eminent feature of the 'American dream.'

As marks of respect and gratefulness, in Warsaw there was Hoover Square in Krakowskie Przedmieście Street; and on 29 October 1922, the Monument of the Gratitude for America, the work of a famed sculptor, Xavery Dunikowski, was unveiled. The Polish dignitaries and diplomatic corps were joined by the crowd of thousands of schoolchildren and all those who gathered to demonstrate their gratitude to Hoover.[11]

The popularization of Hoover's food missions was facilitated by the economic and political weakness of Poland, as well as the fascination with the overseas republic and everything American. It was manifested by letters of congratulations and gratitude to him and his collaborators from the ARA, honorary titles, medals, etc. The humanitarian aid to millions of children, mothers, orphans, and the sick established the closest, most positive and emotional link between the US and Poland. Hoover, along with President Woodrow Wilson, became a popular American hero, recognized and cherished in Poland. He was awarded honorary degrees at three Polish universities and citizenship in several Polish cities and the Polish Republic.[12] Undoubtedly, a large group of Poles held a certain dose of friendliness and appreciation to him, and America in general, for the humanitarian aid.

However, it seems that sometimes the extensive popularization of the benevolent activities of the ARA and Hoover himself were motivated by

---

10 Parafianowicz, *Zapomniany prezydent*, 58–59.
11 For more see, Halina Parafianowicz, 'The Legend of Herbert C. Hoover in Poland in the Period between the Two World Wars', in: *In the European Grain. American Studies From Central and Eastern Europe*, ed. by Orm Øverland, 159–68, Amsterdam: VU University Press, 1990.
12 Halina Parafianowicz, *Zapomniany prezydent*, 59–60.

tactical reasons and hopes of gaining American help in solving Polish complications. The sometimes naïve, subservient or obsequious tone of certain writings proves the low level of professional journalism of the time.

In 1926, several initiatives to celebrate the 150th anniversary of US independence were undertaken in Poland. A special book dedicated to the United States was published.[13] The extraordinary gift of 111 volumes of a beautifully ornamented album with a declaration of admiration to America signed by approximately 5,500,000 Polish citizens was presented to President Calvin Coolidge on 14 October 1926 at the White House as a token of gratitude. Hoover, as the Director of the ARA and member of the government, was the one to whom the thankfulness of the Poles was addressed personally.[14]

'Economic wizard' in the Department of Commerce

As the head of the Department of Commerce, Hoover efficiently promoted not only American products and commercial expansion, but also its values and the superiority of its political and economic system. In the 1920s, he practically implemented his major foreign policy ideas and became extremely effective and influential in policy-making ('economic wizard'). Obviously, the success of US food, money and technical know-how, as well as Hollywood cinema which was very popular in Europe, propagated the rich and prosperous country and cultivated American prestige, especially in East-Central Europe. In the early 1920s, the agents of the Department of Commerce were successfully selling a large amount of American products abroad.[15]

Certainly, numerous people in Poland, as well as in East-Central Europe, were fascinated by the United States's economic, political, ideological and industrial power. Exhausted by the war, disillusioned with their own societies,

---

13   Dzwon Wolności, *1775–1926. W rocznicę narodzin Stanów Zjednoczonych Ameryki. Księga zbiorowa wydana staraniem Komitetu Centralnego Obchodu 150-lecia Niepodległości Stanów Zjednoczonych*. Warszawa 1926.
14   '10 lat aktywności Towarzystwa Polsko Amerykańskiego' // Archiwum Akt Nowych (hereafter, AAN), Ambasada RP w Waszyngtonie, 596. Warsaw, Poland.
15   See, William Barber J., *From New Era to New Deal: Herbert Hoover, the Economists, and American Economic Policy, 1921–1933*. New York: Cambridge University Press,1985; Joseph Brandes, *Herbert Hoover and Economic Diplomacy: Department of Commerce Policy, 1921–1928*. Pittsburgh: University of Pittsburgh Press, 1962; Ethan Lewis Ellis, *Republican Foreign Policy:1921–1933*, New Brunswick: Rutgers University Press, 1965; *Herbert Hoover as Secretary of Commerce*, edited with introduction by Ellis W. Hawley, Iowa City: University of Iowa Press, 1981.

Europeans considered whether they should adopt the efficient ways of the prosperous Americans (e.g. the Ford system). Not only were American products needed in Poland, they were also greatly expected and desired; the trademark 'made in America' became a synonym of high quality products, a benchmark.[16]

The development of Polish-American relations in the early 1920s raised hopes and expectations for more intensive and closer trade and financial relations with the 'republic over the ocean.' Yet, quite soon, Poland as well as the countries which expected closer political cooperation and/or disinterested assistance of the United States had to modify their expectations. Hoover, as a member of the government, became deeply involved in the expansion of US trade and finances abroad. Poland, with its limited possibilities and potential, could not be a partner and was not of special but rather of minor interest for American traders, industrialists and, generally, the whole world of business. Moreover, American sympathy and support for Poland at the end of World War I indicated certain decline. For the Americans, Poles appeared as politically immature, difficult to comprehend and confrontational.[17]

In legitimate and factual reports of 1922, Hipolit Gliwic, the Polish Commercial Attaché in Washington, skilfully analysed and presented the US role in international affairs and the Polish place in it. He emphasized that, for the US, Poland was neither an essential element, nor an obstacle in foreign policy. Poland 'represents no special interest' to America, and one 'cannot even hope to gain America directly for our policy.' At the same time, as he reasoned, America – as a world power and a financial centre – was vital to the Poles, and they ought to adjust and arrange ways of influencing American policy makers. It should be based, as he continued, on concrete conditions and realities, not illusions or sentiments.[18] This opinion did not lose its power in years to come and easily applies to the Polish-US bilateral relationship during Hoover's administration. Regrettably, now and again it seemed as if Polish officials forgot about Gliwic's diagnosis.

---

16   For more see, Halina Parafianowicz, 'American Exceptionalism: The American Dream and the Americanization of East-Central Europe', in: *World and Global History. Reseach and Teaching. A CLIOHWORLD Reader*, edited by Seija Jalagin, Susanna Tavera and Andrew Dilley, 107–21, Pisa: CLIOHWORLD 2011.
17   *The New York Times* in the 1920s provided rather negative image of Poland and its matters. It is worth mentioning that there was no American correspondent in Warsaw, then frequently the information was taken from American correspondents in Berlin and Vienna, which made the interpretations quite critical and hostile to Poland.
18   Hipolit Gliwic, 'Zasadnicze wytyczne polsko-amerykańskiej polityki', 19 July 1922 // AAN, Ambasada RP w Waszyngtonie, 228. Warsaw, Poland; Wandycz, *The United States*, 178.

In the early 1920s, Hoover was remembered mostly as the organizer of the ARA, a 'Wilsonian' (although, as a matter of fact, conflicts happened as with his activities in the Republican administration) and 'a true friend of Poles and Poland.' The occasional information in the magazines and newspapers, books and pamphlets on the ARA or the Quaker literature assured Polish readers of his friendly involvement in Polish matters.[19] Not surprisingly then, Polish-Americans, traditionally pro-democratic, were divided in their sympathies between him and the Catholic and Democratic presidential candidate, Alfred Smith. Eventually, Polish-American voters supported him by a significant proportion in the presidential campaign of 1928, and the president-elect could genuinely be happy with the support he received. Jan Ciechanowski, the Minister in Washington, reported that he used the opportunity to remind some of his American colleagues that Polish Americans contributed to his presidential victory. Optimistically and naïvely, the Minister wanted a more cordial approach to Hoover and his administration and the bilateral relationship between Poland and the US.[20]

In a letter to President-elect Herbert Hoover in November 1928, the American Minister in Poland, John B. Stetson wrote:

> Your name is second only to that of President Wilson in the minds of the Polish people. Their feeling for President Wilson is abstract; for you it is personal because of the tremendous services you rendered in supplying the population with food and other necessary articles immediately after the armistice.[21]

Polish-American relations during Hoover's presidency

By and large, Hoover's victory was favourably received in the Polish press. Once more, he was portrayed as a 'humanitarian' and 'internationalist,' who played an active and important role in the reconstruction of post-war Europe and Poland. There was a general expectation that, as a president, he would not neglect Europe and its matters. There were hopes (or perhaps wishful thinking) about the possibility of a more active US in cooperation with the

---

19   Stanisław Arct, *Projekt odbudowy Polski przy pomocy amerykańskiej*, Warszawa 1920. In 1921 a special issue of '*Świat*' ('The World') was published, fully devoted to America and American friends. There was part dedicated to Hoover in recognition of his humanitarian activities with very emotional yet naïve poem '*Herbert Hoover żywiciel*'.
20   Jan Ciechanowski to the Ministry of Foreign Affairs, 21 November 1928 // Hoover Institution on War, Revolution and Peace (hereafter, HI), Poland. Ambasada (US), Box 7, Stanford, USA.
21   John B. Stetson to Herbert Hoover, November 1928 // Hoover Presidential Library (hereafter, HPL), Pre-Presidential Papers. West Branch, USA.

League of Nations and the World Court.[22] Interestingly enough, his years as a Secretary of Commerce, US expansion and more nationalistic tendencies under his guidance occurred, supposedly due to tactical reasons.

On 24 July 1929, Hoover proclaimed the Treaty for the Renunciation of War (Kellogg-Briand Pact). It was a grand ceremony, with the participation of former President Calvin Coolidge, Secretary Frank B. Kellogg and some former and present Cabinet members. As the Polish *chargé d'affaires* in Washington, Stanisław Łepkowski reported, according to the intention of the organizers, that the event was supposed to be a great or even epochal moment.[23] It raised new expectations for more active US involvement and international cooperation in preserving world peace.

Following World War I, Hoover became a critical supporter of the League of Nations and US participation in the World Court, hence demonstrating a kind of cooperation in keeping the world at peace. Some Americans supported the World Court, yet a large portion of public opinion perceived membership in it as the first step to membership in the League of Nations, which the isolationists were strongly against. Hoover's policy was termed by Joan Hoff Wilson as 'independent internationalism' in a sense that the US should collaborate in world affairs when it could not solve a certain problem through unilateral actions.[24]

Hoover took a nationalist position by favouring high protective duties, particularly on farm products (Hawley-Smoot Act, 17 June 1930) and restriction in the immigration policy. During the Depression years, Polish war debts turned out to be an increasing worry in the bilateral relations. Hoover's moratorium of 1931 as a bulwark against worldwide economic crisis neither worked well nor satisfied most Europeans, Poles included.

In December 1931, Hoover proposed to the Congress a temporary readjustment of the debt to the countries devastated by the Depression, but Congress refused any concessions. The correspondences between Polish and American officials prove that Poles tried to receive a reprieve of interest that was due December 1932.[25] The Polish decisions on the war debt payment were dependent largely upon the action of France and the countries

---

22   *Gazeta Warszawska*, 15 November 1928, 3; *Ilustrowany Kurier Codzienny*, 9 November 1928, 1; *Wyzwolenie*, 18 November 1928, 12; *Robotnik*, 10 November 1928, 3.
23   Stanisław Łepkowski to the Ministry of Foreign Affairs, 30 July 1929 // AAN, Ambasada RP w Londynie, 697. Warsaw, Poland.
24   Robinson and Bornet, *Herbert Hoover*, 106–7.
25   *FRUS, 1932*. Volume 1, 799–807.

that followed the French and British approach. The ultimate effect was a practical rejection of the war debts by the debtors (with the exception of Finland) and the consequent American loss of any payments.

Some of Hoover's activities on the international scene worried Warsaw. The Americans regarded the Geneva World Disarmament Conference (opened in February 1932) as an essentially European affair since the US was interested mostly in naval limitation. President Hoover sent a delegation to Geneva and, shortly after the conference opened, Hugh Gibson presented an American proposal for the limitation of the armaments, which – as it was perceived by the Poles – openly favoured Germany and ignored the requirements of European security.[26] The conference was a failure (later labelled by a scholar 'an unmitigated nuisance') for there was no understanding and agreement among the participants on the fundamental issues. As a price for its armaments reduction, France demanded security and a 'consultative pact.'

The Poles had made various efforts to retrieve some wartime pro-Polish sentiments during Hoover's presidency. To begin, the president himself was considered and called 'a true, good friend.' At the beginning of his term, Polish-American relations seemed cordial and close and – symbolically – were strengthened by a few acts of the Hoover's administration. On 10 April 1929, Tytus Filipowicz, during the presentation of his credentials to President Hoover as Poland's new Minister in Washington, expressed the hope of his government and nation to build more cordial relations and finalise talks on the Treaty of Friendship, Commerce and Consular Rights.[27]

In April of 1929, Hoover issued a statement for the *Chicago Tribune* on the international exhibition in Poznań in which he praised Polish achievements. It is worth noticing that, at the opening ceremony of the exhibition on 16 May 1929, his bust was unveiled in the American Pavilion.[28] Filipowicz, in the interview, emphasized:

> The United States and Poland have always been good friends and they are so today (...). The work of the Hoover relief committee during and after the war has cemented a bond of friendship which it will be impossible to break. Many individual

---

26 Gen. Stanisław Burhardt-Bukacki's report, June 24 1932 // HI.Poland, Ambasada (US), Box 2. Warsaw, Poland; Głos Narodu, 25 June 1932, 1. Many diplomatic reports from Washington, London and Paris showed the sympathetic approach of Americans towards German demands.
27 *The New York Times*, 11 April 1929, 21.
28 Since the beginning of May 1929 *Kurier Poznański* informed daily about the exhibition; *Herbert Hoover and Poland*, 35.

Americans are still helping my country, and we certainly feel very grateful to America for the helping hand which she has extended to us in our hour of need.[29]

In 1929, on the occasion of the 150th anniversary of the death of Kazimierz Pulaski and in recognition of his fight for the independence of the American republic, the Congress established 11 October as a national holiday (the Pulaski Day) to commemorate the Polish-American hero. On 9 October 1929, Poland's President Ignacy Mościcki (1926–39) sent a message to President Hoover expressing a 'deep appreciation and gratitude for the manner in which the name of this Polish and American hero is being honoured by the United States.' Minister Filipowicz, as a Special Ambassador at the coming observance, joined the Polish delegation for the White House ceremony. President Hoover, in his message to President Mościcki, acknowledged: 'The memory of this young Polish nobleman (...) will always be cherished in the hearts of American citizens and their heartfelt appreciation of his signal service in acquiring American independence will never die.' He also reiterated his 'country's gratitude and friendship for Poland.[30]

Professor Roman Dyboski of the English Department of the Jagiellonian University, a former scholar of the Kościuszko Foundation and a member of the Polish delegation, delivered – on the occasion of Pulaski's anniversary – a dozen speeches mostly addressed to the American audience. He talked about Polish culture, history and achievements focusing on the post-war years and building the independent country.[31] His important and useful role in the popularisation of Poland and strengthening its prestige was highly recognised by Polish Americans and acknowledged by Polish officials as well.[32]

At the same time, on 30 October 1929, there was an impressive ceremony honouring Madame Marie Curie by the National Academy of Sciences. President Hoover spoke about her achievements and presented her the gift from the women of America – a bank draft for $50,000 for the purchase of one gram of radium for the research institute named after her in Warsaw. Satisfied and affected, Marie Curie assured him and the audience that 'in my native

---

29   *The New York Times*, 25 May 1929, 2.
30   Herbert Hoover: Exchange of Messages with the President of Poland on the Pulaski Sesquicentennial Celebration', 11 October 1929. Online by Gerhard Peters and John T. Woolley, The American Presidency Project http://www.presidency.ucsb.edu, accessed 23 July 2018.
31   Roman Dyboski, *Stany Zjednoczone Ameryki Północnej. Wrażenia i refleksje.* Warszawa-Lwów 1930, 21.
32   Witold Wańkowicz to Leopold Kotnowski, 2 November 1929 // AAN, Ambasada RP w Waszyngtonie, 822. Warsaw, Poland.

land, your name is revered for having saved, by your humanitarian work, a large part of the young generation. Your kind work of today will add to the gratitude of the Polish people toward you.'[33] The gesture and honours presented to Marie Curie were received enthusiastically by the Polish American community who revered Marie Curie for her Polish roots and her maiden name – Skłodowska.

Filipowicz, getting the support of Polish-American leaders, galvanized by the recent events and proud of the heritage, took an opportunity to popularize the idea of elevation of the rank of the diplomatic missions. The Poles considered the step an important and prestigious act, all the more so because the US conducted diplomatic relations at the ambassadorial level with only six European countries (Belgium, France, Germany, Great Britain, Italy and Spain). After the fall of 1929, Filipowicz explored the chances for the approval of such a concept and talked with some influential politicians, e.g. George H. Moses (Chairman of the Senate), Hamilton Fish (Congressman from New York) and Stephen Porter (Chairman of the Committee of Foreign Affairs at the House of the Representatives).[34] It is worth emphasising that, at the beginning, Secretary Henry L. Stimson – who was not sympathetic towards Polish matters and disliked Filipowicz – was not involved in those discussions.

The Polish-American media and the Polish press connected the decision on raising diplomatic posts to embassy level personally with President Hoover. A semi-official daily, *Gazeta Polska*, optimistically wrote about such a prospect, which would provide 'real chances for closer and deeper' Polish-American relations. Such an expectation and wish – as the author argued – was based on the argument that America was ruled by a 'great statesman and true friend of Poland.'[35]

Congressman Fish, supporting the rising of the diplomatic posts, in report on 15 January 1930 to the House of the Representatives emphasised,

> The Republic of Poland stands fifth among the European nations in the population, and there is no nation in Europe

---

33   Tytus Filipowicz to the Ministry of Foreign Affairs, 19 November 1929//HI, Poland. Ambasada (US), Box 24; Herbert Hoover,'Remarks on the Ceremony Honoring Madame Marie Curie', 30 October 1929. Online by Gerhard Peters and John T. Woolley, The American Presidency Project, http://www.presidency.ucsb.edu, accessed 23 July 2018.
34   Filipowicz reports to the Ministry of Foreign Affairs, 8 October, 16 October, 18 December 1929 // HI, Poland, Ambasada (US), Box 4, f. 4. Stanford, USA; Parafianowicz, *Polska w europejskiej*, 69.
35   *Gazeta Polska*, 13 December 1929, 1.

which has a more friendly and cordial feeling toward the United States than Poland, for the aid given the American delegates at the peace conference toward the establishment of the present Republic of Poland. In addition, there are in the country, several millions of American citizens of the Polish origin who have done much to promote the development and progress of our own country. (...). It is only fair and right that we should recognize the freedom and independence of the Polish people by exchanging ambassadors with the present well-established and powerful Republic of Poland.[36]

Finally, in 1930, the legations in Warsaw and Washington were elevated to the rank of embassies. On 4 March 1930, Tytus Filipowicz, during the presentation of his credentials as the first Polish ambassador to US, emphasized that it was 'a new step tended to strengthen the friendship, increase the volume of trade and add to the feeling of security in East-Central Europe.'[37] President Hoover shared sentiments and expectations of the most cordial relations between the nations and countries. Two months later, on Polish National Day (3 May 1930), he sent the earnest wishes of friendship and good understanding. Another event, although not special but rather symbolic, was the Convention for the Prevention of Smuggling of Intoxicating Liquor signed on 19 June 1930 in Washington by Stimson and Filipowicz.[38]

A year later, after years of occasional talks and negotiation, the Treaty of Friendship, Commerce and Consular Rights was signed on 15 June 1931 by Secretary Stimson and Ambassador Filipowicz in Washington.[39] The Polish media occasionally commented that it was a small achievement in bilateral relations.

On 4 July 1931, when President Wilson's monument, donated by Paderewski and sculpted by Gutzon Borglum,[40] was unveiled in Woodrow Wilson Park in Poznań (named so in 1926), Hoover sent a cordial message on the occasion, read by Ambassador John N. Willys during the ceremony. The president expressed special interest in the observance owing to his 'good fortune to

---

36   *House Reports, 71st Congress, 1st and 2nd Sessions (April 15, 1929–3 July 1930)*, Report No 197, 1–2.
37   *The New York Times*, 5 March 1930, 2.
38   *FRUS, 1930*. Volume 3, 764–7.
39   *FRUS, 1931*. Volume 2, 938–55.
40   It needs to be emphasised that the famous sculptor presented Wilson as a 'peacemaker and Polish friend' in a symbolic pose and gesture. He stood at the pedestal beneath stone map of Poland with its established borders after the World War I. The powerful idea of the monument was above all the justification and reminder of American presidential support for Polish borders. There was also, according to comments in mass media, true hopes and expectations of Poles distressed by the German revisionism for American support for the *status quo*.

visit Poland (...) to meet illustrious citizens of Poland to whose inspiration this gathering is due.' He assured,

> It is, therefore, peculiarly touching to us that a ceremony such as this should take place in Poland, on the anniversary which stands first in our calendar. In the name of the people of the United States, as in my own, I wish to give voice to our profound appreciation of so notable a mark of remembrance, sympathy, and friendliness.[41]

A special guest, Edith Wilson, the widow of the late president, was received at the Castle by President Ignacy Mościcki and amiably honoured by Poles. During the ceremony, attended by Polish officials and the diplomatic corps; the President of Poznań, Cyryl Ratajski, delivered a speech in recognition of Wilson's role in the rebirth of Poland and America's support for the newly restored country. Hoover's name, as one of the friendly Americans, was repeated several times during the ceremony, talks and meetings. Mrs. Wilson was touched and pleasantly surprised by the words of love and gratitude toward her husband and deep appreciation of America for its role and friendship.[42]

On 4 July 1932, in Warsaw, the statue of Col. Edward M. House, a close aide of Wilson and a 'true and devoted friend and supporter' of Poland and its independence, was erected.[43] Such events and gestures, as their initiators and organizers intended, showed not only the gratitude of the Poles but also hope that bilateral relations with the United States would be strengthened.

In 1932, Charles Dewey, a former financial adviser to the Polish government, revisited Poland and Gen. Gustaw Orlicz-Dreszer went for a visit to the US. In August 1932, Gen. Douglas McArthur, the Chief of the General Staff, visited Poland for a few days,[44] which was noticed in the Polish press as a most direct and genuine American interest in East-Central Europe. According to Piotr Wandycz, it was McArthur's 'campaign to strengthen the United States army by pointing at the unsettled state of affairs in Europe.'[45]

---

41   Herbert Hoover, 'Message on the Unveiling of a Statue of Woodrow Wilson in Poznań, Poland, July 4, 1931. Online by Gerhard Peters and John T. Woolley, The American Presidency Project, http://www.presidency.ucsb.edu, accessed 23 July 2018.
42   *Kurier Poznański*, 1 July 1931, 1; 2 July 1931, 1; 3 July 1931, 1–2; 4 July 1931, 1.
43   *Gazeta Polska*, 5 July 1932, 8.
44   *The New York Times* informed briefly that it was 'purely a military affair' (8 August 1932, 21; 11 August 1932, 23).
45   Wandycz, *The United States*, 215.

Obviously, Polish-American relations, apart from the above-mentioned acts and sympathetic gestures, were largely one-sided as Poland was of marginal importance to the United States. The bulk of trade exchange, apart from expectations and attempts to involve Polish-Americans in the promotion and stimulation, was quite small in the inter-war period – especially during the Depression. In 1931, Poland was not present on the list of 58 US exporters, and – as an importer – it was shown almost at the bottom of the list (49th place). According to Polish statistical data, export to the US (in terms of amount and percentage) was insignificant and symbolic. The trade balance was unfavourable for Poland since it imported 14 times more products from the US. The import was dominated by cotton, food (including canned food), furs, a small contingent of cars and some machinery. In some years, the Polish cotton industry was predominantly (80–90%) based on American cotton.[46]

During the Depression, Hoover had much less time for European or, specifically, Polish matters, which were treated as an element of the American political game, mostly in connection with Germany and the stabilization of Central Europe. The rising American media criticism of the Polish-German border issue and the repetitive remarks on the 'Corridor' 'unjustly' taken from Germany in prestigious newspaper dailies, brought about considerable anxiety for Polish officials.

Danger of revisionism

But the main problem, which preoccupied Poles and particularly Polish officials, was the growing tendency for the revision of Polish-German border. Soon after Gustav Stresemann's death, German revisionism became more aggressive and noticeable – also abroad, even in the United States. Revisionism became truly perilous for the Poles, as in the economic crisis circumstances, the Americans reasoned that it could not be overcome until the European disorder was pacified. As many US diplomatic reports from the European capitals suggested, peaceful revision, e.g. return of the 'Corridor' to Germany would ease growing tensions and thus stabilize the political-economic situation of East-Central Europe. It was not only that Hearst's press informed about the 'great injustice' that was the existence of the 'Corridor' but also the *New York Times* occasionally published similar comments on the above topic.[47]

In the American administration there were several prominent persons

---

46   Parafianowicz, *Polska w europejskiej*, 78–80.
47   *The New York Times*, 17 August 1931, 4; 1 September 1931, 20; 8 September 1931, 4; 25 September 1931, 2.

interested in some settlement of the Polish-German border conflict. First of all, Henry L. Stimson, the Secretary of State, was sympathetic towards the German revisionist policy and the idea of a peaceful revision. His papers, namely *Diaries, Speeches, Writings and Statements*, prove – without doubt – that he seriously considered a revision of the Versailles Treaty and, above all, the Polish-German border.[48] To naturalise the speculations and comments that he favoured Germany over Poland, the Secretary of State occasionally repeated that the Polish-German frontiers were a purely European problem. Yet his approach towards a possible solution, which he presented in his announcements, memoranda and talks, was clear. Another pro-German official was William R. Castle, influential chief of the Western European Division at the Department of State, who was close to Hoover and, after the death of Joseph P. Cotton in mid-March 1931, Undersecretary of State. Both of them were closely associated with several journalists, some of German origin, who openly and successfully lobbied for the Weimar Republic's causes. Certainly, the German ambassadors in Washington, particularly Wilhelm von Prittwitz und Gaffron, played an active and consequential role in establishing more cordial US-German relations.

Through diplomatic channels, meetings and official talks, the above-mentioned people impacted bilateral German-American relations. Their close connections with the German-American community were also utilised for the improvement of American-German relations and a better image of Germany 'unjustly punished' after the Great War. American ambassadors in Berlin (Alanson B. Houghton, Frederick M. Sackett) were quite sensitive and sympathetic towards Germany and its problems. Such a situation worried the Polish officials and diplomats in Washington who were unable to change the general approach and viewpoint of American decision makers on the situation of Germany and especially on its Eastern border. The Poles were ineffective in attracting any American support for the European *status quo*.

It should be remembered that the US did not ratify the Versailles Treaty and thus did not oblige itself to defend the treaty or see the status quo as essential or necessary for the stabilization and security of Europe at that time. Rather opposite, Stimson repeatedly pronounced, during and after his summer visit in July and August 1931 in Europe, that the peaceful solution of the Polish 'Corridor' was essential for the political and economic stabilization of Central Europe.[49]

---

48   Henry L. Stimson Papers, Speeches, Writings, Statements Group, No 465, Series No III, Box 181, Yale University Library (hereafter, YUL). New Haven, USA; Ferrell, *American Diplomacy*, 201–3.
49   The diplomatic correspondence showed a great anxiety among Poles who were deeply worried about such a perspective of strong and constant propaganda focused on the revision mainly of Polish border.

According to diplomatic correspondences, in the summer of 1931, Stimson became active in various talks and discussions on the possibilities of Versailles Treaty revision. After the talk to the French Chargé, Jules Henry on 10 September 1931, Stimson wrote,

> I then repeated my attitude towards the peace suggestion, applying it to the revision of the Versailles Treaty and telling him that we expressed no opinion as to the questions of revision which were being urged by Germany but only that we were deeply interested in having any such revision if it was made by peaceful methods and not by war (...).[50]

In reports in September and October of 1931, Ambassador John N. Willys wrote about the growing Polish concern over the attitude of the American press in respect to the Polish-German borders. In a telegram of 20 October 1931, Willys mentioned that,

> Recent articles in the Baltimore Sun, the Washington Star and the New York Times, have particularly wounded Polish sensibilities. (...) The belief obtained in Poland that the United States is so concerned over the security of its financial commitment in Germany that American influence is being aligned on the side of the Reich as against Poland. Press dispatches from America reporting that conferences had taken place between the President, Secretary Stimson and the late Senator Morrow, in which the 'Corridor' was discussed, were looked upon in Warsaw as conformation of these forebodings.[51]

The press comments and supposed support for the revision of the Polish borders caused a great disappointment and anxiety in Poland and among Polish-Americans. The annoyed Poles reacted to such unfriendly comments, all the more so as it was during the stay of Marshal Philippe Pétain in America and on the eve of the French Prime Minister Pierre Laval's visit to the US. On 21 October 1931, Ambassador Filipowicz sent a protesting note to the US government.[52]

Pierre Laval came on an official visit to the US between 22–25 October 1931

---

50   *FRUS, 1931*. Volume 1, 525.
51   *FRUS, 1931*. Volume 1, 597–8.
52   The immediate and categorical reaction of Polish government sometimes was interpreted and attributed to the idea so-called the preventive war.

to discuss the world economic situation. During several meetings and talks with hosts, mostly with Hoover, Stimson and some other officials, particularly on 23–25 October, the situation of Central Europe and the countries of the region were discussed. For dinner, Stimson invited several politicians and senators, including William E. Borah, the influential chairman of the Foreign Relations Committee. It does not look incidental and seems out of the question that during these meetings and discussions, the 'Corridor' issue was taken up.

On 24 October 1931, Senator Borah, in his interview, publicly declared at a press conference the need for changes of the European borders. He stated there would be no disarmament in Europe as long as such problems as the 'Corridor' existed. He said: 'Then I would change the Polish Corridor if it was possible to do so; and I would change the situation with reference to Upper Silesia if I could.'[53] In spite of his qualifications, efficiency and political experience, he made a drastic and undiplomatic statement which caused quite a sensation and rapid response in both the American and Polish press.

The press announcement of Sen. Borah shocked Poles, who did not believe it was only his private opinion. All the more so as he met both Hoover and Stimson and also Laval and potentially talked about it. Exactly how much Sen. Borah's opinion was also Hoover's was not yet fully established or sorted out. Still, there is evidence indicating that several of the president's close co-operators had already declared and supported in some way the idea of revisionism. It is unlikely that President Hoover's opinions, at least private, were diametrically different. It is doubtful that he was surprised or discouraged by Borah's opinion since those matters were discussed quite often in government circles.

Officially though, the president and his administration did not share the senator's views presented in the interview for *The New York Times*. On 25 October 1931, the White House officially and publicly commented: 'A press statement that the president has proposed any revision of the Polish Corridor is absolutely without foundation. The president has made no suggestions of any such character.'[54] The public *dementi* did not, and could not, dissolve the true fears, distress, anxiety and disappointment of Polish officials and public opinion.

Walter Lippmann, the prominent journalist, sympathetic and supportive to the idea of a peaceful revision of the Versailles Treaty, noticed that Sen. Borah said publicly what 'responsible statesmen were saying privately.' He wrote:

---

53 *The New York Times*, 24 October 1931; Wandycz, The United States, 213.
54 *FRUS, 1931*, 603.

The time is probably not ripe, therefore, for a solution of the question, but it may not be too early to go to the Poles and ask them to begin considering whether the unmodified Corridor is not an unmistakable example of one of these 'international conditions,' referred to in the Article XIX of the Covenant of the League of Nations, whose continuance might endanger the peace of the world. To say that to Poland would be not an infringement of the dignity.[55]

Interestingly enough, the sensational episode with Sen. Borah's statement is almost unnoticed or it is at least only occasionally remarked in a few of words in the historical writings on Hoover.[56]

Public opinion in Poland, as seen in the comments of diverse newspapers, was outraged by such unfriendly remarks from somebody influential and close to the administration and President Hoover himself.[57] Also, Polish-Americans were shocked and organised several meetings in protest, and undertook an extensive press campaign to defend the permanence of the Polish borders and European *status quo*.[58] In months to come, also during the November visit of Dino Grandi, Italian Minister of Foreign Affairs (1929–32), the Polish government took energetic steps to stop the 'Corridor' discussions, particularly in the United States.[59]

The 'Corridor' became a timely and hot issue on the American scene for several more months and in1932 – Polish officials were constantly distressed and bothered by its notoriety. Poles abroad were also quite united and helpful in defending their borders and the current situation in Europe. They counteracted the intensification of the anti-Polish revisionist campaign. In the prestigious quarterly *Foreign Affairs*, the Polish Ambassador Jan Ciechanowski published an article on the historical background of Pomorze (Pomerania), the region publicly popularised by German propaganda as the so-called Polish 'Corridor'.[60] Ignacy Paderewski, at a meeting of the Polish-

---

55   Walter Lippman, *Interpretations, 1931–1932*. Selected and edited by Allan Nevins. New York: The Macmillan Company, 1932, 228; Wandycz, *The United States*, 213.
56   Fausold, *The Presidency*, 189 ('some excitement ensued during visit'); Meyers, *The Foreign Policies*, 183 ('undiplomatic speech' of Borah).
57   *Gazeta Polska*, 30 October 1931, 1; *Ilustrowany Kurier Codzienny*, 26 October 1931, 12; *Głos Narodu*, 25 October 1931, 7; *Gazeta Warszawska*, 25 October 1931, 3; *Robotnik*, 25 October 1931, 1; *Zielony Sztandar*, 1 November 1931, 3.
58   *Herbert Hoover and Poland*, 38–39; Parafianowicz, *Polska w europejskiej*, 140.
59   Jan Ciechanowski reports from the autumn of 1931 // AAN, Ambasada RP w Waszyngtonie, 242. Warsaw, Poland.
60   'The Polish Corridor: Revison or Peace?' *Foreign Affairs*, 10/4 (October 1931–

American Chamber of Commerce and Industry in New York, on 18 May 1932, delivered a powerful speech in which he brilliantly defended Polish rights to Pomerania and the European status quo. In conclusion he emphasised,

> We will not accept so monstrous an injury, no matter by whom inflicted. The territory restored to us is justly ours and we will stand by it. We are peaceful and peace-loving people. We need peace more than any other country in the whole world. (...). Do not believe those fortune tellers, who predict a return to prosperity provided the corridor be given back to Prussia. That is a tale for children. A new partition of Poland would be an evil deed.[61]

Sen. Borah's interview and the discussions about the Corridor had been referred to for several more months. This time, mainly under Polish actions, some more favourable comments also appeared in the America media. *The New York Times* published various articles and comments, including those defending Polish rights, such as from E. De Kleczkowski, who wrote,

> The demand, therefore, of some German propagandist for territorial changes in this Polish province in favour of Germany is to commit one of the gravest of injustices that could be perpetrated in an age of self-determination of nations. The whole Polish nation, numbering 32,000,000, is unanimous on this point and will make any sacrifice to keep it within the present Polish frontiers as established by the Treaty of Versailles. No Polish statesman conscious of his responsibility would dare to suggest any territorial alterations in the present state of affairs.[62]

The 'Corridor' propaganda and issue raised so loudly and soundly in America during Hoover's presidency became a sore problem for Poland in the bilateral relations with the US. The extensive and successful revisionist, mostly German, propaganda found quite sympathetic conditions on American ground. It worried Poles, as reflected in diplomatic correspondences, and soured and shadowed Polish-American relations in those years.

Certainly, the Depression did affect the foreign policy of the US during

---

July 1932):558–72.
61   *The New York Times*, 19 May 1932. Paderewski speech was later published – Ignace Jan Paderewski, 'Poland's so-called Corridor,' *Foreign Affairs*, 11/3 (October–July 1933): 420–34.
62   *The New York Times*, 29 January 1933, 5.

Hoover's administration. Experienced and personally interested and well-informed in the international situation, President Hoover was challenged and tested on many fields. Over the decades, his foreign policy was generally explained as a 'combination of the influence of Quaker pacifism, the rising time of depression, and the overriding strength of Secretary of State Henry L. Stimson.'[63] To some extent, it is true; nonetheless, these generalities missed the mark widely as he was well-equipped to direct US foreign policy and became quite active in policy-making, regardless of the strong influence of Secretary Stimson.

The Great Depression modified US policy, including the relationship with Europe in general and with Poland in particular. First of all, it caused American retreat from economic and financial expansion. The US demonstrated no interest in European political problems and controversies and declared official *désinteressément* in solving the developing tensions in the 'Old World.' On the other hand, after the spring of 1931, America intensified consultations with European politicians in order to reconstruct world finances and the economic system. Then came Hoover's moratorium and Stimson's visit to Europe in 1931.

I share the opinion of those scholars who emphasise that the European policy of the US neither favoured nor opposed Polish interests; rather, it did not perceive them or even ignored them.[64] America paid some attention to Polish issues only in connection to and in the context of the stabilisation of East-Central Europe in general. The statements on the need and/or possibility of a peaceful revision of the Polish-German borders, which gained more and more advocates and supporters in the United States, became a real peril for isolated Poland in defending its position and the *status quo*. In the short run, the strong Polish response and protest turned out quite effective.

I agree with Neal Pease, who wrote,

> With paradoxical irony, however, the advent of a more vigorous American foreign policy under the stewardship of a figure renowned for his humanitarian service to Poland coincided with the growth of Polish misgivings concerning the effects of US diplomatic efforts in Europe.[65]

---

63 Martin L. Fausold, *The Presidency of Herbert C. Hoover*. Lawrence: University Press of Kansas, 1985, 167.
64 Pease, *Poland, the United States*, 166; Winid, *W cieniu*, 175.
65 Pease, *Poland, the United States*, 130.

In conclusion, I would like to add a few words on Hoover's visit to Europe before the outbreak of World War II. In the late 1930s, the ex-president, as a hostile critic and opponent of Franklin D. Roosevelt and his policies, decided to go on a 'sentimental trip' to Europe. In February-March 1938, he visited several countries, e.g. Germany, Austria, Czechoslovakia, Poland, Latvia, Estonia, Finland and Sweden. On 19 March 1938, he was met at the Polish border by Michał Kwapiszewski of the Polish Ministry of Foreign Affairs to travel together. The Poles arranged 'a great program of hospitality' through Hoover's journey, on a special train, to Poznań, Cracow and Warsaw. Hoover had opportunities to discuss the problems of the times with local officials and university professors. He had an impression 'that freedom was disappearing in Poland' and that it was 'in a "nutcracker" held by Hitler and Stalin.' Summing up, the president wrote:

> Eighteen years before this visit to Warsaw, the democratic Polish regime under Ignace Paderewski had been overthrown by the dictator-minded Chief of State, Jozef Pilsudski, and a half-Fascist regime had been installed. He was succeeded by a group of his supporters (the 'Colonels') who were in effective control of Poland at the time of my visit.[66]

Hoover had the opportunity to talk with over a hundred officials, professors, business leaders, etc., including President Ignacy Mościcki, Prime Minister Felicjan Sławoj-Składkowski (1936–39), Vice-Minister of Foreign Affairs Jan Szembek, the Minister of Education Wacław Jędrzejewicz and Marshal Edward Śmigły-Rydz. All of them argued that a strong government 'was necessary to save Poland from Communism.' They, as he emphasized, recognized the dangerous situation in the country and of the gloomy prospect of future conflict.[67] Hoover noticed that the Poles organized 'a great army, hoping they could hold both enemies at bay.' He concluded:

> Despite the authoritarian trend of the regime, the Poles in 1938 had more freedom than the Germans. There were no concentration camps or liquidations, and there appeared to be a fairly free press. The most cheerful aspect of Poland was the astonishing cultural and economic expansion under the sunlight of independence given her at Versailles. On the other hand, the entire political structure of the country at this time seemed to me very weak.[68]

---

66   George H. Nash (ed.), *Freedom Betrayed. Herbert Hoover's Secret History of the Second World War and Its Aftermath*. Stanford: Hoover Institution Press 2011, 74.
67   *Freedom Betrayed*, 74.
68   *Freedom Betrayed*, 75.

Hoover was bitterly disappointed by world affairs and European tensions; he became an ardent isolationist. However, his 'sentimental journey' to Europe could not revoke the legend of his humanitarian and benevolent activities.

Note on Indexing

E-IR's publications do not feature indexes. If you are reading this book in paperback and want to find a particular word or phrase you can do so by downloading a free PDF version of this book from the E-International Relations website.

View the e-book in any standard PDF reader such as Adobe Acrobat Reader (pc) or Preview (mac) and enter your search terms in the search box. You can then navigate through the search results and find what you are looking for. In practice, this method can prove much more effective than consulting an index.

If you are using apps (or devices) to read our e-books, you should also find word search functionality in those.

You can find all of our e-books at: http://www.e-ir.info/publications

www.ingramcontent.com/pod-product-compliance
Lightning Source LLC
Chambersburg PA
CBHW032252150426
43195CB00008BA/429